The Narrative of
Realism and Myth

The Narrative of
Realism and Myth

Verga, Lawrence, Faulkner, Pavese

GREGORY L. LUCENTE

THE JOHNS HOPKINS UNIVERSITY PRESS
Baltimore and London

*This book has been brought to publication with the generous
assistance of the Andrew W. Mellon Foundation.*

Library of Congress Cataloging in Publication Data

Lucente, Gregory L.
  The narrative of realism and myth.

  Includes bibliographical references and index.
  1. Myth in literature. 2. Realism in literature.
I. Title.
PN56.M94L8   809.3'915   81-2084
ISBN 0-8018-2609-8   AACR2

for Randy and Marty

Contents

Preface

This study began several years ago at the convergence of two separate yet related incidents. The first of these occurred in Madison, Wisconsin, as I listened to a heated discussion between a friend and Fredric Jameson. A novel by Balzac was under consideration. At a certain point, Jameson ended his side of the conversation with an exclamation cast at least rhetorically as a question. If I recall correctly, his words were, "You say 'sense of myth.' But where is the myth?" At that time, the apparent assertion that these two things — the feeling or aura of myth and myth itself — were separable or even different disturbed me. My reactions to this formulation, which I took to be central to the discussion that day, serve as the basis for Chapters 1-3 of the present study.

The second incident occurred during a discussion with David Hayman and others about French Naturalism. In the course of the conversation, one of the more voluble participants asserted that there were no mythic underpinnings whatever in the major novels of Zola's Rougon-Macquart series. It was not long before the imprudent speaker was repenting his folly, as Hayman ticked off Zola's favorite myths one by one and demonstrated their presence in the specific events of the narratives. As I listened, I began to wonder whether a close reading of novelists from differing periods and cultures (yet whose works demonstrated a strong interest in some aspect of representation) might not yield a storehouse of myth as rich or even richer than Zola's.

In light of this later discussion, the issues at stake in the first one became clear. The important point to be educed from each discussion does not concern only realism or myth but also the interrelations of both. Such a formulation is more complex than the conventional opposition between realism and myth. It involves a series of relations, at various levels, between components of realistic and mythic discourse. Despite the complexity of this phenomenon, or perhaps because of it, there has been very little work devoted to the combination of these fundamental aspects of modern narrative. The course of my own investigation can be traced in Chapters 4 and 5. It has run from the work of the nineteenth-century Sicilian, Giovanni Verga, through that of D. H. Lawrence and William Faulkner and ends with the last major novel of Cesare Pavese.

Throughout these later chapters, as I hope I make clear in Chapter 3, the focus of inquiry remains centered on the interaction of realism and myth rather than on the discrete functioning of one or the other, because, for me, the two are finally inseparable. But that is getting ahead of the story, which now must speak for itself.

Acknowledgments

I would like to thank the University of California Press for permission to include the text of "The She-Wolf."

An earlier version of Chapter 2 appeared as "The Creation of Myth's Rhetoric: Views of the Mythic Sign," *Comparative Literature Studies* 18, no. 1 (March 1981): 50-68. The first three sections of an earlier version of Chapter 4 appeared as "The Ideology of Form in Verga's 'La Lupa': Realism, Myth, and the Control of Passion," *MLN* 95, no. 1 (January 1980): 104-38. Each is reprinted here with the publisher's permission.

The Narrative of
Realism and Myth

1

Mimesis and Verisimilitude: The Theory and Practice of Realism

Perhaps no other theoretical construct has been used to justify as many contradictory positions as has realism. In traditional philosophical discourse, it has carried two opposite meanings, one empirical, the other metaphysical. At times it has meant the immediate perception of the material world (the "naïve" realism advanced as a corrective to nineteenth-century idealism), and at other times it has been used to indicate the transcendence of everyday particulars, pointing to a system held to be truly universal and so more "real" (the realm of Platonic forms, the Scholastics' divine source, or the developmentalists' preadolescent "moral realism").[1] In literary theory and practice, realism has historically been invoked to sanction "revolutions" in both style and subject matter, though neither the form nor the ideological content of "realistic" fiction is necessarily revolutionary.

Despite these confusions in theoretical terminology and practice, the historical dialogue concerning realism has consistently focused on two central topics: first, on the subject-object relationship, and second, on the existential position of both subject and object in regard to an external source of meaning. In literary theory, discussions of *mimesis* (or imitation) and *verisimilitude* (or the narrated semblance of truth) have repeatedly turned to a privileged topic, the problematic relationship between words and things. For the moment, mimesis may be construed as the faithful reflection of the world's surface, and verisimilitude as the narrative's obedience to deeply ingrained cultural models for character motivation and plotting. It should be clear from the outset, however, that neither mimesis nor verisimilitude would be possible without some adherence to established convention. Since language constantly forges and reforges our perceptions not only of ourselves but also of the world, realism's literary re-creation of the world's truth is able to operate only through the prior conventions of communication. It is important, therefore, that realism be viewed as an object of rhetorical as well as of epistemological and moral concern.

1

Plato's analysis of artistic production, presented most concisely in a famous passage of book 10 of the *Republic*, is a critique of value based on trustworthiness.[2] According to Socrates' formulation, the ideal bed is real and "one only," not particular (597c-d). The carpenter, following the transcendent model, produces a particular material bed that only then may be reproduced in imitation by the painter and the poet. By conflating the categories of the real and the true under the valorized concept of the essential, and then temporalizing the example, Socrates demonstrates how far the poet lags in the "descent" of the three beds. Poetic imitation is "thrice removed" from the truth across an irrecuperable distance that is at once epistemological and existential (597e). Because the poet is likely to be especially skilled in persuasion, his reflecting imitation is considered not only inaccurate but also dangerous. In book 3, Plato is careful to distinguish between imitation (mimesis) and allowable simple narration (diegesis), but such a distinction provides little comfort for the creator of complex fictional discourse whose product involves both mimetic and verisimilar effects.

It is true that on occasion Plato reformulated his criticism of poetic production, but the primary thrust of his argument remained constant. For the moment it is sufficient to make two points. First, the example of the three beds demonstrates a necessarily problematic relationship between meaning and verification. By placing the referent of all discourse (including *in nuce* the carpenter's material re-production) in a transcendent realm, Socrates counters the atomist/empiricist conception of the progression of artistic meaning. His argument then further separates the *signatum* (the particular bed) from the *signans* (the artist's imitation). This does not mean, however, that Socrates takes the step of cutting loose the system of artistic signs to create meaning among the signs themselves in an interminable world of reflections. Their relationship to both the ideal ("real") and the material realms is seen not as contingent but as necessary, even though in the *Republic* that relationship is construed as negative. Artistic signs are merely the deceitful shadows of prior meaning, produced by those who are incapable of creating actual value in praxis—which is to say, in the service of the State (599c-e).

Since the *signans*, placed in a negative relationship with the *signatum* and barred from connection with the transcendent referent, is in no case verifiable, its valuation in the Platonic formula is in contradiction to that of literary realism's nineteenth- and twentieth-century apologists. Moreover, the mitigating possibilities of a necessary relationship between linguistic signs and inherently meaningful sounds, or between naming and named, is put in doubt, though not finally refuted, in the *Cratylus*. In the Platonic critique, as the appearance of artistic imitation becomes more convincing, it also becomes more treacherous, and this development entails the diminution of any potential for social value. The simulacrum thus represents not the height of artistry's achievement, but its most despicable product. Not only rhetorical embellishment (as for Locke) but imitation itself is seen as inevitably corrupt and corrupting. For Platonic society, based on caste priorities within a sharply limited market economy, the meaning of social discourse is portrayed as residing not in the necessarily soiled and potentially disruptive material world of everyday life, but rather in relation to an ideal source external to, yet generating, all worldly endeavor. The first full-blown critique of mimesis in the West was thus profoundly negative, and in precisely those terms that the continuing dialogue on realism has not yet succeeded in discarding or fully clarifying.

Aristotle's concern with mimesis in the *Poetics* was at least equal to Plato's;[3] however, by describing imitation as a natural instinct that is predominantly human (4.1448b), Aristotle foregoes speculation regarding metaphysical sources and focuses instead on the worldly phenomena of art's creation and use. For Aristotelian poetics it is crucial that poetry, considered to include both drama and verse, is the imitation not of an object but of an action. This concept of dynamic imitation has special ramifications in both Renaissance and contemporary theories of representation, primarily because of the tremendous strategic advantage Aristotelian imitation gains over the earlier Platonic model. Once imitation is seen as an essentially active process, the inner relations of the parts of the created object may then be viewed as creating meaning themselves, no matter what relation they might bear to an external source. The procedure of bracketing the source of poetic meaning and focusing instead on its locus is a logical maneuver that occurs with cyclical regularity in the history of formalist aesthetics, though its emphases and implications differ significantly with each recurrence. By positing imitation as a human instinct worthy of investigation in and of itself, Aristotle frees his discussion for the subsequent inquiry into the other source of poetry, the "instinct for 'harmony' and rhythm" (1448b). Poetry may then be evaluated solely in terms of the ways its creation and presentation correspond to the initial thrust of these two "causes." The poetic product thus becomes a practical phenomenon with a privileged social value for both pedagogy and "cleansing" (catharsis).

No longer is art seen as inherently inaccurate or necessarily deceitful. On the contrary, it may provide a special source of unity in the rapidly expanding and shifting Hellenic world. With Aristotle, the quest for a perfect artistic and social language becomes not an endless longing for the barred past of an ideal and static unity (in which art as such would be useless), but an inquiry into the progressive refinement of existing models. What *is* remains constantly open to comparison with what *should be*. Description and prescription balance each other, and both appear essential to poetry's creation and critical assessment. Though the prescriptive function of aesthetics may seem antithetical to realism, this is not the case either in Aristotle's analysis or in subsequent empiricist programs. Far from successfully eliminating prescription, realism has historically incorporated this function into its vision of the material world, since description itself necessarily involves selection and evaluation. Aristotle's shift away from the epistemological and temporal perspective of Platonic analysis is central to all subsequent discussions of art's integrity and value, and it will prove especially useful in considering the poetics of both nineteenth-century Naturalism and twentieth-century Socialist Realism.

One element of Aristotle's definition of tragedy has special implications for the practice of realist narrative. In the *Poetics*, tragedy is defined as an imitation of an action that is not only serious and of a certain magnitude but also "complete" (6.1449b). By insisting on the artistic "unity of plot" in direct contrast to the "infinitely various" incidents in human life (8.1451a), the *Poetics* sets a standard of aesthetic effect which for centuries will confuse discussion on the nature of verisimilitude. Rather than uniting poetry and history, Aristotle sets one against the other. By asserting the value of aesthetic unity, Aristotle underscores the factitiousness of art, which pleases not because it is true to the disordered surface of human existence, but because it selects and arranges privileged elements to satisfy the given instincts of harmony and rhythm and the artistic criterion of wholeness ("one action," 8-9.1451a-b).

Denied the possibility of the exact representation of worldly life, Aristotelian poetry then resorts to a "superior" form of realistic effect, substituting the aesthetic truth of conventionalized unity for Plato's realm of transcendent forms. Again, the Aristotelian source of meaning is neither abolished nor entirely concealed within the locus of experience, but merely shifted toward an empirical realm that is both psychological and moral. For Aristotle, the essential truth of poetry and that of worldly existence remain two distinguishable though overlapping concepts. It is true that the *Poetics* deals at greater length with tragedy than with comedy. It should be noted, however, that the overarching conception of unity as the motivation for the construction of plot and presentation of character poses genuine difficulties for *any* approach to the notion of imitation. Aristotelian formalism thus slays one guise of "naïve" realism, the material, only to engender another, the psychological-moral, in an adjacent realm.

These problems of mimesis and verisimilitude may be clarified further by contrasting Herodotus, the "father" of realistic effect, with his purposefully different successor, Thucydides. It is impossible to read even part of the *Persian Wars* without being struck by the effort Herodotus continually makes to characterize his sources of information. His vignettes, culled from his own travels or from others' reports, begin with a precise ascription ("I saw myself," "I was told by," "They claimed") often followed immediately by the professional disclaimer ("but I do not believe it"). In his enthusiasm for the breadth and variety of life, Herodotus intends to record everything of note that he has seen, heard of, or read, regardless of his belief in his sources' veracity. This material is all viewed as being a part of natural life and thus both inherently interesting and significant. The result, especially in the introductory books, is a collection of moral anecdotes (Croesus and the oracles from Delphi, Solon/Croesus/Cyrus), tales (Gyges and Candaules, Helen in Egypt), and *faits divers*, many of which make fine short stories, but none of which is ordered in accordance with an overriding organic unity. In the abundance of geographical and social detail, direct representation of speech and act, and the occasional interest in psychological grotesquerie, Herodotus wants to be, and more than any other writer of his period succeeds in being, a mirror of his times.

In the *History of the Peloponnesian Wars* there is none of this. For Thucydides, "scientific accuracy" meant the exclusion of all material irrelevant to the inquiry's central thesis, the Spartan-Athenian conflict and its outcome. The chatty and often eccentric chronicler's reportage of Herodotus and the early logographers is replaced by another standard of narrative trustworthiness: subordination of character and event to an internal unity of meaning. This unity is an instance of narrative verisimilitude, because within the guidelines of Thucydides' project, the only means of achieving historical truth was precisely through the exclusion of disunified and naïvely true-to-life material. This is a historian's version of what will later become Aristotle's precept for poetry, and, to that extent, Thucydides' project may be regarded as the first "poetics" of history. Thucydides' program even led him to the point of arranging the set speeches to demonstrate the various situations more clearly as they *should* have been. It is essential, then, to bear in mind these distinctions between the standards of Aristotelian verisimilitude and Platonic mimesis. This is especially true in the assessment of a heterogeneous form such as the nineteenth-century novel, in which the narrative requirements of long-range plotting and character motivation may both depend on, and conflict with, equally significant aspects of cultural description. In the process, such narratives may reveal unexpected ideological stances in their subordination and resolution of realism's opposing claims.

In the section of Aquinas's *Summa Theologica* which defines the four levels of allegory in Scripture (1a.1.10), there is a typically precise assertion that will prove central to the semiotics of realism. Since the author of Scripture is God, who has the power to signify His meaning not only by words (as man can do) but also by *things*, scriptural exegesis must take both these aspects of divine discourse into full account: "hoc habet proprium ista scientia quod ipsae res significatae per voces etiam significant aliquid."[4] In this combination of metaphysics and empirical representation, speech represents a transitional but not a unique operation in the world of discourse. Words are a special order of signs that can contain but not exhaust the total meaning of divine communion. Far from attempting to counter the adage "individuum est ineffabile," Aquinas preserves the "quidditas rei" by making it the concrete base in which the divine source of meaning is actively manifest. With other writers' extensions of the Scholastic method beyond Holy Writ, the tertiary discourse of secular exegesis could evaluate the representation of even the lowliest elements of the material world as having special significance. Unlike the Platonic conception of poetic meaning, late medieval exegesis did not proceed as though the surface of artistic discourse were itself inherently deceitful. Indeed, the relation between *signans* and *signatum* was guaranteed by the transcendent perfection of the Christian world's divine referent.

But only within the Scholastic dialectic were Aquinas and later Dante indicative of the rise of Western literary realism. As Erich Auerbach notes, perhaps the strongest source of medieval realism was not the private experience of the individual writer, but the dramatically shared tales of the Old Testament and the Gospels, and especially the story of the Savior, with its combination of worldliness and transcendence, passion and intellection, tragedy and consolation.[5] The Mysteries did not, of course, represent the beginning of linguistic and psychological realism in Western drama, as a reading of Old or even Plautine Comedy immediately demonstrates. Medieval verse, too, tended to embody certain popular elements of lexical register and social behavior, particularly at the beginning of literary movements before the forms became thoroughly conventional. (Guillaume d'Aquitaine, Cecco Angiolieri and the Tuscan realists, and, in the north, François Villon are cases in point.)

Though knowledgeably realistic narrative had well-known precursors prior to the Italian Trecento, with Boccaccio the realist mode gained full development in both stylistics and ideology. The immense shift in economic, political, and cultural life that occurred around the year 1300 in Tuscany was crucial for early Renaissance realism. The development of the town as the center of economic and social life, together with the astronomical rise of the Florentine banks, meant the decline of the feudal system and the old Guelf-Ghibelline loyalties, and the substitution of a radically different system of social organization and values. At the same time, the ancient contrast between country and city life took on a new and much more compelling meaning. Increased trade between major centers brought the need for travel, encounters with different cultural groups and, through ensuing reflection, the development of a conscious sense of local identity. The need for a common language gave strong currency to simple and direct forms of speech, and the necessity for precision and punctuality in exchange created a new awareness of measurement in general and of time and place in particular. Indicators that had previously appeared natural because they were a part of nature (dawn, noon, dusk for time, landmarks for space) or embedded in "immemorial" and sanctified custom (the tolling of the bells at canonical hours, the position of the castle, fields, or crossroads as place markers) were challenged and, in part, replaced by the code of the clock and the compass. It would be an exaggeration to assert that the quickening of interest in worldly affairs eclipsed the concern with the life to come (if nothing else, the extraordinarily graphic apocalyptic art of the Pisan Traini and others following the Black Death of 1348 would be enough to refute this). It is true nonetheless that the new fascination with man himself affected every area of human endeavor, from political thought to social life and art.

In many respects, however, these developments were not entirely new. There had been severe social disjunctions in previous eras in the West, and many of these had resulted in cultural manifestations focusing on man's dealings in the everyday world of passion, wit, and profit (the *Satyricon* is perhaps the best example). It is thus important to note that Florentine life of the Trecento was essentially different from that of the Greek or Roman town in two ways. First, Florence was not a caste-bound society based on slave labor, and second, the simple hegemony of an established upper class was no longer a basic, unchallenged assumption in the organization of the city's bitterly factional society. These new circumstances, generally speaking, shaped a society that was open not only at the bottom but also at the top and that provided the opportunity for profit and loss across the full range of its social system.

For artistic production, the implications of this new situation were extraordinary. Like Petronius, Apuleius, and the *jongleurs*, Boccaccio describes and values worldly knowledge and practical endeavor, but, unlike his predecessors, Boccaccio is able to valorize these attributes from *within* the milieu of his work. No longer is the clever servant doomed to remain a servant despite his wit. While at the other end of the scale, gone is the use of satirical cunning merely as an outlet for the frustrations of a trapped or hopelessly decadent upper class. Unlike Petronius's tricksters, Boccaccio's heroes are able to work upward from *within* their class, and the knowledge they gain is positive in both individual and social terms. Andreuccio da Perugia (2.5) thus represents not a rustic lout rising inexplicably to prominence amid the Dantesque "gente nova," but a new being from first to last, the "town" hero whose goals and victories are so fantastic (the gold, the night journey, the Bishop's ring) precisely because so narrowly prescribed. Ser Ciappelletto is a saint, not despite his thorough "notaio" knowledge, but as a result of it, and because he never leaves his own everyday moral realm to gain his success.

The *Decameron* may also be set apart from another element in its cultural lineage, what Mikhail Bakhtin terms the carnivalistic.[6] Many features of folk culture still color the early Renaissance novella (the language of the marketplace, festive imagery, more or less overt description of bodily functions), but this material is no longer regarded exclusively as a means of escape during special celebrations, appropriate only on determined occasions and only in contrast to established — and quickly reinstated — norms. As opposed to earlier carnivalistic narrative, the actions of the *Decameron*'s most strikingly realistic heroes are not restricted by seasonal or ecclesiastical festivities. On the contrary, the world inhabited by Boccaccio's individualized and willful characters is itself seen as normative, and the greatest success they can achieve is learning to live and maneuver within its newly formulated bounds. Andreuccio's *descensus ad inferos* into the worldly knowledge of the Bad Hole ("Malpertugio") may thus be seen for the positive victory it represents. For the young hero, this journey assumes a value precisely opposite that of Dante's pilgrimage, not a spiritual *ascensus* out of the world's marketplace, but a fortunate fall into it.

One aspect of Florentine culture that made this artistic situation possible was simply the presence of a new audience. Though there had been a homebound reading public as early as the Greek romances, this type of audience had never attained the numbers or the social variegation that it did during the Italian Renaissance. Thus it was not merely fortuitous that in his proem and conclusion Boccaccio dedicated his collection to "le donne" (in part the "deserted" women of Dante's lament in *Paradiso* 15.118-20), those who would read his book not so much because they wanted to as simply because they could, the new bourgeois audience created by the very culture so thoroughly embodied in the most realistic tales of the book. Along with this developing audience came a radically new relationship between the producer and his public, in which the artist as an individual strove to free himself from prior tradition in order to make his individually produced and privately consumed commodity new enough to warrant special attention, though not so strange or outrageous as to be utterly unmarketable.

In Boccaccio's work, the dual exigencies of conformity and novelty take a noteworthy form. It is easy to emphasize the abundance of freshly forged realistic detail in lexical register, specific composition of place, social customs, and incipient psychological individuation (all especially evident in the city-oriented stories of Florence, Naples, Palermo, and Venice). It is equally important, however, to point out Boccaccio's dependence on the conventional and highly didactic forms of traditional medieval narrative.[7] Rather than discarding the Romantic matter of France and Britain, or the pointedly allegorical exempla of the *predicatori*, the anecdotes of the *Novellino*, and the tales of the *Gesta Romanorum*,

Boccaccio's work recodes the symbolic valuation of these elements for special use in a new world. Nor are the traditional elements confined to the courtly frame story or to overtly Romantic tales like those of Trancredi and Ghismonda (4.1) or Lisabetta and the pot of basil (4.5). Andreuccio's gold is replaced not by another easily measured and exchanged sum, but by the symbolic ring of fable itself, preceded only briefly by the explicit warning of the two thieves who assure him of the naïvely unrealistic nature of his quest to recuperate his loss ("Ma che giova oggimai di piagnere? Tu ne potresti così riavere un denaio come avere delle stelle del cielo").[8] In this way, Boccaccio's narrative exploits the symbolic load seen as preexistent in the forms of *use* as well as in those of *exchange*. The ring becomes the symbol of knowledge gained in the ways of the new system. The allegorical elements are conserved within the most realistic notations of the text and add an aura of stability and duration to realism's apparent spontaneity. Indeed, the Bishop's name, the monetary value of the ring, and the historically accurate location of the cathedral are all supplied. The patently *allegorical* elements are now used to focus the *worldly* point of the tripartite story, which is at once strikingly new and, on closer examination, extraordinarily conventional.[9]

It is important to emphasize that this process of recoding occurs within the narrative fiber itself, not as an appendage attached a posteriori to a finished product. The self-effacing nature of this procedure distinguishes early Renaissance realism from previous and contemporary syncretist forms, such as patristic allegoresis or the self-consciously transendental verse of the first *stilnovisti*. In this way, the Renaissance novella, once established as a self-sufficient form, tends to avoid open display of certain of its most conventional literary qualities.

These symbolic underpinnings indicate the particular richness of Boccaccio's combination of mimetic effect and narrative verisimilitude. For the first time since the fall of the Empire, primary accumulation of capital—in conjunction with severe factional disruption of political allegiances—had advanced to such a point that there existed on a large scale the genuine possibility for social rise within an individual's own lifetime. Competitive worldly knowledge in sexual and monetary exchange provided one key to the newly available treasures, but not the only one.[10] A thorough awareness of the old modes of perception could now be included *within* the intellectual and material ambience of the *umanisti*, and in such a way that the former consciousness of the world could be retained as positive if utilized within this new and all-encompassing synthetic framework. Andreuccio's success is itself indicative of this unity of new and old. In biographical terms, it is especially significant that Boccaccio began his career writing traditional, elegantly romanticized verse while representing the banking interest of his father and the Bardi in Naples at the magnificent Angevin court of Robert the

Wise. For Renaissance financial practice, with its compelling drive to master both new *and* old procedures, there was no single lesson of greater moment than Edward III's exercise of traditionally power-based royal prerogative in England's dismaying repudiation of its debts to the Florentine banks. It was only after the financial disasters and the plague that Boccaccio, once again in Florence, turned definitively from the elaborate Romances of the early period to compose the knowledgeably eclectic novelle of the *Decameron.*

There is one other type of allegorical procedure that should be mentioned in connection with Boccaccio's realism. The decisively new relationship between the artist and his audience entailed a further modification of major importance for literary production, this in the relationship between the artist and his own product. Increasingly set apart from the audience with whom he once shared the very space of production, and deprived of direct contact with a spiritualized first Cause, the artist began to turn to his own work for both subject matter and sustenance. Cut off from the immediately visible effects of his work in the material world, the bourgeois artist began to take speech and specifically fictional discourse as privileged topics, in a circular process that was at once allegorical and ironically self-conscious.

Boccaccio's self-consciousness as an individual storyteller in the world of the markets is perhaps most obvious in his polemical response to his critics, which he included in a remarkable excursus preceding the fourth day. In the course of his response, Boccaccio balances the forces of fame, hunger, and fiction ("fama," "fame," and "favole") without denying the reality of any of them. In a concluding passage, he clarifies his attitude toward the powers of fictional discourse. His text interweaves idealistic and commercial terms in order to show the truth and utility of fables and the deceit of his supposedly sincere detractors:

> Ma che direm noi a coloro che della mia fame hanno tanta compassione, che mi consigliano che io procuri del pane? Certo io non so, se non che, volendo meco pensare quale sarebbe la loro risposta se io per bisogno loro ne dimandassi, m'avviso che direbbono: —Va' cercane tra le favole.— E già più ne trovarono tra le loro favole i poeti, che molti ricchi tra' loro tesori, ed assai già, dietro alle lor favole andando, fecero la loro età fiorire, dove in contrario molti nel cercar d'aver più pane che bisogno non era loro, perirono acerbi.[11]

This passage is polemical, but throughout the excursus it is clear that at this point in his career Boccaccio feels the need for the sustenance of both bread *and* poetry. Although he never denies the importance of these two requirements for his life in the material world, he ridicules the blind materialism that would deny the power of fables ("nel cercar d'aver *più* pane che bisogno non era loro"). He also claims that poetry represents not so much a means of material fulfillment as of transcendence into the special knowledge that will *then* feed back into the world of men ("fecero la loro età fiorire").

For Boccaccio, therefore, fictional discourse itself, once set free as an object in the world, has the power to regenerate its own meaning and value. This point is demonstrated within the stories as the "saint's tale" of Ser Ciappelletto is efficaciously repeated first by the credulous confessor and then by the congregation at large ("e chiamaronlo e chiamano san Ciappelletto, ed affermano, molti miracoli Iddio aver mostrati per lui e mostrare tutto giorno a chi divotamente si raccomanda a lui").[12] This novella concludes in a delicate pas de deux, with the narrator himself (Panfilo) assuming the tone and formulaic phrasing of a medieval preacher, followed by the briefest reminder of the organizing intelligence immanent in the narration of all the tales:

> E per ciò, acciò che noi per la sua grazia nelle presenti avversità ed in questa compagnia così lieta siamo sani e salvi servati, lodando il suo nome nel quale cominciata l'abbiamo, lui in reverenza avendo, ne' nostri bisogni gli ci raccomanderemo, sicurissimi d'essere uditi. — E qui si tacque.[13]

The narrative, which began with the clear distinction between discourse and meaning or, more precisely; between naming and knowledge (Cepparello→Ciappelletto), moves through Ciappelletto's use of discourse as "inganno" and concludes with Panfilo's subtle demonstration of knowledgeable language in action. The irony of Ser Ciappelletto's sainthood thus becomes the allegory of the worldly manipulation of both ignorance and knowledge through discourse. Like sex and money, language itself is now viewed as a crucial medium of exchange in the world, and, in the *Decameron*, it takes its role as an object of study and manipulation as well as a means of risk and gain.

Within the most realistic tales, the narrating subject is seemingly removed as an actively evaluative participant to be reconstituted only as the voice charged with the duties of representation, as a presence that strives to appear solely as absence. This self-effacement of both the framing intelligence ("E qui *si tacque*") and the narrating personae is, of course, merely another aspect of the exquisite narrative game. The resituation of the dual narrators *within* the layers of their own narration resembles Michel Foucault's description of the self-consciously skillful technique of Velázquez's portraiture in the nascent codes of European realism.[14] It is important, however, to note that this indirect appeal to the reader had begun in the socioeconomically advanced centers of the early Renaissance, well before either Velázquez's portraiture or the *Don Quixote*, and that it was intimately connected with both the worldly isolation of the individual subject and the status of the knowledgeably interpreted text as a valuable entity in its own right. Indeed, it is precisely the *telling* of the Siciliana's courtly tale of adventure which creates the backdrop for Andreuccio's first fall. It is this same tale that the knowledge-able narrator characterizes as skillful but incredible "favola" ("così ordi-natamente, così compostamente detta da costei"), thereby denying the value of misinterpreted fable in the very moment of "Andreuccio"'s narration. On the level of stylistics as well as ideology, the *Decameron* thus serves as a unique document in the two-fold rise of European realism, a testament both to cunning wit and to knowledge raised to the second power, a degree of intelligence that is fully capable of taking itself not only as its own subject but also as a suddenly valuable commodity in a new world.

There was revived interest in Aristotelian unity after Francesco Ro-bortello's 1548 edition of the *Poetics* and the spread of Italian literary theory through France and England. But it was not so much in form as in psychological analysis that the practice of realism in seventeenth- and eighteenth-century narrative differed most radically from that of previous fiction. This shift in emphasis did not take place primarily in Italy. Throughout the Italian Renaissance, *imitatio* had had two meanings; first, the conscious imitation of prior artistic models, and second, the imitation of nature. Despite the empirical interests of Leonardo, Machia-velli, and the *umanisti* who had preceded them, the narrowly court-centered culture of the High Renaissance city-states (Milan, Ferrara, Venice, Urbino) continued to value the first of these two meanings over the second. Until well into the late sixteenth century, Horace was the preeminent theorist, with undisputed emphasis on established literary models and the cautious if elegant imitation of *aurea mediocritas*. Even in the comparatively popular ambience of Florence, the developing interest in man as a newly valid subject was not free from reactionary opposition, and the syncretist reinterpretation of prior forms of knowledge in the hands of Pico, Ficino, Lorenzo, and others was ardently attacked as heresy from Savonarola's pulpit.

It was primarily in the northern countries, far less vulnerable to the dead hand of the Tridentine decrees, that literature developed its new psychological interests. Poetic creation could, of course, include imitation of prior models, but it entailed reflection of man's reactions to the con-temporary world as well. The Reformation's violent assertions of the moral integrity of the individual subject went incalculably further than the earlier Italian academics' most speculative discussions of the dignity of man and of *libero arbitrio*. The resituation of post-Copernican man not only as an objectified sign within nature, but also as a privileged entity worthy of internal investigation, gave special significance to the representation of psychological processes. Long-range focus was thus free to expand and develop *within* the characters, a phenomenon antici-pated by Boccaccio's *Fiammetta* and the *Don Quixote* and fully evident in Madame de Lafayette's masterpiece of consciously mediated desire, *La Princesse de Clèves.*

As Ian Watt has suggested, the primacy of the interior operations of the individual subject, given most clearly in the Cartesian *cogito,* was to have immense importance for the development of realism in the early novel.[15] In narrative fiction, not only verbal elements but also characters and settings came to be regarded as fully meaningful signs. The remnants of the Scholastic dialectic were thus refocused within the everyday world. With the undisputed hegemony of the marketplace in the daily life of the nineteenth century, realism's developing codes became capable of manipulating the audience's shared knowledge of the environment to make the *appearances* of both things and people psychologically meaningful. Selection of the details to convey psychological meaning became crucial, with special priority given to "typical" elements, which, from a middle-class perspective, were at once representative and noteworthy.

The concept of typicality in fiction has been revived as a touchstone for critical analysis in this century by Georg Lukács, but its lineage extends back through Hegel to the Scholastics and Aristotle. Lukács himself has been most active in condemning both his early handling of the concept and the Hegelian slant of the work in which it first appears, but the notion of typicality is never really abandoned in his writings and reappears as a crucial element—in combination with the necessity for purposeful intratextual criticism—in his discussions of "critical realism."[16] The basic concept, that characters are at once concrete individuals and representations of what Fredric Jameson terms "something larger and more meaningful than themselves," was already present in the exchange of letters in 1859 between Marx, Engels, and Lassalle concerning Lassalle's historical drama *Franz von Sickingen.*[17] In Luckács's formulations, characters are free to represent both the concrete moment within the fictional world and the broader historical concerns of the ongoing struggles that define their class, thereby mediating the rival claims of the particular and the universal. Through the inherent temporality of narrative, in combination with the infinite play between character and narrator consciousnesses, the realist text is capable of developing and critiquing its own ideological underpinnings in one multilayered operation, a process that Lukács shows to occur consciously in the novels of Thomas Mann and that Marx and Engels had detected at work in Balzac's profound ambivalence toward the nineteenth-century French aristocracy.[18]

The great realist narrative of the nineteenth century can be characterized in part by this worldly plentitude of the realist sign, its assertion of the very capacity to mean or, in Roland Barthes's terminology, the classical quality of the "lisible."[19] This realism was much more thoroughgoing than the superficial reproduction of "local color" or the mechanical observation of social *bienséances*. The diegetic unity of plot combined with cultural motivation and mimetic description to form a narrative that was both traditional and new, deeply rooted in the rich soil of its literary antecedents, yet burgeoning with the life and feel of its own time. Along with long-range character focus and slowed pace, it is not difficult to list some of the other salient characteristics of the nineteenth-century realist novel: the inner logic of the text, which arranges itself in the easily identifiable beginning-middle-end of narrative suspense, taking the characters from illusion to disillusion while drawing the reader into the text and leading him to forget his own potentially critical situation as "reader"; the tendency to transcend the view of any single character, integrating individuals first into an internally ordered group and then into a larger social world, which nonetheless remains subordinated to the all-embracing knowledge of the narrator; language that avoids calling attention to itself once the register of everyday discourse has been established (a norm that may then be breached in distinguishing extraneous individuals or groups); precision in measurement for systems of work and exchange as well as for spatial and temporal orientation (again, in regard to plotting and representation); and finally, the insistence on naming, both in character identification and in the inventoried detail of scene.

These characteristics combined to buttress the overall view, essential to epistemological realism, that the world of matter and the senses had meaning and that literary art could communicate its significance. In contrast to Hegelian idealism and Platonic realism, early and middle nineteenth-century realism did not regard artistic language as problematical or deceptive so much as functional, the key moment of communicable transition between the world of the senses and that of the intellect. Of course, this is not to say that all nineteenth-century writers of realist fiction shared this entire list of characteristics. To take the example of inventoried description, Balzac tends to arrange the objects of perception in hierarchical order according to the predetermined *idées fixes* of the characters' personalities, thus establishing the environmental backdrop against which the narrative drama unfolds; Flaubert organizes lists of details that work subtly against the established priorities of the protagonist's conscious desires, thereby introducing the disturbance of irony within the text; and Verga orders description according to the internal dynamics of the Sicilian peasants' affective "logic" and thus creates active sympathy for even the simplest characters.[20]

It is important to remember that the realist exploitation of irony was not entirely new. Part of Boccaccio's method had involved breaking with the conventions of oral narrative, in which what a character does *is* what he knows, by employing verbal irony to signal the active separation of the experiential and cognitive levels. In "Andreuccio," for example, the narrator's ironic commentary begins with the descent into Malpertugio ("la quale quanto sia onesta contrada, il nome medesimo il dimostra") and does not completely subside until the concluding sequence, during which Andreuccio catches up with the previously delimited group of narrator and reader, who have possessed the requisite knowledge of the world's organization from the very beginning.[21]

This technique recurred in early nineteenth-century social irony. As long as the source of irony remained clearly localized within the figure of the narrator, as for example in Jane Austen's *Emma*, these effects could be used to valorize the withdrawn, knowledgeable "teller" in relation to the only gradually demystified objects of narration. The overt subjectivity of the structure of Romantic irony thus served to organize the cognitive functions of realist narrative and to glorify the persona of the fiction's producer in the first full era of economically competitive and commercially dependent publication. Again, as in Boccaccio's most realistic narratives, early nineteenth-century realism tended to conceal its necessary dependence on prior literary forms. The author thus established for himself both favored subjectivity and creative freedom. In this way, the *ultimate* source of artistic invention could be located not in the "real" world and even less in the traditional models of literary convention, but instead in the individual "reflecting" genius of the speaking subject.

In Flaubert's work, however, there occurred a major shift in the narrator's relation to the world of his own narrative, again demonstrated most clearly in the changing use of ironic effect. With the progressive development of technique, the distance created by the spontaneous thrusts of verbal and situational irony became so pervasive as to create an unbridgeable gap between the narrator and the world of his creation. With Flaubert's extended utilization of the *style indirect libre*, the readily identifiable position of the narrator began to disappear, creating the sustained impression of a multicentered text that worked from the inside against the apparent priorities of its own characters (as occurs most noticeably in *Madame Bovary*, *L'Éducation sentimentale*, and *Un Coeur simple*). The result was no longer a knowledgeable critique of the fictional world carried on from without, but a progressive dissolution from within, accomplished through the problematical mixture of subject and other which is the hallmark of the *style indirect libre*. By means of this self-effacement of the figure of the narrator, Flaubert restored the sense of objectivity to his depiction of the world. At the same time, however, through the purposeful diffusion of ironic effect, his seemingly most realistic work made that world appear to collapse. As Northrop Frye has suggested, mimesis can and often does turn to irony.[22] But far from being the fruition of mimesis, this turn represents the final dissolution of mimetic imitation. Indeed, it was only with the elimination of conscious irony that Zola's Naturalism was able to reset the second cornerstone of its announced program, establishing a method for investigation based on objective observation and on the assumptions of scientific determinism, and thereby restoring the apparent integrity of both the observer and the world.

Zola's Naturalism represented a codified version of the literary practice and the scattered theoretical theses of his nineteenth-century realist predecessors. Elements of his essays and prefaces derive from Taine, Flaubert, the Goncourts, and even Hugo. At the same time, Zola's "method" borrows at least as freely from contemporary scientific and sociological investigations, especially from Comte's Positivist tracts, Prosper Lucas's treatise on the heredity of nervous disorders (1847-50), and Claude Bernard's *Introduction à l'étude de la médecine expérimentale* (1865). Through his polemical opposition to post-Kantian Romantic and Symbolist doctrines of artistic autonomy, Zola played a central role in the continuing debate on the nature and validity of realism.

The two basic tenets of Zola's Naturalism, objectivity and determinism, had been part of philosophical investigations since Comte's *Cours de philosophie positive* (1830-42). Like Vico and Hegel, Comte had described the progression of human intellectual and social existence as passing through three broad "états": the theological (or fictive), the metaphysical (or abstract), and the positive (or scientific). Comte claimed that the third state was in the process of being achieved; moreover, the key to its comprehension lay neither in the errors of man's prior conceptions of his past nor in an idealistic approach to a perfected future. For Comte, the past was of interest only *as* past, and the idealist conception of continuing progress was more a methodological encumbrance than a goal ("Ne voulant construire aucune utopie").[23] In order to discover the laws governing man's "positive" condition, the investigator needed only to observe and record the elements of the world around him with scientific rigor. Comte's Positivism required an objective accumulation of data, with a view to eventual discovery of the set of laws that organized the existing environment. Positive existence was thus regarded as static rather than truly progressive, even though knowledge of its organization was necessarily postponed until *after* the accumulation of data was complete.

In a fashion similar to Aristotelian formalism, Positivism concentrated on the locus of meaning in the world of sense and matter; however, rather than merely deferring discussion of a potentially external or transcendent source of meaning, Positivism regarded such inquiry as both misleading and futile. All that can be known is the created world as it is (Vico's *verum ipsum factum*); practical laws of organization thus replace essences as the objects of investigation. This maneuver is typical of modern realism and demonstrates the "revolutionary" power that its conception of the world claims.

It is nonetheless crucial to note that Positivism does not do away with the source of meaning. Instead, it centers that source within the worldly locus itself, in the relationships between things. This explains, in part, the extraordinary vitality that internal relations may demonstrate despite the overall stasis of the Positivist framework. It was no coincidence that both the founder of Positivism and the chief exponent of Naturalism passed through two clear phases in their work, each turning away from the deterministic objectivity of the initial writings, one to found a religion of Humanity itself, the other to compose narratives of the social force of *Germinal* and *La Terre*. This progression represented not an internal contradiction, but the development of the tendencies inherent, though suppressed, within the original systems, a movement from the mere accumulation of detailed evidence to full acknowledgment of the radiance hidden within data.

Zola's clearest explanation of his method, "Le Roman expérimental," appeared as an essay in the *Messenger of Europe* (*Vestnik Evropy*, Saint Petersburg) for September 1879, collected in 1880. Following the outspoken prefaces to the second edition of *Thérèse Raquin* (1868) and *L'Assommoir* (1877), this essay was programmatic enough to please not only partisans, who quickly elevated it to the status of a prescribed text, but also detractors, who found in it ample grounds for counterattack. The elements of the essay most in need of reconsideration today are those serving to demonstrate Zola's position and at the same time to mask its underlying assumptions, which turn out to be not so much empiricist as a heterodox blend of empiricism and idealism. The method's "scientific" procedure is specified almost immediately: "le romancier est fait d'un observateur et d'un expérimentateur."[24] Zola credits Bernard's work and admits, with a frankness that would be ingratiating if the implications were not so disturbing, "Le plus souvent, il me suffira de remplacer le mot 'médecin' par le mot 'romancier'" (p. 1175). His polemical opposition to the proponents of Romanticism and idealism is evident from the outset: "Le déterminisme domine tout. C'est l'investigation scientifique, c'est le raisonnement expérimental qui combat une à une les hypothèses des idéalistes, et qui remplace les romans de pure imagination par les romans d'observation et d'expérimentation" (p. 1183).[25]

Insisting on the "caractère impersonnel de la méthode" (p. 1197), Zola proceeds to outline an inductive program for social investigation through the agency of precise artistic representation. The goal of the scientifically refined "experimental" novel is the discovery of the underlying mechanisms to be found at work within what Taine had termed the "dépendences et . . . conditions" of race, milieu, and historical moment.[26] These mechanisms are held to generate and organize the observable phenomena of existence, but even as Zola posits the presence of such mechanisms, he takes care to leave in abeyance the ultimate determination of their essential nature ("sans me risquer à formuler des lois," p. 1184). In this way, Naturalism, like Positivism before it, valorized the seemingly random, objective accumulation of data at the same time as it sought to formulate the proper questions of social meaning:

> Et c'est là ce qui constitue le roman expérimental: posséder le mécanisme des phénomènes chez l'homme, montrer les rouages des manifestations intellectuelles et sensuelles telles que la physiologie nous les expliquera, sous les influences de l'hérédité et des circonstances ambiantes, puis montrer l'homme vivant dans le milieu social qu'il a produit lui-même, qu'il modifie tous les jours, et au sein duquel il épreuve à son tour une transformation continue . . . [comme] romanciers expérimentateurs, aller du connu à l'inconnu, pour nous rendre maître de la nature. (Pp. 1184-85, 1189)[27]

Even within Zola's essay, however, the pretense of scientific objectivity is qualified:

> Le romancier expérimentateur est donc celui qui accepte les faits prouvés, qui montre dans l'homme et dans la société le méchanisme des phénomènes dont la science est maîtresse, et qui ne fait intervenir son sentiment personnel que dans les phénomènes dont le déterminisme n'est point encore fixé, en tâchant de contrôler le plus qu'il le pourra ce sentiment personnel, cette idée *a priori*, par l'observation et par l'expérience. (P. 1203)[28]

It is important that rather than abandoning the experimental method's claim to objectivity, Zola simply makes this another goal, an end attainable through the progressive methodological refinement that is not merely probable but predetermined ("que dans les phénomènes dont le déterminisme n'est *point encore* fixé"). In this way, the program's most vulnerable element is subsumed as an object of inquiry within its own ongoing investigations. This move protects the method's apparent integrity both from external attacks and from potentially disruptive self-knowledge. Subjective artistic quality thus preserves its special claims to validity within Naturalism's "scientific" framework at the same time as it acknowledges its subservience to objectified worldly quantification.[29]

In seeking out the mechanisms hidden within the environment, Naturalism logically began with what it regarded as the simplest, most fundamental objects of investigation. This predilection explains the extensive focus on the lower classes, although the Romantics's open sympathy and their covert belief in the unique genuineness of "the folk" was to be expunged ("le plus qu [e le romancier] le pourra"). Despite Naturalism's claims to observation of characters' internal functions ("les rouages des manifestations intellectuelles et sensuelles"), interior analysis of logical and emotional processes was effectively prevented by the representational barrier of "scientific" objectivity, accompanied by Zola's own strictly middle-class background and by the class values immanent in French fiction after the bourgeoisie's 1830 triumph. This is essentially the point made by Arnold Hauser in his *Social History of Art*, although, as he notes, the example of Zola remains a complicated one.[30] In place of

individual or class motivation, Zola's narrative substitutes the ideologically formulated "mécanisme" of passion—amatory, gustatory, or
bibulous. This is especially evident in Zola's depiction of the Lantier-
Gervaise-Coupeau relationship in *L'Assommoir* and in the hereditary
weaknesses of their progeny. Indeed, Nana's furtive presence at the seduction following the famous orgy of chapter 8, with her large eyes "d'enfant
vicieuse" lit with sensual curiosity, exemplifies Zola's limitations in the
handling of lower-class motivation. By treating the functional attributes
of social behavior (irresponsibility, shiftlessness, alcoholism, illiteracy) as
inherited causes, Zola turns distinctions of class into those of caste, thus
providing a sense of destiny in the inevitable deterioration of his characters' moral and social lives. Though it is true that an element of sympathy
is incorporated within the narrative through the assignment of guilt to
realms beyond the individual character's immediate control (heredity,
environment), this does not mean that an actual alternative to decline is
seen to exist *within* the early and middle novels of the Rougon-Macquart
series, prior to Zola's acute reaction to the "Manifeste des Cinq" of 1887.
The single logical exit, that of changing not the characters but the organization of the world itself, was the one possibility that both Positivism
and Naturalism had programmatically discarded from the beginning.

As in the early Renaissance novella, nineteenth-century realism elevated
competitive worldly knowledge to the status of a prized commodity,
making its symbolic attributes the objects of an ideologically intellectu-
alized fetishism. This very knowledge was valued only as it served to
facilitate movement (social, political, economic) within the existing
borders of the bourgeois world in the century of middle-class agitation.
Significant social change not only entailed a prohibitively great individual risk; it also required the type of active causal analysis that Positivist
knowledge continually deferred in favor of the ongoing accumulation of
worldly data. For both Positivism and Naturalism, the individual was
too dependent on external forces, and the organization of society too
vast—and "as yet" insufficiently understood—for anything beyond the
maintenance of the present "état." Comte's emphasis on the crucial role
of an ordered, family-centered "vie domestique" as an antidote to post-
Revolutionary disruption was a manifestation of this attitude.[31] Even
Zola's later defense of Dreyfus represented not so much a call to revolution as an attempt to make the State fulfill its prescribed function. The
rare moments of pleasure in the midst of this pervasive pessimism were
themselves seen as the results of incoherent, uncontrollable passion, and
thus either short-lived, destructive, or both. In this way, the apparently
secure status quo of the stable world of matter and sense became not just
a fact but a self-perpetuating goal.

Although the temporal perspective of Positivist Naturalism appears
suited to the study of the actual world with regard to man's potential for

progress, its effect is instead the solidification of the present in a pre-determined circularity that resembles timelessness. This perspective gives Zola's most effectively detailed description an aura not only of gradual accumulation but also of a continual repetition approaching the atempo-rality of myth, as Giacomo Debenedetti perceived in *La Terre*.[32] Along with asyndetic parataxis, the temporal technique central to this effect is the extensive use of the imperfect, in what Gérard Genette terms the iterative style.[33] This style emphasizes the dependable repetition of action. By reinforcing the sense of destiny noted earlier on the levels of plot and character, the introduction of this "mythic" temporality into the de-scriptive passages of Zola's texts creates the illusion of a development that is progressive but also predetermined. All life is seen to exist within the established synchronic boundaries of this state. In this way, the present is conceived of as being at once inevitable and endlessly repeated under the frozen gaze of destiny itself. The constant utilization of con-ventional mythoi even in Zola's most original narratives regularly rein-forces this effect.

In addition to having a favored class of social objects, Naturalism also had a privileged mode of perception, that of sight. The direct visual ex-perience of the material world plays a large part in Zola's characteristic metaphor of the human environment as a scientific laboratory. The artist thus presents himself as an objective observer/reporter rather than as a subjective creator. Of course, the late nineteenth-century interest in the objective-subjective functioning of vision was not an exclusive property of narrative fiction. It formed the basis of far more subtle investigation for the Impressionist painters, for Zola's friend Cézanne, and for the growing art of photography. Truth was conceived of as residing in the immediate perception of the world, seemingly obviating the reflective agencies of Stendhal's mirror and George Eliot's shiny bead of ink.

Though not a completely new artistic effect, the accurate representation of speech was one of the openly polemical elements of Zola's manifesto. It must be noted, however, that, like sight, auditory phenomena were subjected to the scientific criteria of Positivist measurement, so that Zola's narratives remain a series of "lower-class" dialogues tied together by a narrator who writes in the prescribed lexical register and logical order of middle-class discourse. It is this combination of middle-class logic and ideologically conceived lower-class irrationality which at times makes Zola's *style indirect libre* appear ungainly; moreover, Zola's *bêtes humaines* consistently avoid the roughest elements of speech theoretically available to them. Even the most sodden and desperate of Zola's char-acters thereby betray the identity of their author, an extremely sensitive man who lived and worked within the confines of solitary quarters and rarely descended into the Parisian streets.[34]

By valorizing the objective accumulation of data, Zola effectively reversed the Platonic conception of mimetic art as inherently deceitful. For Naturalism, the representation of detail was motivated not by the Scholastic assertion of its value in necessary relation to an external source, but by its inherent importance as a constituent element in the laboratory of the world. This does not mean that in practice Zola was able to follow his theoretical guidelines, as both the knowledgeable utilization of narrative illusion and the lack of fully accurate reportage indicate. Indeed, the unquestioning adoption of the Aristotelian unity of plot poses as many internal difficulties for Zola's practice of mimesis and verisimilitude as it had for classical historiography and Renaissance narrative.

In professing to value the representation of all life, Zola eliminated the need to motivate plot through a single character's continuing desire or through the supposedly accurate portrayal of an established (and subsequently allegorized) historical period. But this new freedom did not entail true objectivity. Both the conventional unity of plot and the very factitiousness of fiction worked against Zola's goal from his project's inception.[35] Like Boccaccio and Balzac before him, Zola could create a full fictional world, but that world could hold together internally only as fiction, not as life. Viewed from this perspective, the literary mode of realism reassumes its guise as a relative phenomenon, revolutionary, but only in relation to prior rigidified codes, connected with life itself, but only through the mediation of consciously fictional discourse.

When European Naturalism hardened in its polemic against Symbolism, it assumed the form of an absolute system, claiming an integrity for itself which belied its necessary relation (positive and negative) to prior literary and theoretical models. Through this process it completed its own self-negation, claiming universal truth and thus denying its previously announced existential relationship with the shifting world of material and sensual particulars. Nineteenth-century realism ended by apodictically asserting the necessity of its own system, valorizing the now unified worldly source over the empirical locus and thus assuming the self-contained certainty of Platonic and Scholastic realism, as the essays of both Zola and his Italian comrade in arms, Luigi Capuana, amply demonstrate.

As it became established in a codified system, realism lost not only the vital thrust of its critique but also the crucial ability to examine and criticize itself. Again, this dual function had traditionally characterized the realist text. In *Moll Flanders*, for example, through the carefully combined agency of the sanctimoniously proper "editor" and the avowedly penitent narrator, the official moral code of middle-class, Protestant England was accurately presented to the reader at the same time as it was ironically undercut by the knowledgeably demystified seventeenth-century *pícara* (who ends up, even after her repentance, sailing to America and dining at the captain's table). As a trope depending for its effect on what remains *unsaid*, irony both demands and rewards a thorough knowledge of the subtleties of the text's realistic world. In Zola's narrative, however, unlike that of Boccaccio, Defoe, or Flaubert, the temporal separation of the experiential and cognitive functions results not in an ironically knowledgeable critique, but in blind assumption of the system's underlying unity. Through the continual deferral of ultimate knowledge, Naturalism's characters are effectively barred from full comprehension of their own state. Even the organizing narrator can only report what he sees and hears in the service of ongoing, objective investigation. The irony in Zola's texts thus represents not an escape into knowledge, but a submission to destiny. With the programmatic depiction of human motivation, the cyclical unity of predetermined decline, and the curtailing of ironic introspection, Zola's novels became not an immediate representation of "real" life, but a coded, uncritical allegory of Naturalism itself.[36] Zola's work thus retained the integrity of the fictional world, but only in allegorized form. For the nineteenth century, this was not the beginning of empirical realism but its end.

Naturalism's special concern with measurement, and its emphasis on sight as the privileged mode of perception and on the present as the single fully measurable and thus meaningful period, accounted for its ideological inability to pass beyond the boundaries of its own system. It could only restate those same boundaries in a polemic that effectively precluded self-knowledge. In refusing to withdraw from the sharply limited focus determined by its uncritical conception of the nature of data, and in steadfastly claiming to value only the mechanical truth of the object itself, Positivist Naturalism was doomed by its own hand to blind repetition of its programmatic version of worldly phenomena.[37]

Marx had been correct, then, as early as *The Holy Family* (1844-45), to point out the extraordinarily conservative stance of Comte's Positivism, which refused to look beyond the surface of the institutions composing contemporary society (such as the private ownership of land).[38] For Positivism, any social change would necessarily occur as measurable movement along a horizontal plane; whereas for Marx, movement was always doubled from its inception, proceeding vertically upward from the economic base as well as horizontally through society's superstructure, creating confrontations and crosscurrents at every level. In terms of Marxian analysis, both Positivism and Naturalism were prohibited from seeing the underlying dynamics of the characters and events they described but could not comprehend. Indeed, they were barred by their own program from critical understanding of the "mechanisms" they professed to seek. This accounts for Engels's initial championing of Balzac over Zola and for the continuing adversary relationship between Marxism and Positivism in this century, even though Foucault claims to see these two analyses as supplementing each other rather than as constituting a true opposition.[39]

Through Marx's and Engels's conception of art as an aesthetic and social product, necessarily connected with a base that is itself concrete yet constantly developing, dialectical materialism began to create the theoretical tools for a full analysis of realistic art. The illusion of artistic autonomy could thus be eliminated, though without destroying the specific nature of art in its unique relationship with the rest of social life. In the 1920s, this insistence on the interplay of material and cultural influences countered the Russian Formalists' idealist notion of the self-determining progression of artistic forms (through the mechanism of *ostranenie*, or defamiliarization). The goals of materialist literary criticism were to unmask apparently self-sustaining ideologies and to demonstrate the underlying and often unconscious motivations determining form and especially content. The historical mode of realism could thus be understood as a fully ideological orientation toward life, one that symbolically codes the material and intellectual elements of its own society at the same time as it recodes those of prior periods. The "rise" of the theory and practice of realism thus appears to be neither an autonomous, self-contained phenomenon nor a separate half of an art/life tandem, as the analyses of Watt and Auerbach tacitly assume, but instead the development of a mode of representation inextricably enmeshed in the dynamics and history of class struggle from the very beginning.[40]

Socialist Realism became the official doctrine of the First Congress of Soviet Writers (1934) and remained strictly in force until the post-Stalin Second Congress (1954) and the Twentieth Congress of the Party (1956), which made de-Stalinization state policy. It is easy to agree with Lukács, Henri Arvon, and others that Socialist Realism was the embodiment of Zhdanov's unfortunately nondialectical desire to reduce art to an officially cheerful administrative function (thus neglecting both Marx's and Engels's explicit reservations concerning mechanistic or tendentious "types"), but even so, important aspects of the theory remain to be accounted for.[41] Although Stalinist controls eventually resulted in rigid codification, in the beginning—even for Gorky—the program was less dogmatic and far more energetically debated than its later enforcement might suggest.[42]

Like Aristotelian empiricism and nineteenth-century realism, Socialist Realism assigns a special value to the artistic representation of the phenomenal world. Fictional discourse is regarded as competent both to record the salient elements of the existing environment and to demonstrate the proper attitude toward social development. Like Marxism itself, Socialist Realism asserts an in-depth analysis of the present material world and a privileged orientation toward the future. Far from being destroyed, the Platonic ideals are transferred from the metaphorization of space to that of time. In certain of its programmatic aspects, Socialist

Realism thus resembles Zola's Naturalism, except for the former's claim to demonstrate *consciously* within itself both truly progressive temporality and a full analysis of the kind of social and economic phenomena which remained a sealed book for Zola (such as the complexly ideological nature of European class antagonisms after 1848, or the pervasive influence of the late nineteenth-century economic depressions).

For Socialist Realism, both capitalist mystification and social demystification are real, since they occur in the world. The first, nonetheless, is a perversion and a stage of consciousness to be passed beyond; only the second is both necessary and true. Socialist Realism professes to represent a return to the concept of quality in art, but now on the level of content rather than form and in the realm of full society rather than in that of the solitary individual. This does not mean the end of formal considerations in narrative theory. A principal result of Socialist Realism is the openly ideological subordination of mimesis to verisimilitude. Platonic realism and Socialist Realism share a polemical distrust of the mere imitation of the random surface of life, but the latter attempts to correct the potentially dangerous errors of representation by prescribing both the contents (*partijnost'*) *and* the diegetic organization of properly realistic fiction. In other words, with Socialist Realism's official triumph of narrative verisimilitude over mimesis, the fictional world once again looks and feels only as it *should*.

By conflating the categories of the real and the true within the socialist future, and by valorizing the source of meaning residing in the worldly base and emanating throughout social life, Socialist Realism assumes its position aş the last great realist program in modern narrative. Even in Soviet aesthetics, the categories and terminology of Platonic reflection were never discarded, but the negativity of Plato's argument was reversed as its focus was shifted from a transcendental to a material realm. Though transcendentalism as a system was denied, the seeds of its utopian potential remained intact in the fertile worldly soil of time itself.[43] In this way, the real was seen to encompass not only the present but also the ideological truth of the Socialist future in a utopia of men and women as well as ideas. Once again, realism took care to guard the capacity for illusion on which it has always thrived.

For the social analysis of aesthetics, it is an especially vexing problem that the institution of Socialist Realism was contemporaneous with the decline, or one might almost say the dying gasp, of realist theory and practice in the West. For the moment, we must defer the question of whether this means the end of Western realism, or whether it simply requires us to look elsewhere for continuing realist products, such as to journalism, television, or film. Nonetheless, the contemporaneity of Socialist Realism and Western antirealism does suggest the possibility that even the most challengingly "meaningless" modern products, like those of Dada and Surrealism, or the contemporary novel of the European academies, do reflect, albeit in dialectical and at times obscure fashion, the helplessly anxious reality of twentieth-century middle-class life encompassed in a narrative structure that is the accurate embodiment of our own times, in the fear and refusal of unified meaning itself. For the theory of realism, the question then would be, in what ways is modernist representation framed and/or distorted by the rhetorical and epistemological functions of both irony and allegory? Such an analysis entails consideration not only of contemporary social life but also of the prior models on which perception is based, and it therefore requires us to develop a means of determining the components of myth as well as those of realism.

2

The Creation of Myth's Rhetoric: Views of the Origins of the Mythic Sign

Myth's lineage in aesthetic and philosophical discourse is as fully established as that of realism, but, like its antagonist, myth remains a problematical entity. A review of commentators as diverse in their assumptions and approaches as Plato, Vico, Müller, Frazer, Jung, and Freud will serve to distinguish the moral and epistemological evaluations inherent in some of the major schools' views of the mythic sign prior to our own day. The goal of this investigation should ultimately be clarification of the current debates on this topic, which invariably arise from a fundamental and at times baffling question, how can we approach the origin of the mythic sign?

Such a historical and theoretical review logically entails an inquiry into the source of myth's rhetoric. Once broached, the question of origins leads to the problem of humanity's vision of itself as expressed in the language it uses to confront and, at the same time, to obscure the "true" nature of its existence. Each school, in revealing and at times contradictory ways, has tried to clarify this relationship between the locus of mythic narrative and some external origin of meaning, a force or ideal invoked as the prime mover of mythic language. These problems of myth's origins and validity have been treated openly in the last two centuries, but they are as ancient as myth itself. Finally, for the study of literature, an attempt should be made to outline the ways in which the signs of myth interact with those of realism to create meaning in narrative fiction.

Traditionally, "myth" has been the term *par excellence* for falsehood, whether intentional or innocent, strategically invoked or blindly accepted, but, at the same time, the word has retained a connotation of higher truth. In this sense, it has been used to combine the functions of *gnoscere* with the privileged vision of *narrare*. Between these two views intervenes the neutral, Aristotelian use of "mythos" in the sense of basic plot, which has been reinstituted in the study of narrative by contemporary American and European criticism.

26

Plato's dialogues demonstrate three attitudes toward myth and its origins.[1] At times, as in the *Ion* and in parts of the *Republic* (especially book 2), all poetic discourse is regarded as necessarily corrupt because of either the untrustworthy nature of poetic inspiration or the inherent limitations of the critic and audience. At other times, in the *Phaedrus* for example, Plato appears to sanction some mythic narrative as long as the *furor poeticus* is sufficiently contained to insure myth's faithful reproduction.

In general, Plato manages to avoid the question of myth's origins by focusing on these problems of myth's *re*-presentation. There are, however, a surprisingly large number of instances when Plato himself generates parables resembling myths in order to develop a position or to resolve a difficulty viewed as logically insoluble either in the arguments of Socrates or in those of the other participants. This method of argumentation occurs in the *Symposium* with Aristophanes' tale of Androgynous and the primeval origins of love's power; in the *Meno* when Socrates, in the midst of an otherwise closely reasoned discussion, adduces first the "inspired" lyric poets and then the myth of Persephone in support of his contention that all learning is recollection; at the end of the *Phaedo* in the "charming tale" of Platonic cosmology and the mansions of the soul, followed by Socrates' strategic but pointedly limited disclaimer ("A man of sense ought not to assert . . . that the description which I have given of the soul and her mansions is exactly true. But I do say . . . that something of the kind is true," 114d); on occasion in the *Timaeus*; and, perhaps most notably, at the conclusion of book 10 of the *Republic*, only a short while after the stringent critique of poetic production, when Socrates uses the tale of Er to explain the central doctrine of the preexistence of the soul. It should be clear, then, that Platonic myths, when knowledgeably utilized as parables within the highly rational dialogues, are regarded neither as misleading nor aberrant, but rather as another means of approaching the goal of truth. The foremost classical opponent of the deceptive reproduction of mythic discourse may also be seen as its consummate manipulator, in a series of discussions that openly criticize mythic representation on the one hand and cunningly utilize it on the other.

Questions of the origins and moral value of myth both preceded and followed Plato's discussions. In the prologue to the *Theogony*, Hesiod had reiterated the caveat attributed to the Olympian Muses: "we know how to speak many false things as though they were true; but we know, when we will, to utter true things."[2] Herodotus, as a not quite disinterested historian, had taken great delight in first reporting and then rationally debunking the "false" myths of his deluded subjects, and particularly those of the Persians. In chapter 25 of the *Poetics*, Aristotle insisted on the special value of poetic representation (explicitly defined as including "tales about the gods"), which he considered to possess a truth that was "greater" precisely because nonhistorical and thus potentially universal. Euhemerus (fl. 300 B.C.), following a line of Epicurean thought and anticipating Vico in certain important respects, reversed the Aristotelian values by locating myth's truth not outside the realm of human history, but precisely in history itself. Mythic tales were considered to originate as the allegorized versions of actual historical figures, used by a ruling class to legitimize "divinely" ordained authority. Though this analysis was one-sided, Euhemerus did strike on an important aspect of myth's origins. The creation of myth in support of political and social ideology is a recurrent phenomenon and is one reason why subsequent interpretations of mythic discourse always carry the potential both for demystification of prior norms and legitimation of current, authentically "knowledge-able" ideologies.

With the work of Giambattista Vico, the study of myth and the origins of the mythic sign nominally achieved the status of a "science." For a century before Vico, the preservation of popular narrative, and especially folklore, had occupied European letters, as evidenced in the influential work of the Neapolitan Basile, Perrault, Mme. d'Aulnoy, and Fontenelle. With Vico's *Scienza nuova* (1725-44), however, both myth proper and the development of mythological narration became the objects of exhaustive theoretical inquiry.[3] Vico's "New Science" represented the first attempt at a full history of mythological perception. From the standpoint of aesthetics, it is of decisive importance that Vico did not share the rationalist biases of Voltaire and the proto-positivist Encyclopedists. Although Vico's work demonstrates a preoccupation with methods of systematizing, his interest in generative rather than static or accumulative relationships, along with his careful attention to the history of class motivations, gives the *Scienza nuova* a perspective closer to that of nineteenth-century dialectical thought than to the post-Cartesian Enlightenment. Vico's writing thus represents one of those happy "sports" in the history of literary theory, a work so ahead of its time that it demonstrates its greatest strengths only by stubborn resistance to the intellectual and material environment that helped to shape it.

It would be misleading to pretend that Vico's system is concisely presented or easily explicated, but it is not difficult to describe some of its salient features. It was primarily the theory of poetic perception which made Vico's work attractive to Herder, Coleridge, and Goethe. For Vico, as later for Rousseau, primitive language originated as metaphor arising from a passion (joy, sorrow, lust, fear) that was itself based on a prior perception, but not necessarily on a simple need. The first languages were monosyllabic, representing as strictly as possible a direct, worldly connection between words and things. For Vico, language began in what Genette and others have shown to be the delusions of cratylism, but Vico's analysis does not stop there. What originated in necessity remained in convention. As language developed, the flexibility of articulation vitiated the original poetic unity of object, passion, and expression and thus appeared to bar the desires of speech from direct connection with the phenomenal world. In each of mankind's three progressive stages (divine, heroic, vulgar), however, language retained its original core of metaphorical meaning. This layered mound of meanings gives rise to the "scientist's" task: the reinterpretation and assessment of truth in the light of his knowledge of historical experience (1.2.58-60). Because this task must necessarily be performed both in and through discourse, the "new science" can know itself only through systematic knowledge of its own roots. This accounts for the obsession with both mythological rhetoric and temporality which underlies Vichian historiography.

As each metaphor was used, reused, and elaborated, it continued to contain its story even beyond the conscious knowledge of the individual speaker: "ogni metafora sì fatta vien ad essere una picciola favoletta" (2.2.1). This is not simple linguistic determinism. Language can and does shape man's perception of the world, but it is in turn shaped by the speaker himself, whose relation to the signs of speech depends on a particularly Vichian mixture of convention, imagination, and naïveté. Because of primitive man's metaphorical imagination and his ignorance of phenomenal causality, the gods were created to explain the otherwise incomprehensible vicissitudes of the natural environment: "La fantasia tanto è più robusta quanto è più debole il raziocinio" (1.2.26). Natural phenomena (the passage of the sun, changes in vegetation, rain, thunderbolts) thus became the signs in the gods' language. The first mythic tales were grand precisely because of the capacity for wonderment in man's primordial, animistic ignorance: "La maraviglia è figliuola dell'ignoranza; e quanto l'effetto ammirato è più grande, tanto più a proporzione cresce la maraviglia" (1.2.35).[4] Vico may thus be seen not only as the first modern historian but also as the first psychologist of aesthetics after Aristotle. This is true because, unlike Bacon, Vico focused not on rational and conscious creation, but on the fears and desires at the origins of mythic discourse.

In Vico's analysis, precritical man created the gods and, at the same time, through active misapprehension of his own agency, believed in them. On this subject, Vico borrows a formulation from Tacitus: "fingunt simul creduntque" (2.1.1; cf. *Annals* 5.10). Primitive man then instituted a priestly class to preserve and administer the formalized "mysteries" of religion. As the theological age passed to the heroic, Achilles and Ulysses became the archetypal heroes, and Homer eventually took his place as the age's poet.[5] For Vico, mythic thought remained as a mode of perceiving the world and continued to generate discursive forms. However, since both the mode and the forms it engenders are not absolute, but historically and epistemologically dependent, subject to the winds of time, mythic discourse is never amenable to Euhemerism's straightforward, one-step interpretation. Though belief fades with the development of reason, the forms of mythic tales survive in language long after faith devolves into the irony of reflection and skepsis; therefore, the *signatum* can never exhaust the possibilities of the *signans*, and the true referents of language are located in the residue of this inevitable disjunction. Mythology should thus be read as the fully symbolic representation of inner passions, natural phenomena, and, with later corruption, legendary class-symbols, in a comprehensive history of human perception.

The poetic "characters" of this linguistic progression proceed from the "fantastic" universals comprising the languages of the divine and heroic periods to the "vulgarized," articulated particulars of the discourse of the third age, in increasing disruption of the imaginative connection between words and things (4.5-6). In this way, Vico explains the ideological potentials of mythological representation while preserving the necessarily "poetic" nature of both perception and expression. The divine hieroglyphs of the priests' secret language became heroic figures, and these in turn became the words of articulated, vulgar speech. The discourse of the poets representative of each age—Orpheus, Homer, and the "vulgar" poets—embodies this progression, though it is important to note that Vico saw these three types of language as interweaving rather than as merely progressing linearly from one to the next. The original passion hidden in the poetic metaphors of myth ("true narration") is seen to evolve first into the metonymy and synecdoche of more reasoned discourse and eventually into the fully demystified irony of realistic prose, without losing the ideological motivations and the experiential base of each progressive state (1.2.53; 2.2.1-5). In this way, mythic discourse and realistic interpretation are considered as distinct but not fully contradictory operations carried on at two historical moments of perception:

> L'ironia certamente non poté cominciare che da' tempi della reflessione, perch'ella è formata dal falso in forza d'una riflessione che prende maschera di verità. E qui esce un gran principio di cose umane che conferma l'origine della poesia qui scoverta: che i primi uomini della gentilità essendo stati semplicissimi quanto i fanciulli, i quali per natura son veritieri, le prime favole non poterono fingere nulla di falso; per lo che dovettero necessariamente essere . . . vere narrazioni.
>
> Per tutto ciò si è dimostro che tutti i tropi (che tutti si riducono a questi quattro), i quali si sono finora creduti ingegnosi ritruovati degli scrittori, sono stati necessari modi di spiegarsi [di] tutte le prime nazioni poetiche, e nella lor origine aver avuto tutta la loro natia proprietà. . . . E quindi s'incomincian a convellere que' due comuni errori de' gramatici: che 'l parlare de' prosatori è propio, improprio quel de' poeti; e che prima fu il parlare da prosa, dopoi del verso. (2.2.4-5).[6]

According to the *Scienza nuova*, man's separation from the original poetic unity of words and things came not with a single fall, but with a progressive movement into articulated, rational discourse. Again, it is important to note that this movement occurred not only in perception and reason, as though it constituted a prior phenomenon manifested subsequently in speech. Rather, it may also be seen in operation simultaneously *within* mythic discourse, in the knowledge that mankind both intelligently expresses *for* itself and unwittingly hides *from* itself in language. This ambivalence between historical and linguistic determinism, the inability to decide whether history creates language or language creates history, shapes all of Vico's arguments and represents the driving force in his mythologized historicism. This is why myth is central to Vichian analysis, since it is the privileged locus where language and history blend. The single escape hatch in Vico's otherwise closely ordered system turns out to be the ambiguous category of "providence" itself.

In its imaginative richness and theoretical breadth, Vico's work anticipated the bounds not so much of any one school as of the entire range of positions in the nineteenth-century debate over the origins and nature of mythology. This debate centered around two major issues, the source of mythic representation and the workings of the primitive mind. Rather than dwelling on the contradictions of the evolution-diffusion debate, with its welter of deterministic and speculative arguments, we might profit more from outlining a few of the disparate theories of myth's origins. Müller argued that myth arose from the insufficiencies preexistent in discourse itself. The philological slant of Müller's work can be explained in part by the fact that he was a student of Franz Bopp and later of the Sanskrit authority Eugène Burnouf. Unlike Frazer's later contention that mythology was based on homeopathic magic and on primitive man's perceptions of the dying and reviving of the seasonal year, Müller's claim was that the true source of mythic discourse lay in "a disease of language."[7] Müller contended that for the speakers of Proto-Indo-European in the "mythopoeic age," the primary index of both spatial and temporal orientation had been the sun, which provided the main source of metaphors crucial to human communication. As language's potential for abstraction developed (somewhat as in Vico's and in Fichte's analyses), the original meanings of the solar metaphors became contaminated and were finally lost, giving rise to a full-blown mythology developed to explain a secondary linguistic misapprehension.

Müller's naturistic "solar mythology" of paeans to the sun was attacked in his own day by Andrew Lang and others, just as Frazer and his evolutionist adherents quickly found supporters and detractors in a polemically charged atmosphere. Nonetheless, the effects of Müller's and Frazer's doctrines and of their comparative methods have been pervasive in this

century. In reemphasizing the eighteenth-century notion of the epistemological dilemmas inherent in myth's language, Müller revived a field of
investigation which was to become central to twentieth-century linguistics
as well as to psychoanalysis. Although Frazer's theory of the "dying god"
no longer commands the respect it once enjoyed, the emphasis that Frazer
placed on magic and taboo has left noticeable traces in the theory of the
origins of mythology as recently as the Anglo-American ritualist school
of Lord Raglan, Theodore Gaster, and Stanley Hyman.

In an early essay on Claude Lévi-Strauss, Edmund Leach sketched a
method of classifying several modern positions concerning myth's origins.[8]
According to Leach, the ritualists and Jane Harrison (on whose work
many of their premises are based) may be described as "functionalists" in
the "assumption of an intimate and direct association between myth and
social action" and in the belief that "the myth and its associated rite are
. . . two aspects of the same unitary whole." Leach also places Durkheim
and Malinowski in this category, contrasting them with a group he terms
"symbolists" (Frazer, Freud, the young Ernst Cassirer, and, eventually,
Lévi-Strauss), who view myth as "'a thing in itself' without any direct
reference to the social context in which it is told," and who claim that
"the meaning can be discovered from a consideration of the words alone."
In this schema, the functionalists, presumably including the rest of the
later Cambridge school and, more recently, A. R. Radcliffe-Brown, are
those who consider the mythic sign to originate as a contingent representation of *something else* within a particular society (a social custom, a
rite, an economic institution); whereas the "symbolists" claim a special
integrity for the body of mythic signs, which gain their meaning not as
referential adjuncts to temporally specific social phenomena, but from
the dynamic of their own interrelations, themselves originating in, and
predetermined by, the universally "given" organization of the human
mind. Whereas functionalism provides a ready means for analyzing myth
on the level of individual cultures, Leach's symbolism (or, in its recent
avatar, Parisian structuralism) establishes a method for the speculative
reintegration of myth into the overall workings of imaginative discourse.

Each of these approaches has the potential to mitigate the mid-nine-
teenth-century view of myth as a specious, vestigial form of social expression, the remnant of a stage of linguistic and perceptual development
to be destroyed root and branch. This negative conception of the primitive
mind was embodied in the first of Comte's three "états" and had played a
role in Vico's analysis as well, even though Vico's valuation of it was
ambivalent. Such an original dialectician as Marx was unable to free
himself entirely from this view of ancient myth. E. B. Tylor's positivistic
conception of primitive animism, Frazer's homeopathic magic, and Lucien
Lévy-Bruhl's law of participation all shared the common evolutionist
assumption of the precritical and thus inadequate nature of primitive
thought. Even the modern ritualists, in their claim that myth originated

in a necessary connection with an ancient rite, shared this basic assumption. It has only been with postwar structuralism and, specifically, with Lévi-Strauss' *La Pensée sauvage* (1962), that the poles of metaphorical (concrete) and metonymical (abstract) conceptualization have been thoroughly reevaluated, in an open attempt to counter the pervasive prejudice in favor of rational discourse since the eighteenth century (despite periodic Romantic reactions).[9] The advantage of this approach is that it views myth as a mode of thought with a distinct relation to the history of ideologies rather than as merely an immature genre. More recent treatments of myth's origins have thus been able to reassert its value both as a significant object of study and as a specially organized, though not autonomous, body of knowledge.

Leach's functionalist-symbolist opposition should be understood only as a convenience for schematization in a forbiddingly complex field; nevertheless, comparison of these approaches serves to clarify a pair of unresolved difficulties in the study of mythology. One is the methodology of data collection, the other the exact nature of the mythic symbol. Of course, the determination of evidence is important in a field that necessarily deals with "materials" that have been transmitted orally. The functionalist approach entails both the accurate collection of data and its grounding in an individual sociocultural setting that includes additional society-specific phenomena (for the ritualists, for example, this comprises not only the myth but also the performance of the rite that is seen to engender it). At midpoint between functionalist and symbolist methodology stand the positivistic procedures instituted by Tylor and Antti Aarne and continued by Stith Thompson and the "Bloomington school," with the seemingly endless compilation of indexed motifs, carefully collected and catalogued, but not culturally exclusive.[10] Finally, the symbolists, content to cull examples from widely divergent sources in order to demonstrate the universal application of their theories, pay less heed to culturally specific phenomena than do functionalists, and far less to detailed field collection than either functionalism or neopositivism. The result, within Leach's propaedeutic framework, is a gradual move from social and historical to literary analysis, accompanied by increasing emphasis on the *independent* capacity of myth to generate meaning. Of course, eclectic positions combining aspects of both functionalism and symbolism do exist. René Girard's view that myth functions as a displacement from the originary violence of the *real* victimage with which society founds its order is at base a functionalist conception. Yet Girard's treatment of mimetic desire, competition, and ritual is equally applicable in analyzing social *and* literary phenomena.[11]

Now it seems to me that the symbolist approach, by asserting the epistemological independence of the body of mythic signs, and then combining this notion with the assumptions of universality, effectively circumvents the standard typologies of mythic discourse. Although the distinctions between myth, fairy tale, fable, legend, philosophical allegory, romance, parody, a posteriori etiological explanation, political propaganda, and other genres are not denied, their differences are subordinated to their underlying similarity, the presence of the mythic symbol. Unlike the functionalists' view of myth as contingent and directly referential (an approach that lends these genre distinctions special significance), symbolism claims not just the symbol's independence but also its logical unity of meaning. In extreme formulations, the symbolist position regards even the positivistic collection of motifs as futile, since the meaning is generated by the organization of the symbol itself, not by the broader social "motif" that supposedly determines its attributes.

The internal unity of the symbol was precisely the issue that Károly Kerényi used to separate Müller's philological approach from Malinowski's functionalism and that appeared as a basic doctrine in the works of Kerényi's mentor and colleague, C. G. Jung.[12] Again, this is a problem of the origins and referentiality of mythic signs construed within the realm of the symbolic, yet involving both psychological and social questions. According to Jung, the symbols recurrent in myth, dreams, folklore, and delusions arise from archetypes in the collective unconscious. Although Jung at times used the term *motif* to designate the figures and situations he regarded as archetypal, it is important to notice the unified, generative principle involved in Jung's initial idea of the symbol, as opposed to the nongenerative, static conception of the neopositivists and the functionalists' assumptions of dependence and simple external reference. Jung described the archetypes as follows:

> I have not been able to avoid recognizing certain regularities, that is, *types*. There are types of *situations* and types of *figures* that repeat themselves frequently and have a corresponding meaning. I therefore employ the term "motif" to designate these repetitions. Thus there are not only typical dreams but typical motifs in the dreams. These may, as we have said, be situations or figures. Among the latter there are human figures that can be arranged under a series of archetypes, the chief of them being . . . the *shadow*, the *wise old man*, the *child* (including the child hero), the *mother* ("Primordial Mother" and "Earth Mother") as a supraordinate personality ("daemonic" because supraordinate), and her counterpart the *maiden*, and lastly the *anima* in man and the *animus* in woman.[13]

These archetypes, along with a few others Jung mentions elsewhere, find their way into all imaginative discourse via the personal unconscious of the creating subject and, underlying that, the collective unconscious of the race: "I am assuming that the work of art we propose to analyse, as well as being symbolic, has its source not in the *personal unconscious* of the poet, but in a sphere of unconscious mythology whose primordial images are the common heritage of mankind. I have called this sphere the *collective unconscious.*"[14] Jung's analysis thus restores the symbol's referentiality by placing the referent not in society, as the functionalists would, but in the barred realm of the collective unconscious. This description of the archetypes raises two crucial questions: where do the archetypes come from in the first place? and, once they have been established, do they necessarily recur at both collective and personal levels, effectively gaining the status of innate ideas? Jung's account of the origin of the archetypes represented an attempt to answer both these questions by reconciling empiricism with universality:

> The primordial image, or archetype, is a figure—be it a daemon, a human being, or a process—that constantly recurs in the course of history and appears wherever creative fantasy is freely expressed. Essentially, therefore, it is a mythological figure. When we examine these figures more closely, we find that *they give form to countless typical experiences of our ancestors. They are, so to speak, the psychic residua of innumerable experiences of the same type.* They present a picture of psychic life in the average, divided up and projected into the manifold figures of the mythological pantheon. But the mythological figures are themselves products of creative fantasy and still have to be translated into conceptual language. Only the beginnings of such a language exist, but once the necessary concepts are created they could give us an abstract, scientific understanding of the unconscious processes that lie at the roots of primordial images.[15]

The psychic result of these "innumerable experiences of the same type" ("psychischen Residuen unzähliger Erlebnisse desselben Typus") is the institution in each individual of a compelling inner drive to imaginative creation. Though this "irrational force" can be channeled and/or suppressed, it can neither be implanted by education nor destroyed by rationality. Both the basic propensity and the boundaries that limit its activity are inherited rather than learned. Imaginative creation is thus seen not only as pleasing but also as inevitable: "one can withhold the material content of primitive myths from a child but not take from him the need for mythology, and still less his ability to manufacture it for himself."[16] Indeed, it is precisely this type of noncritical and fully "symbolic" artistic creation that produces the most valuable evidence for the inquiry into the functioning of the collective unconscious, since conscious personal artistry "far from making a work of art a symbol, merely turns it into a symptom" (which Jung then polemically leaves to Freud and the ex-master's "purgative methods").[17]

In response to the attacks on the claim of innate ideas, Jung divided his formulation of the archetype into the archetype per se (*primitive Vorlage*) and the "archetypal image" it generates. Jean Piaget has commented on this distinction, claiming that although it clarifies the theoretical underpinnings of the system, it reduces the power of Jung's avowedly symbolist argument;[18] however, the theoretical basis for this type of distinction occurs with a fair degree of consistency throughout Jung's work. Indeed, it was only by this maneuver that Jung could allow for the actual diversity of imaginative creation and at the same time affirm the (re)constructive value of speculative analysis. The following passage dates from 1922:

> There are no inborn ideas, but there are inborn possibilities of ideas that set bounds to even the boldest fantasy and keep our fantasy activity within certain categories: *a priori* ideas, as it were, the existence of which cannot be ascertained except from their effects. They appear only in the shaped material of art as the regulative principles that shape it; that is to say, only by inferences drawn from the finished work can we reconstruct the age-old original of the primordial image.[19]

Beyond the basic equivocation, it was perhaps the hesitancy of this and later explanatory passages which continued to attract critical attention ("Ideen a priori gewissermassen . . . das heisst nur durch Rückschluss"). By making the archetypes derive from "inborn possibilities of ideas" ("angeborene Möglichkeiten von Vorstellungen") rather than from original images, Jung attempted to rejuvenate his theory's symbolist stock by grafting upon it what today we would call a structuralist scion. In certain respects, the "inborn possibilities" now would appear to correspond to the deep-structure "kernels" of Chomskian linguistics. This position does not necessarily negate Jung's occasionally repeated conception of the archetypes as "not whimsical inventions but *autonomous elements* of the unconscious psyche which were there before any invention was thought of."[20] But it does place far greater emphasis both on the structural (and so potentially explicable) organization of the unconscious and on the *relative* freedom of the creating imagination. In this way, the symbolic effects of the archetypal "originals" (themselves the results of the prior "possibilities" of human psychic experience) become fully subject to a posteriori analysis on both the individual and racial levels.

For Jung, the source of human meaning continued to reside in the internalized, self-reproducing, and as yet barred realm of the collective unconscious ("only the beginnings of such a language exist"). Both the primitives' *mana*—the power residing in the unconscious yet externally objectified through psychic projection—and the symbolic language of modern aesthetic creation are expressions of a compelling inner force whose universal essence and empirical attributes resemble an internalized combination of Vichian deities and transcendent, self-perpetuating Platonic forms.

Jung thus maintained the determinism of racial and individual heredity by making the objects of inheritance originally the "possibilities" and only then the archetypal images, while he reasserted the symbol's universality and autonomy by describing its basic structure as *absolutely* universal and its attributes as only *relatively* autonomous. Like Vico and

Rousseau, Jung conceived of mythic discourse as indirectly referential, representing internal passions through the mechanism of metaphors apparently directed toward external objects. However, Jung placed the source of these passions not in the traceable past of the individual's worldly and emotional life, but in the barred prehistory of the race, giving the archetype an origin that is both empirical and psychic, but that is at the same time thoroughly hidden from view. With his repeated claims for the experiential origin of the "roots" of psychic life, Jung opened the door to a method that could have been at once speculative and empirical, open to theoretical inquiry yet grounded in history. But by keeping these origins in a realm from which concrete investigation continued to be blocked, Jung's position remained a willful mystification even in the midst of his attempts to clarify its precepts.

There is a further aspect of Jung's theory of artistic production which needs attention. Although in his writings on art Jung generally preferred to deal with the macrocosmic phenomena of myth and folklore, at times he did turn to consciously individual literary products in order to develop his theories. His conception of the relation between formal art and social life was principally a psychoanalytic version of Hegelian dialectics, with the archetypes providing the charged transition between creation and aesthetic perception. In one respect, however, Jung's theory was surprisingly contemporary, for the relationship between the single artist and his society was seen as predominantly negative:

> The impact of an archetype, whether it takes the form of an immediate experience or is expressed through the spoken word, stirs us because it summons up a voice that is stronger than our own. Whoever speaks in primordial images speaks with a thousand voices. . . .
>
> That is the secret of great art, and of its effect upon us. The creative process, so far as we are able to follow it at all, consists in the unconscious activation of an archetypal image, and in elaborating and shaping this image into the finished work. By giving it shape, the artist translates it into the language of the present, and so makes it possible for us to find our way back to the deepest springs of life. Therein lies the social significance of art: it is constantly at work educating the spirit of the age, *conjuring up the forms in which the age is most lacking. The unsatisfied yearning of the artist reaches back to the primordial image in the unconscious which is best fitted to compensate the inadequacy and one-sidedness of the present.* The artist seizes on this image, and in raising it from deepest unconsciousness he brings it into relation with conscious values, thereby transforming it until it can be accepted by the minds of his contemporaries according to their powers.[21]

In the phenomenology of the origins of modern, fully individual artistic production, the one area that Jung usually felt obliged to leave to the "purgative methods" of Freud and his disciples, Jungian theory hints at the potential richness of its own dialectic. It does so in a theoretical scheme that opens itself both to the modernism of Walter Benjamin and the negative dialects of T. W. Adorno and the Frankfurt School.

It would be inaccurate, then, to maintain that Jung's system was merely a reaction to Freud's insistence on the analysis of the individual subject, that it represented a secondary development rather than an independent theory with an integrity of its own. Nonetheless, for all its avowedly cross-cultural methodology and impressive rhetorical presentation, Jung's discussion of the origins of mythic symbols was neither as incisive nor, finally, as subtle as Freud's. Freud borrowed certain important configurations from mythology (Oedipus, Narcissus, Eros) and reworked others (the primal horde, the band of brothers, the founding of civilization); however, many of his formulations most readily adaptable for the aesthetics of mythic creation occur not in his discussions of society's organization, but in his description of symbol formation itself, and particularly in his theory of dreams.

The analysis of the origins of symbols in *The Interpretation of Dreams* is well known. The manifest content of the dream represents the originally unconscious content adjusted to pass by the psychic barrier of "censorship."[22] Some symbols (sticks, houses, the act of climbing stairs) are so pervasive as to appear universal, in direct "symbolic" (emblematic) relation to specific psychic elements (6.E.350-404). But most of the manifestation in dreams can only be interpreted in strict connection with the history of the individual dreamer. In this way, the signs in the dream include, but are not restricted to, universal symbols. These symbols themselves may be used by the "dream-work" in highly individualized ways. It is only as all the manifest contents come together in interpretation that Freud's analysis, in contrast to Jungian theory, then leads back to the basic unconscious drives (propagation, sustenance) seen as inherent in the race. Although dreams are extremely personal expressions of internal conflicts, these same forces of "unconscious ideation" give rise on a broader social level to folklore, myths, legends, idioms, proverbs, and even jokes (6.E.351). Rather than embodying a mechanical repetition or reflection of a prior symbol, the signs in Freud's theory of the dream stand in a dynamic relation with those tensions—individual and social—that cause their formation. In terms of aesthetics, Freud's theory is thus one of true symbol formation rather than allegorical reproduction, with the few exceptions noted earlier. This is why the rhetorical analysis of the language of dreams remained important even as Freud's theories of psychic organization developed and changed.

All dreams represent "the fulfilment of a wish" (2.121), creating pleasure by reducing excitation and protecting the dreamer's sleep (7.E.588-609). Libidinal energy is thus dissipated, but not destroyed. For Freud, as opposed to Jung, the interpersonal psychic struggle itself, and not an archetypal image, represents the origin of the symbol's meaning. Symbols are thus formed and re-formed by the individual psyche rather than repeated as mere reflections of a body of collectively shared imagery.

The dream's perception and subsequent recollection (its "text") may be endlessly complicated by "secondary revision,"[23] but the basic mechanisms of representation, beyond direct symbolism, are only two: condensation and displacement (6.A-B.279-309). *Condensation* is the creation of a single, combined formation in the place of previously contradictory elements, whereas *displacement* is the progression along a chain of signifiers individually linked by similar attributes but, in terms of psychic energy, "overdetermined" and so imbalanced one to another (6.B.307-8). These active transformations, carried on within the individual psyche and entailing necessary difference, give the manifest content its symbolic form. This is how Freud explains the depth and force of symbolic representation without resorting to an absolutely barred or transcendent origin.

As has been suggested in various reassessments of Freud's work, his terminology can be divided fairly easily into primary rhetorical figures. The principal means of psychic representation are metaphor (condensation) and metonymy (displacement), with the supplementary additions of allegory (direct symbolism) and irony (reversal, or representation by opposites). Although allegorical symbolism is most common in myth proper and other types of cultural representation (6.E.351), and outright reversal is only occasionally present in dreams, all of these figures are constantly available in the production of each form of imaginative discourse. Therefore, figural representation invariably refers to its source in the unconscious, but in disguised and ambiguous ways. Vico's rhetorical analysis of discourse's historical development is thereby refocused within the generating faculty of the individual psyche. What the dream represents on the individual level, the myth repeats on the level of society, though with broader use of direct symbolism and in more polished form, as has been described in Otto Rank's description of the birth of the hero, Ernest Jones's and K. R. Eissler's analyses of *Oedipus* and *Hamlet*, and Melanie Klein's discussion of the *Oresteia*.[24] Like representation in dreams, mythic discourse may thus be seen to express and momentarily placate the deepest struggles of the psyche in its relationship with the world, but only through illusion, fabrication, and indirection.

Despite continuing debate over the content of the theories of Freud, his work on the origin and the mechanisms of psychic representation remains invaluable for literary and linguistic analysis. It is, however, important to note that even as he denied the presence of a "collective unconscious" beyond the level of the individual unconscious, Freud was unable to refute the existence of an origin of meaning external to the locus of the individual psyche. He simply placed that meaning in the structures of bourgeois society itself and thereby kept alive myth's historical potential for both internal *and* external reference. The entire question of Freud's

"Oedipal" historiography of individual development is currently the subject of a great deal of research in both psychoanalysis and anthropology. Nonetheless, even if Oedipus and the oppositions his story embodies turn out to be the Viennese doctor's hypostatization of patriarchal, willfully rational, family-centered man, the methods of expression available to the psychic apparatus may nonetheless remain intact, subject to energy generated from fully new social oppositions and organized according to different priorities. Indeed, this is one explanation for the constantly renewing force of myth, which has originated radically new forms in every culture at the same time as it has revitalized and recoded older ones. The primitive cult figures, the Olympian deities, the Judeo-Christian heroes, and even the recent figures of political and cultural legend may thus be seen to represent the same indestructible drive to symbolic expression on a level that strives toward timelessness, idealization, and universal truth.

In this way, contemporary criticism may understand mythic discourse as originating not in opposition to the seemingly demystified worldly knowledge of realism, but in interaction with it, in an ideological tandem involving the history of perception and expression. Both myth and realism may then be seen to represent fictional modes as well as special genres of literary products. This position obviates the facile, allegorical reading of myth's signs which would rob the mode of mythic discourse of its power to *create* meaning as well as to reflect it. In narrative fiction, the transcendent fullness of myth, which locates its significance not in the world of time and matter, but in a realm beyond temporal and spatial limitation, thus complements the worldly plenitude of the realist sign, as it recodes on an idealized level what realist representation codes on the material one. Realism's dependence on the conventions of shared worldly knowledge mixes with myth's requirement of shared belief in a transcendent system of signs. While both myth and realism claim exclusive ethical and epistemological validity within their separate spheres, neither can hide its roots in the realm of the other, though each is driven to attempt this subterfuge by the inner logic of its own system. The oppositions of truth and falsehood may finally be seen at work within the representation of *both* the real and the mythic. In the novel, this complex lie at the beginning of fictional discourse becomes a means of organizing a version of truth which claims to be worldly and transcendent, empirical and imaginative, equally capable of reflecting and generating meaning. This intricate play of illusion is given constantly renewed life by the same initial disjunction between words and things, subject and object, from which the originating desire of all discourse springs.

3

The Interaction
of Realism and Myth

Mythic and realistic discourse each have a privileged moment in cultural history (the early stages of social communion for myth; the nineteenth century for classical European realism), and each have a special stance toward the material environment (transcendence; immersion) as well as a favored trope ("poetic" metaphor; "analytic" metonymy). Of course, realism and myth have often been treated as separate modes or genres,[1] but the important point for literary analysis is the combination of realism and myth, each of which may be seen as necessarily operative on all levels of narrative, though with radically different emphasis in every historical period. Each may be seen as a *mode* of discourse (realist or mythic) which, when preponderant, produces a recognizable *genre* of literary product. Moreover, it must be remembered that realism and myth are aesthetic categories and that only by understanding them both in terms of symbolicity can we recover their workings in reality.

Attempts have not been lacking in recent studies to distinguish the means by which the logical possibilities preceding narrative elements combine to form complete fictional discourse. These schemes have placed unnecessary weight on either the semantic apsects of the literary sign, such as Jung's archetypes, which spring into literature with a full-blown vocabulary all their own, or on the syntactics of organization, such as the formalists' functions or the structuralists' "isotopies," which may appear to produce meaning solely from their interrelations within the text. The utility of this second kind of analysis, like the first, has often been demonstrated in literary criticism. Unless it is carried. on in a critically evaluated context, however, this kind of analysis leads to a reification of the text itself and thus vitiates the force of history. Our investigations might profit, then, from focusing on the ways in which symbols are created within a culture's self-perception and then re-created in narrative as the motivated energy-source of desire is "re-entelechized" in fantasy to produce meaning in social and literary discourse.

41

As aspects of the ideological constructs of both perception and expression, mythic and realistic components precede the text, though they only become operational as literary elements in the process of re-creation within the narrative itself. In this way, literary discourse may be seen as only one aspect of society's presentation and necessary misapprehension of itself; but it remains true that such discourse has a unique relation to the fabric of social life in both validity and knowledge. These two types of components, when combined in different measure and accompanied by varying degrees of belief, may be seen at work in all forms of fictional narrative, from myth, tale, legend, and saga, to the comic-book story and the novel, as well as in the ritualized presentation of professional sports, advertising, and political campaigns.[2] Establishment of the criteria for distinguishing between forms thus becomes a matter of logical and affective organization rather than determination of a progression along an increasingly valorized line of development, since both the components and the energy organizing them are necessarily anterior to literary (though not to aesthetic) form.[3]

The components of both myth and realism fall within the major categories of time and space, character and plot, and belief. Although historical consideration of audience response is of most importance in the category of belief, in which it is coded into the text, the influence of history itself may be seen as operative in every category and at all levels of narrative organization. Indeed, in much of the extended narrative of the nineteenth and early twentieth centuries, the intratextual metaphor of history, grounded in the consciousness and experience of the central characters, provides a basic transition between the text's mythic and realistic components.

Briefly, then, mythic components are those repeating elements of narrative which approach an existence apart from the specificity of space and time, which at their core involve unified and idealized figures, and which establish and depend upon a relationship of unquestioning belief. By contrast, realistic components are made up of those elements that claim a clear and definite position in space and time (and so in culture), that involve figures whose relation to experience is not idealized, and that invite an attitude of analysis or even skepticism rather than immediate faith. Again, the central interest of literary aesthetics lies not in the discrete and thus distorted functioning of these two series of elements, but in the dynamics of their requisite interaction.

From the outset, realist discourse assumes the possibility of worldly representation. Realism's attempt to capture the "true to life" aspects of a constantly shifting society accounts for the revolutionary power of its program. This attempt also gives rise, however, to its vulnerability as a relative phenomenon, new and different, but only in relation to what has gone before. Since Socrates' critique in book 10 of the *Republic*, the willful conflation of the categories of the real and the true, coupled with either positive or negative valuation, has been a favorite strategy of realism's detractors as well as of its advocates (Zola is a primary case in point). When valorized, this maneuver indicates the importance realism places on being in the world, which is also demonstrated in the worldly plenitude coded into the realist sign. To put this in other terms, the world of matter and sense is seen as possessing meaning, and language is considered capable of reproducing its significance. This distinctive plenitude finds expression in all of the elements of realistic presentation: linguistic, material/physical, historical, moral/cultural, psychological, and attitudinal. The first three of these groups of elements deal primarily with expression and thus make up the criteria for mimesis, whereas the last three stress full cultural perception and so create the effects of verisimilitude.

Under the auspices of an overarching narrative voice, linguistic realism may spread throughout the narrative. In other cases, it may be limited to certain characters or groups either in dialogue or, through the *style indirect libre*, in descriptive passages. This includes slang and regional dialects, since any class in a particular society will have characteristic means of expression of thought and feeling as well as a distinguishing discursive register. It is important to note that dialects provide a central link in the realist text between individuated idiolects and the communal formulae of myth. Once the parameters of linguistic presentation have been established, however, realism tends not to call attention to the text's language as such, but instead to the shifts in individual character or class that varying idiolects and group registers indicate (as witnessed, for example, by Flaubert's programmatic self-effacement of the position of the narrator in relation to the characters he portrays). Language is thus seen as the tool with which the shared meaning of the real world is reproduced in narrative discourse, a crucial yet dependable transition between perception and expression rather than a problematic agency with its own epistemological ambiguity. This might seem to put a premium on linguistic "competence" instead of artistic virtuosity. However, realism's drive to portray the true life of the present, or of the carefully delimited past, makes accurate representation of linguistic phenomena a part of its worldly program and thus a fully valued goal rather than a mere means to an end. Since language is at one and the same time a part of the represented world and the sole means of representation, realism tends to reestablish the narrator's virtuosity through indirect means, such as irony or conscious linguistic refinement, even as it claims to restrict his task to direct narration.

The representation of the material/physical environment, the "naïve realism" of the world of matter and sense, is accomplished through precise attention to spatial and temporal measurement, consistency in naming, and ordered presentation of descriptive detail. Ideological motivations are betrayed within the realist text's principles of selecting and ordering descriptive inventories, just as they may be traced in the spatial and temporal organization of setting and "scene." Despite realism's polemical claims of objectivity, material objects, natural and made, carry symbolically charged significance even in the most objective realist presentations. At the same time, the standard realist emphasis on vision as the privileged faculty of perception demonstrates the ideological conservatism inherent in realism's programmatic depiction of the mirrored surface of the world as it is. This conservatism is also evident in nineteenth-century realism's attempts to represent that world as an ordered universe in which characters and even whole environments predictably reappear and in which the laws of time and matter are always in force (in opposition to Brecht's realism, which claims to be true precisely because its universe is ordered and *moving*).[4]

The distinctively historical aspects of realistic presentation include the institutions that make up and regulate social life: military, legal, political, economic, and academic institutions, as well as class organization and the forms of labor in a particular period. The narrative may demonstrate knowledge of any or all of these on either a superficial or deep (and so possibly ironic) level; however, once the bounds of knowledge have been set within the narrative, realism attempts not to overstep them. The reason for this caution is that if such transgression were sustained, it would entail potentially fantastic interpretations of the depicted world. As in all elements of realist presentation, historical realism thus tends to draw the reader into the authentic and in some ways familiar world of the narrative, inducing him at times to forget his position of exteriority and its accompanying potential for criticism in relation to the text. Even in seemingly objective literary description, history thus becomes a determined part of nature and is idealized.

The moral and cultural elements of realistic presentation function on diegetic as well as mimetic levels. They serve to create the verisimilitude of social behavior as well as that of culturally realistic plotting. It is important to note, however, that realistic representation is only one aspect of character behavior and plotting (Herodotus's version of realistic representation as opposed to Thucydides'), since mythic components also affect the plots of even the most realistic narratives, lending them an aura of unified necessity rather than randomness or contingency.[5] Whereas historical realism depicts the institutions of a society, moral and cultural realism demonstrates the ways in which society and individuals react to those institutions. In addition, it is important to note that cultural motivation, fully as much as the confusion of history and fiction itself, necessarily represents an ongoing puzzle constructed and reconstructed among the motivated perceptions of the fiction's producer, the divergent claims of historical representation, and the shifting social norms of the audience.

The development of psychological realism, which plays a central role in conceptions of the novel as divergent as those of Auerbach, Frye, Watt, and Lukács, represents the principal discovery of eighteenth- and nineteenth-century realistic narrative. The emphasis on the individual subject, seen as belonging to—yet in conflict with—his own society, shifts the locus of presentation progressively deeper inside the characters. This shift, accompanied by the established narrative techniques of long-range focus, slowed pace, and prolonged suspense, permits realistic narrative's presentation of internal psychological processes. It is important, however, that this kind of presentation is not so much a function of mimesis as of verisimilitude, because the accuracy of psychological depiction is a matter of convention just as much as that of social behavior and is therefore fully subject to ideological motivation in regard to perception and expression. It is also important that the realist novel's emphasis on psychological development does not result in total separation of the fictional subject from his society, since mental processes themselves, especially in the nineteenth century, are seen as both individual and socially shared phenomena.

In terms of attitude, realism has two crucial moments. The first of these occurs with the narrative's portrayal of worldly knowledge as valuable in itself, independent of any connection with a transcendent realm. The second appears initially as an outgrowth of the first, a logical extension that begins as a difference in degree but ends as a difference in kind. As empirical knowledge itself becomes valuable—a process that occurs in a world of material and social flux and in which this type of knowledge can lead to appreciable gain—the very function of knowing begins to take itself as its own subject. The source of life's meaning is then seen to reside in the self-consciously controlled will of the individual subject. As Foucault has demonstrated, this process begins to occur throughout Europe during the late Renaissance. It can, however, be traced in the economically and socially advanced regions of the south, such as Boccaccio's Florence, as early as the fourteenth century. In literature as in life, the rise of competitive capitalism may thus be seen to create solitary, apparently self-sufficient individuals, and not vice versa. Realism's inquiry, then, may lead both to self-consciousness and to self-doubt, instilling in realistic narrative the epistemological disturbance of irony. As long as the irony is openly controlled, this disturbance is not the end of worldly investigation, but a function inherent in realism's program from its inception. Indeed, it is this very development that permits realism's discourse to continue by opening a space for increasingly knowledgeable narration, as demystification itself becomes both the "spontaneous" origin and the programmatic goal of realistic presentation. Again, though this procedure moves the realist text ever further from the world of shared experience which produced it and which it claims to depict, it does not finally entail cutting the worldly ties seen as both anterior and necessary.

Among other possibilities, the destructive/recuperative functions of irony may find their locus in the persona of the narrative voice (as in *Emma*, or in certain of Boccaccio's novelle); in an identified narrator (Conrad's Marlowe, Hemingway's Jake Barnes); within a principal character (Pirandello's Mattia Pascal); in disjunctive arrangement of ironically contrasting narrative segments (such as the inserted stories in the *Princesse de Clèves*); or in conflicting attitudes embedded within the *style indirect libre* (as in *Madame Bovary*). These are, of course, very general descriptions of irony's subtle and extensive functioning in such narratives. In any case, realism's irony protects the validity of the pursuit of knowledge by building essential uncertainty into its program from the beginning. Indeed, it is only through acceptance of the fundamental ambiguity of time and chance that realism can reassert its interest in preparation for the future through knowledge of the present, as well as its continuing allegiance to the values that gave birth to its inquiries in the first place. All this occurs in a world seen as constantly changing, and in which the present itself is merely a contingent development in the finally unknowable progression of time, of metonymy's continual difference.[6] The seeming spontaneity of irony (as opposed to full satire) thus represents the recurrent hedge that permits realism's worldly bet to continue, just as the constancy of tacit belief protects the temporal sleight of hand of myth.[7]

Although myth is strategically subordinated in realism, its influence is nonetheless pervasive. Its idealized realm influences the conventional abstractions of material environment, institutional organization, and social behavior; however, myth's most important effects on the formal presentation of the realist text may be found in verbal register, plotting, and character configuration. In this way, myth, too, contributes to narrative's distinctive unity of voice, action, and character. Its presence may be indicated within the text by direct reference to, or even by piecemeal adoption of, myth proper, as in Eliot's "mythical method" and similar approaches.

But the effects of myth go much further than this. Freud's writings on the subject of mythic perception were scattered and at times ambiguous in their approach; though suggestive, they never came together in a full discussion of the symbolicity in human communication. Nonetheless, in a passage describing the "omnipotence of thoughts" in his essay, "The 'Uncanny'" (1919), he came closest within his system to accounting for the continual force of mythic discourse, seen as operative on all levels of social life:

Our analysis of instances of the uncanny has led us back to the old, animistic conception of the universe . . . characterized by the idea that the world was peopled with the spirits of human beings; by the subject's narcissistic over-valuation of his own mental processes; by the belief in the omnipotence of thoughts and the technique of magic based on that belief; by the attribution to various outside persons and things of carefully graded magical powers, or *"mana"*; as well as by all the other creations with the help of which man, in the unrestricted narcissism of that stage of development, strove to fend off the manifest prohibitions of reality. It seems as if each one of us has been through a phase of individual development corresponding to this animistic stage in primitive men, that none of us has passed through it without preserving certain residues and traces of it which are still capable of manifesting themselves.[8]

One aspect of this animistic state, seen as culturally anterior, but re-capitulated and then potentially reactivated in the life of each individual, is the compulsion to repeat. This has been recognized as a key element in the ontology of mythic expression at least since Plato and has recently been discussed by Mircea Eliade and Lévi-Strauss, among others.[9] For Freud, the need to repeat occurs not just in relation to pleasurable experiences, but to seemingly painful ones as well. This argument recalls Kierkegaard's, except that for Freud repetition is not so much a matter of moving forward as backward, not only a process but also an instinct. In *Beyond the Pleasure Principle* (1920), after describing the "compulsion to repeat" as instinctual, Freud notes that instincts themselves may be seen as "an expression of the *conservative* nature of living substance" (*SE* 18:36; emphasis in the original).[10] This does not mean, however, that repetition is strictly passive and negative. Despite the appearance of de-structiveness and withdrawal, the instincts are protective mechanisms designed to reassert active control over the external environment in place of passive submission to the unknown. This phenomenon involves both temporal and ontological inversion: *"an instinct is an urge inherent in organic life to restore an earlier state of things* which the living entity has been obliged to abandon under the pressure of external disturbing forces; that is, it is a kind of organic elasticity, or, to put it another way, the expression of the inertia inherent in organic life" (*SE* 18:36, emphasis in the original).[11]

Freud's critique of human perception—which appears to proceed forward by willfully reintegrating the external reality of time and chance into stable modes of consciousness which are always prior—is antici-pated, in a section added in 1915 to the *Three Essays on the Theory of Sexuality* (1905), by an equally radical reassessment of "the instinct for knowledge" (*SE* 7:194). Repetitive childhood "research" is defined as a "sublimated manner of obtaining mastery," spurred by previous libidinal energy in the child's drive to express and understand his own sexuality (here related to scopophilia). In Freud's later formulations, the instinct for mastery through knowledge becomes intertwined with the compulsion to repeat, in a procedure designed not to confront the "disturbing forces" in the "manifest prohibitions of reality," but to subsume them within the ego.

Since man is physically unable to exist on his own for an extended period after birth (in sharp contrast to other animals), he learns to live in a world in which he is both dependent and vulnerable. Even mature, apparently "rational" self-protection, on both individual and social levels, entails the continual reworking in fantasy of the patently grandiose aspects of the story of Narcissus. Man thus takes not only the self and others but all of external reality to be constantly recurring images in the service of a being seen as safe because both *whole* and *prior*.[12] In a fundamental way, the increasing accumulation of worldly knowledge serves to reinforce and repeatedly authenticate that story, the protective structure man depends upon in order to live in the world, since the fiction is begun and continually reenacted not only with perception and judgment but also with social knowledge itself. To put this another way, as Peter Brooks has pointed out in regard to Freud's text, just as desire entails temporality, so Freudian knowledge depends on the basic repetition of "plot."[13] Although it is important to remember the profoundly deterministic cast of much of Freud's thought, his analysis of the organization of human knowledge and perception remains invaluable in understanding myth's means of representation and its power to frame our conception of life itself.

In terms of temporal development, myth attempts to freeze the metaphorical moment and then to repeat it in ritualized circularity. It thereby adds the certainty of future promise through connection with a signifying object embodying a truth that is unchallengeable because already past. Mythic discourse thus depends on the illusion of a temporality that is fixed yet predictably mobile (in the cyclical repetition of metaphorical identity, or "condensation"), as opposed to the incrementally progressive repetitions of Romance or the seemingly linear "displacement" of realism's metonymy. In this way, mythic narrative possesses a privileged means of structuring and emphasizing its discourse: reiteration in recurrent cycles. There is, furthermore, a preexistent force that denies the necessary difference of repetition in favor of identity through the temporal legerdemain of willful blindness masquerading as knowledge. This force is faith itself. As Enrico Castelli has described, the ancient Greeks' *mythos* thus represents the

> racconto di una continua richiesta dell'evento sovrannaturale nell'invocazione che prende corpo attraverso il contatto con un oggetto che continua la narrazione senza data. Una storia fuori di un tempo determinabile è un "sempre" sui generis, perché è dell'origine, il *sempre stato* che non può essere significativo di un *per sempre*, ma della insufficienza originaria. Un altro aspetto dell' infallibilità sacra.[14]

Again, it is precisely in what Castelli terms the "insufficienza originaria," filled by the primeval *horror vacui*, that the mythic sign establishes its true referent. This referent is found in the Vichian residue of mythic discourse created by the inevitable insufficiency of the *signatum*, which can approach but never exhaust the *signans*. Each rebeginning appears as another approach to that universal and timelessly valid origin. As in Freud's description of the "animistic" stage of individual perception, Castelli's analysis demonstrates the manner in which social myth promises the future and sanctifies the contemporary by repeatedly locating its truth in a realm whose "present" is perpetually pure because always past ("il *sempre stato*"). Because of their dependence on repetition and belief, myths tend to be more culturally specific than fairy tales, which do not require groups of the devout in order to perpetuate the internal meaning of their conventions.[15] Although myths may, and often do, live on as tales, such perpetuation is accomplished only through a radical shift in the relationship between the myths and the audience that creates them.

Though not known for its theoretical formulations, ego psychology has developed a series of crucial distinctions between myth and its generic companion, the fairy tale. Bruno Bettelheim distinguishes between myth and fairy tale in both content and plot structure. According to Bettelheim, myth is made up of easily allegorized god-heroes who inhabit a realm unattainable to human beings.[16] Their stories are pessimistic and end in tragedy, as Géza Róheim has also pointed out, and thus embody the negative strictures of the Freudian conscience, or superego.[17] By contrast, Bettelheim describes the fairy tale as representing the integrating powers of the developing ego, involving figures who display important elements from everyday life and whose stories end happily. The fairy tale thus entices its audience into the complexities of the phenomenal world, whereas the myth counsels the futility of dealing with the true nature of that world, except through specially ritualized practices and, most importantly, through tacit faith. In this way, the tale begins and ends in speech, the myth in silence.

Although both genres embody contradictions active in the unconscious mind, myths treat these issues on the broadest level of social organization and interdiction, whereas fairy tales take them up as constituent parts of a single personality in the midst of a laborious initiation into social life. While mythic elements combine to represent a full set of social prohibitions, the components of the fairy tale come together to make up just one psyche. Myth thus elicits awe; fairy tale invites identification. On the level of character, mythic figures are idealized and barred, supplying the answers that claim to lead the devout out of the world, whereas those of the fairy tale are symbolically "realized" and accessible, posing the questions that draw listeners into the world. Both types of figure are incomplete and demand energetic elaboration within the imagination of the participating audience, but one type is a partial formation only in its forebodingly superhuman unity of traits, while the other is incomplete in its subhuman (or, more accurately, childish) lack of cognitive and affective development. Though both myth and fairy tale may adopt supernatural devices, the former portrays these as normative aspects of its world, whereas the latter depicts them as special privileges on loan from another realm. As a narrative form, the tale thus represents a movement away from the apparent purity of myth, a rudimentary step toward the worldly complexity of the novel.

It is not surprising, then, as the theories of Adorno and Max Horkheimer suggest, that society may be typified in standardized myths that turn the *boundaries* of partially perceived sexual and temporal vulnerability (incest, eternal omnipotence) into authenticated yet proscribed strengths. Myths serve, then, as the illustrative yet protective reminders of the *hidden* violence and the ritualized limits past which social man, in real life, may not go.[18] It should not disturb us that, in certain periods, knowledge of material reality itself takes on the fetishistic value of myth, as it does occasionally in Boccaccio's novelle as well as in Balzac and Zola. Indeed, this is one way of understanding Lévi-Strauss's *bricoleur*, to whom any concrete object at hand, no matter how random or how mundanely "real," can be seen as endowed with special significance through its revealed relationship with a source whose realm is transcendent, but only partially barred, and to which the now fully symbolic object provides an empirical bridge.[19] The apparently empty neutrality of the material object is thus filled with energy from the perceiving subject, who, through ritualized misapprehension of his own position as creator, invests that energy with the unifying power of supernatural meaning.[20] Within the order of the "omnipotence of thoughts," the most real objects may thus be seen to be the most radiantly symbolic as well, traces of absent transcendence ritually reinvested with an aura of authenticity *first* coded and *then* perceived by the initiated or, in terms of Freud's argument, the repeatedly self-initiated subject.

The myth thus serves to protect the subject by ideologically focusing his perceptions of reality's otherwise threatening chaos, endowing the objects of those perceptions with an origin *in illo tempore* and a story that forever approaches the perfect knowledge that is at once silence and stasis, man's continual beginning in desire and his perpetually repeated end. The mythic symbol, then, does link the unknown with the known, but it does so only through constant regress, by forever effacing both the conventionality and the worldly contingency of its sign, as may be seen in Boccaccio's and Zola's seemingly unconscious incorporation of standard mythoi into their most realistic narratives. It is from the traces of this maneuver that both the speaking subject and the myth he tells are formed, in a constant process of symbolic re-creation. In this way, social knowledge necessarily precedes individual perception, which is indeed only a handmaiden to the prior faculty, itself spurred by energy from an unconscious source not its own. The basic symbolic oppositions that organize mythic narrative thus represent a reworking of materials whose prototypes must be sought in discourse but not in literature, precisely because they are first formed by the driving desires of the unconscious only to be re-created within the forms of literature. In this way, as Vico saw, even myth leads back to history — to the perceived origins, nature, and destiny of man, in the processes of initiation and cyclical renewal — but it does so in necessarily devious and ambiguous ways.[21]

In terms of linguistic register, the mythic knowledge that society has "always" possessed is depicted in the realist text through a privileged means of expression, the proverb. The prenarrative oppositions giving rise to mythic discourse are thus transformed to be reembodied in the simple oppositions of proverbial speech, the one type of verbal expression that is in essence communal, sanctified, and "timeless."[22] Mythic characters are idealized types representing fundamental but grandiose and impossibly unified anthropomorphic qualities. They reflect the primary oppositions of life-death, male-female, self-other, rational-irrational (culture-nature), and ruler-ruled (class organization). These oppositions are split among mythic figures and then reorganized and linked with necessary tasks to form the functional polarities in developed narrative. As in Vico's and in Saussure's conceptions of the enduring metaphors constantly recoded in discourse, mythic characters (those of classical Greece as much as those of Asia, Africa, and America) are made up of prior components that are realized and perpetuated in the narrative.

As combinations of preexisting elements, mythic characters carry their own stories, which they set in motion to be completed in narrative through repetition, modification, or opposition, as in Frye's four master mythoi or even Claude Bremond's elaboration of possible roles.[23] Because of the cyclical unity of mythic plotting, it is important to note that patterned mythic components combine with the apparent contingency of realism to create the full effects of verisimilitude; and, in this sense, the *vraisemblance* of unified plotting can be seen as a matter of both cultural motivation and literary convention. Nonetheless, once the components of myth have been established, the narrative is free to play within their bounds and is therefore capable of creating genuinely new and intentional combinations even while working with a limited number of basic models.

Through modification of Roman Jakobson's analysis of the various levels of discourse, it is possible to describe five major levels on which mythic and realistic components combine to form the narrative, grouped within the three broad divisions of narration, plot, and character.[24]

Division into five levels is, of course, an aid in conceptualization rather than a formula. It must not be forgotten how complicated the passage from theory back into critical practice always is. The goals of such a schema must remain expansiveness and flexibility rather than the creation of rigid compartments. These five levels, with their realistic and mythic components, are shown in Figure 1.

Figure 1.

Narrative Division	Discursive Levels	Myth	Realism	Principal Components
Narration	Textual Surface	Repeated Formulae	Environmental Specificity	Tone _____ Mimesis
Plot	Full Plot	Aesthetic Unity	Cultural Motivation	Verisimilitude _____ Diegesis
	Phrases	Belief	Skepsis	Textual Attitudes _____ Character Interaction
Character	Individual Characters	Idealized	Individuated	Social/ Psychological
	Logical Elements	Prenarrative Oppositions		"Phonemes/ Morphemes"

The primary elements (narrative "phonemes" and "morphemes") that precede the level of individual characters represent the basic prenarrative oppositions described earlier. These same oppositions, though with constantly varying emphasis, give rise to the aesthetic components of both myth and realism. In the narrative, these elements come together to make up the psychologically individuated characters, which may nonetheless be fully developed or merely sketched, complex or simple, "round" or "flat."[25] The "phrases" within narrative action come about as characters begin to interact with each other and their environment in the key moments of narrated exchange: discussion, deceit, sex, and violence. Textual attitudes are created and reinforced in faith, or countered in irony and parody, by the progressive development of these phrases. This progression eventually gives rise to the articulated sentences of the plot in the full force of the historical, cultural, and literary influences that contribute both to plotting and to its perception by the reader. The surface of the narrative includes all of the lexical elements, which combine to form the anthropomorphic "voice" and tones, or verbal attitudes, of discursive narration, along with the overt notation of environmental detail (psychological and social as well as material/physical).

It is worth reemphasizing that realist narrative begins and proceeds only through the combination of the basic components of myth and realism on all five of these levels, which are themselves constantly interacting to produce full narrative discourse. As in Otto Jespersen's original conception of "shifters," the delicate game of realistic fiction achieves its fullest effects during the vertigo of uncertainty as both the text and the reader are required to guide the narrative through its transitional moments.[26] In realism, such moments occur at precisely the points of intersection as mythic and realistic elements come together to form the seemingly self-accreting monster that is fictional discourse. As though by conflation of the two positions in Plato's *Cratylus*, the language of realism is thus both natural and conventional, displaying its dependence on the everyday world and on the realm of aesthetic convention. It is perhaps not surprising, then, that at the hinges of history we find myth, just as surely as we recover history's code through—and only through —myth's enduring power.

4

The Ideology of Form in Verga's "La Lupa": Realism, Myth, and the Passion of Control

As a literary movement, realism came later to Italy than to France or England. Doubtless, the slower development of the middle-class reading public and the lack of a unified tradition of national journalism—not to mention a national spoken language—contributed to this tardiness. By the 1870s, however, Italian *verismo* was taking form in the same crucible of polemic and counterpolemic that typified literary and philosophical debates throughout the rest of nineteenth-century Europe.[1]

Luigi Capuana's manifesto, *Il teatro italiano contemporaneo*, appeared in 1872, although Capuana had composed many of the essays it contained in the 1860s in his capacity as drama critic for the Florentine newspaper, *La nazione*. In Italy, interest in realism rose steadily. Verga's *Nedda*, the "bozzetto siciliano" that inaugurated *verismo*'s Sicilian *stil novo*, was published in Milan in 1874. *Vita dei campi* appeared six years later. "La Lupa" was the second novella in the collection.[2]

It is true that the novella's natural descriptions are generalized and very brief, betraying the use of the "scissors" which drew D. H. Lawrence's objections.[3] Moreover, the language has been homogenized into the standard forms of the recently unified kingdom, purged of the local expressions of *Nedda* and even the few remaining Sicilianisms of "Cavalleria rusticana" (the collection's opening narrative). Nonetheless, at its appearance "La Lupa" was regarded as so strikingly realistic as to be utterly unlike its predecessors in nineteenth-century Italian fiction. Indeed, Capuana, Verga's Sicilian friend and *verismo*'s most active polemicist, claimed to have had personal knowledge of the central character. Capuana later bestowed upon this story, one of his favorites, the borrowed badge of French Naturalism's programmatic approval: "*La Lupa* si potrebbe dire un semplice *fatto diverso*."[4]

Depicting character interaction and plot as deriving from the culturally influenced perceptions and desires of the central characters is a primary strategy of realist narrative. The utilization of unified mythic components to shape the novella on both diegetic and discursive levels serves realism's

54

ends, as a method of reinforcing the ideological foundations of its discourse. In general, Verga's narrative furnishes especially useful examples of the dynamics of this combination, thanks both to his technical mastery and his choice of subject matter. Nineteenth-century Sicily remained one of the places in Europe where in the minds of the populace, as well as in the image presented to the outside world, even the old myths seemed to retain a measure of their power. "La Lupa" is therefore an especially relevant text for realist aesthetics not despite, but because of, its depiction of *meridionale* passion and the extraordinarily basic nature of the oppositions that organize it. The reader has access to the network of mythic elements only through their necessary combination with the components of realism.

Though the specifically Sicilian aspects of Verga's narration have been suppressed or, more accurately, translated into literary Italian, all evidence of the justly renowned *siculità* has not been removed from the surface of the text. As in the narratives following "La Lupa," Verga's language has undergone only a partial transformation from regional caste to national class, retaining in literary discourse the remnants of generally *meridionale* popular and rural linguistic register on the level of lexicon ("*gnà* Pina . . . una *lupacchiotta* . . . lingua a *strasciconi*," pp. 145-48), as well as grammar and syntax ("Cosa *gli* date a vostra figlia Maricchia? . . . Andrò dal brigadiere, *andrò*," pp. 146-47). This slight shift in emphasis is also evident in the proverbs embedded within the narration, which appear as normalized versions of locally characteristic figures of thought.[5]

The partial nature of this transformation is important. Even though the forms are standardized, the knowledge that the proverbs express is presented as especially Sicilian, as both the methods of temporal reference ("fra vespero e nona," pp. 146-47) and the tacit belief in the supernatural ("il diavolo quando invecchia," p. 146) indicate. In this way, Verga manages to broaden the area of his subject matter without losing the aura of authenticity in terms of specific populace as well as moral precept. In Verga's text, both regional and class elements are thus presented as contributing factors in narrative representation. Neither class nor region is finally determinant, however, since human destiny is seen as universal and prior to all categories of individual existence and action, including, as we shall see, literary narration itself.

Whereas physical and material details are not lacking in the story, there is only a trace of the photographic accuracy that linked *verismo* to other European realist programs, such as Zola's Naturalism and late nineteenth-century schools of painting. When particular mimetic details do appear, they are unfailingly turned back into the symbolic framework of the story. In this way, the notation of the "seno fermo e vigoroso da bruna" functions initially as a marker of class and sexuality rather than as primarly personal individuation, and the realistic redness of the "labbra fresche e rosse" leads to the openly symbolic "papaveri rossi"—once again accompanied by the eyes "che vi mangiavano"—of the narrative's conclusion. In similar fashion, as Giovanni Sinicropi has shown, the striking depictions of the natural environment, the burning stones and stubble of the immense fields stretching toward Etna, serve to extend and reinforce the correlative passion constantly aflame within la Lupa, "sotto al fustagno del corpetto."[6]

The frame of temporal reference within the narrative is determined more by social and religious customs (Natale, Pasqua) and by the passage of the seasons than by hours and days. The story first creates a generalized aura of perpetuity, punctuated only by brief encounters, and then suddenly narrows the dramatic focus of spatial and temporal orientation in the final scene.[7] Although the reckoning of time and space by socially typical methods is itself realistic, the incorporation of narrative events into unified cycles is a matter of literary and dramatic convention, or verisimilitude, rather than mere mimesis of the superficially "true to life." In this way, individual acts, no matter how strong, are reintegrated into the established pattern of rhythmic recurrence, portrayed now as authentically cultural as well as conventionally literary. Far from abrogating this pattern, action itself only reaffirms the predetermined logic of Verga's carefully constructed wheel of destiny.

Of particular interest is the narrative's apparent suppression of direct historical reference. There are occasional indications of the political and economic institutions of post-Risorgimento Sicily: the continuation of the feudal system of ownership and production, now in the hands of the bourgeoisie ("e mieteva il fieno con lei nelle chiuse del notaro," p. 145); the militarization of the State with the consequent increase in travel and social experience ("un bel giovane che era tornato da soldato"); the increasingly complex legal apparatus, officially extended to cover women and peasants ("—No!— rispose invece *la Lupa* al brigadiere —Io mi son riserbato un cantuccio della cucina per dormirvi, quando gli ho dato la mia casa in dote. La casa è mia," p. 148); and the continuing importance of the Church. These references find their way into the text only indirectly. Whenever indications of historical institutions do occur, they are immediately subsumed within the functions of localized social and cultural verisimilitude, so that they appear to originate and remain as individual and local phenomena instead of indices of national or even regional (provincial) developments. Although Verga's language is recast in nationally conventionalized forms, his depiction of political and economic phenomena in "La Lupa" remains either universally human (in the affective responses of the characters) or strictly localized (in the individual reactions to village institutions). The resultant suppression of class and nation in favor of either individual or universal moral analyses marks not only "La Lupa" but also the rest of the 1880 edition of *Vita dei campi*.[8]

Rather than making the extremely limited world of the story appear deficient, this meticulous suppression of external reference gives the village itself an integrity that it would not easily retain if put in direct comparison with the outside world. Nanni's return from the military may thus be seen as significant not in reference to the official militarization of Italian society but as an indication of his own virility and social freedom. This partially explains the absence of any notation of Nanni's family even in the midst of a culture organized around the stability of the "focolare." As a young demilitarized soldier, Nanni enjoys perhaps the greatest breadth of sanctioned choice in popular Sicilian society, at least during the transitional period of his unmarried manhood; whereas Maricchia, as a maiden, is utterly bound by the will of her mother and the legal inheritance from her father.

As an aspect of cultural verisimilitude, la Lupa's use of the law in connection with the dowry and the house demonstrates not only her singular will and "sagacia contadinesca" but also the great distance between herself and the social norms that organize the village.[9] As opposed to Nanni, she utilizes the law and the "true" servant of God as an outsider, driven away from the sustaining sympathy of social life by the anathema on her activities as a sexually aggressive widow spurred by an all-consuming passion. Described repeatedly as "diavolo," "spiritata," "satanasso," enchantress, vampire, and succubus, she nonetheless does not fulfill even the socially acceptable role of *strega*, since she has no clients, only victims (herself included). Indeed, as Maricchia becomes fully socialized into the adult life of the community ("coi figli in collo"), even she turns on her mother in the exact moral and religious terms of the rest of the community: "—*Scellerata*. . . . Mamma *scellerata*! . . . Ladra!" (Latin s/celestus, barred from the heavens). Here, as elsewhere, the indirect reference to religious and social institutions serves less as a concise analysis than as a convenient means of thematizing the pervasive powers of patriarchy and Catholicism within the "timelessly" given social and moral organization of the village.

The narrator of the story establishes positions both inside and outside the parameters of village knowledge, shaping the localized perception of characters and events while not appearing to evaluate or judge those perceptions except through the selection and organization of his own discourse. *Verismo*'s program of "dispassionate" impersonality, similar to that of Zola and even Flaubert, tended to distance the narrator from the events he describes at the same time as it permitted his authentic, seemingly objective knowledge of the characters and milieu.[10] Although much of the narration is introduced as originating in village sources ("Al villaggio la chiamavano *la Lupa"*; "la gente andava dicendo"), each of the two major sections begins with statements of "fact" independent of privileged village knowledge ("era alta, magra"; *"La Lupa* era quasi malata"). Verga often uses sensory notation to establish the internal perspective of presentation ("Nanni spalancò gli occhi imbambolati"; *"La Lupa* lo vide venire"), but this is by no means always the case. The constant use of dialogue serves again and again to break up the easily attributable origins of presentation.

Through the appearance of objectivity combined with the intimate knowledge of event and social custom, the narrator of "La Lupa" manages to focus the essentially contradictory perspectives of the story without becoming openly subservient either to la Lupa's driving passion, Nanni's repeated expressions of ambivalence, or patriarchal Catholicism's sustained condemnation. Though the characters are passionate and the events violent, as elsewhere in Verga's Italianized depiction of Sicilians' self-perceptions, the narrator himself appears removed throughout. He eschews even the technical closeness of the fully individual *style indirect libre*, which would clearly be available and is so much in evidence from the opening paragraphs of "Cavalleria rusticana" ("Dapprima Turiddu come lo seppe, santo diavolone! voleva trargli fuori le budella dalla pancia, voleva trargli, a quel di Licodia! però non ne fece nulla").[11]

This is not to say, however, that the narrative is flatly objective, or even that it could be. This mitigation of objectivity is demonstrated in the selection and organization of the language itself, and especially in the proper nouns. The function of naming in Verga's narrative is perhaps more complex than it may first appear. La Lupa receives her name, of course, because of her devouring passion, which forces her to wander "con quell'andare randagio e sospettoso" like a hungry wolf, "la sola anima viva che si vedesse errare per la compagna." That her passion is a force that has totally possessed her and over which she, as gnà Pina, has no control, is indicated by Verga himself in a letter to his Swiss translator, Édouard Rod, in which she is described as subject to a "passione cieca, carnale, brutale anche se volete, ma quasi fatale."[12] Whereas Verga habitually associates passion with the process of creation, and creation with life itself (in the introduction to "L'amante di Gramigna" and elsewhere), in "La Lupa" passion is seen as a blindly destructive force, past all hope of control and leading to death ("quasi fatale"). Just as it has consumed la Lupa, so she must continually devour others for its momentary appeasement. Once this chain of events has been set in motion, there is no apparent escape except through subjugation of the force itself, through repeated and violent contest with the destroying power.

As Vittorio Spinazzola has remarked, la Lupa thus represents the greatest conceivable threat to the patriarchal community, "la divoratrice di uomini."[13] The description of the blood-red lips and the continual reference to the eyes "che vi mangiavono" support such a denomination. These descriptive effects immediately connect la Lupa to superstitions of possession (lycanthropy, vampirism), as her dual naming would also indicate: "ella si *spolpava* i loro figliuoli e i loro mariti in un batter d'occhio, con le sue labbra rosse." They also show her affinity to the *femmes fatales* of the nineteenth-century feuilletons and their Gothic predecessors, as well as to a host of Mediterranean and European figures (Lilith, the Sirens, Theocritus's Sicilian Sorceress, La Belle Dame sans Merci). But why, with all this painstaking thematic development, should Verga risk choosing a name that carries connotations that, far from strictly negative, are at the least profoundly ambiguous in Italian tradition?

Of course, it is no explanation to say that the narrator exculpates himself in the choice of such an obviously symbolic name by using a favorite strategy of the realist text, denying complicity in the matter by attributing the function of naming to the authoritatively hypostatized communal voice: "Al villaggio la chiamavano *la Lupa*." Nonetheless, the ascription to a communal origin is of particular interest. Indeed, the positive Italian connotations of the word *lupa*, from Roman to Sienese, are all connected with the founding and nurture of the patriarchal community. A solution to the dilemma presented by these interfering meanings may perhaps be found in the wonderfully mythologized pages of Livy's *History*. Livy describes the typically heroic two-fold salvation of Romulus and Remus, first by the she-wolf who gave them suck and cleansed them with her tongue, and then by Faustulus, the king's herdsman who took the twins to his wife Larentia to care for in his hut. Livy is unable, however, to restrain himself from offering a more logical variant of the story, reporting that some thought the origin of the fable was the circumstance that Larentia was a common prostitute and was called "wolf" by the shepherds: "Sunt qui Larentiam volgato corpore lupam inter pastores vocatam putent; inde locum fabulae ac miraculo datum."[14]

As in the thematic development within Verga's novella, the oppositions underlying Livy's account are clear. The natural hunger of the she-wolf to achieve self-gratification while subordinating external stimulus to her own needs represents a positive benefit, as long as it is controlled and organized, in its second stage, by the sustaining values of patriarchal society. This is accomplished not through the annihilation of animality but through the transformation of its energy in service to the patriarchal order. Verga dissociates his "heroine" from the potentially positive connotations of her epithet by turning her repeatedly against that order, in a maneuver similar to Livy's second, ideologically rationalized reading of the foundation legend. The positive attributes of the she-wolf do occur in Verga's narrative, but they are not clustered around gnà Pina. Instead, they accrue to Maricchia, though only after she has accepted Nanni as a husband and has begun to produce and protect potentially patriarchal offspring ("Maricchia piangeva notte e giorno, e alla madre le piantava in faccia gli occhi ardenti di lagrime e di gelosia, come *una lupacchiotta anch'essa*," p. 147). Just as in Livy's first version, the stabilizing power of the she-wolf is emphasized by direct transformation of her powers in obeisance to patriarchy, with Livy's notation of the motherly tongue (neutralizing the otherwise destructive teeth) and Verga's playful combination of suffixes ("lupacchiotta").

The ideological systems basic to Livy's and Verga's narratives should be apparent, when irrational, female passion is seen as leading to the death of society unless taken over and channeled by rationally ordered, male-dominant institutions (male royalty in Livy; the Church, laws, and town in Verga). Again, the dispute over the ownership of the house is of primary significance, since la Lupa uses the law not to sustain but to thwart the values of patriarchy. It is nevertheless clear that this is only a holding action. La Lupa has sown the seed of her own destruction by submitting to Nanni's initial demand and sacrificing her daughter to the socializing institutions of the established community ("l'amava anche lei quel marito che le *avevano* dato per forza").

• Over the long term, Maricchia's socialization represents, in a very special way, la Lupa's defeat. As we shall see, however, it does not and cannot represent la Lupa's destruction. It is important, then, that legal institutions in and of themselves are by no means adequate to win this battle. Beyond the utilization of social forms and community support, "volontà" will also be required, as Nanni eventually discovers, and as the others in the village ("tutti i vicini e i curiosi") appear to have known all along. In both Livy and Verga, the supposed repository for this knowledge lies precisely in the time-honored sayings of popular (though again, ideologically male-dominant) discourse: "called 'wolf' by the shepherds"; "Al villaggio la chiamavano *la Lupa*."

Traces of popular discourse are also apparent in the expressive effects of oral narration ("due occhi grandi così"; "Una volta *la Lupa*"), in the "ritmo binario" of the descriptive passages, in the organizational trebling evident throughout the narrative, and in the proverbs.[15] Of the two proverbs that serve major functions in the text, the elements of the principal one are repeated three times: "*In quell'ora fra vespero e nona, in cui non ne va in volta femmina buona*. . . . —No! non ne va in volta femmina buona nell'ora fra vespero e nona!— singhiozzava Nanni'. . . . Quando tardava a venire anzi, nell'ora fra vespero e nona, egli andava ad aspettarla." The proverb itself repeats and organizes the thematic elements already present in the characteristics of naming: the hunger perpetually driving la Lupa to wander "in volta" at all hours, in the traditional imagery of lust (*cf. Inferno* 5); the separation from ecclesiastical and social mores, "nell'ora fra *vespero* e *nona*," when women should be tending to their duties in the home, away from the overwhelming power of the burning sun; and the major antagonism underlying the dual organization of the proverb—secure patriarchal Catholicism in opposition to straying woman.[16] Once again, within the proverb and the entire narrative, only women are presented as irredeemably errant, and only certain pejoratively denominated women at that ("femmina").

The earlier proverb embedded in the narrative ("il diavolo quando invecchia si fa eremita") also carries the distinctive linguistic turn of localized custom and organizes themes that extend beyond the limits of contemporary village life. In this way, it, too, serves to sanctify the prevailing moral and religious ideology with the authenticity of timelessness. Besides the continued emphasis on the dangers represented by the solitary, nonsocialized, and nonproductive recluse, this proverb also embodies a second notation that gains particular significance in the symbolic organization of the story—that of age. It is important that la Lupa is so vexing to the village, and especially to "le donne," precisely because she is long past the stage of effective socialization. She thereby represents a unique threat for the elaborate yet precarious structure of social constraints to which the other women have, at least in appearance, submitted themselves.

The proverbs thus combine with the other effects of popular discourse to lend the narration an aura that is at once popular and universal, established in time and place yet transcending the very boundaries that help to create its authenticity. Once the knowledge implicit in the proverbs has been depicted as emanating from legitimate communal sources, the narrator then repeats this knowledge in connection with la Lupa as though it were a timeless and necessary given, rather than an attribute deriving from her previous activity: "la gente andava dicendo che *il diavolo* quando invecchia si fa eremita" (p. 146); "E meglio sarebbe stato per lui che fosse morto in quel giorno, prima che *il diavolo* tornasse a tentarlo e a ficcarglisi nell'anima e nel corpo" (p. 148). This assumption of the predetermined givens of the individual personality is, of course, a part of nineteenth-century Darwinism, which also influenced Zola and the Parisian Naturalists. It is important, however, to note that even though Verga was subject to a profoundly stoical pessimism, he was not so fully deterministic as this depiction might imply, since the transmittable phenomena are always seen to be matters of essence but *not* of form, as the distinguishing force of the *lupacchiotta's* inherited will clearly indicates. Moreover, the repeated progression of belief from popular attribution to unquestioned essence—or from identification to identity—is not the only movement that the proverbs of the text undergo.

The central proverb is formally stressed through italicization and repetition. Though this progression reproduces and sustains communal knowledge, it does so in a very strange way, affirming the idealized unity of

belief in relation to la Lupa and creating the distance of pointed evaluation in regard to her imperfectly socialized victim.[17] In this way, Nanni's
very freedom works against him, since the special separation from village
restraints which makes him desirable also renders him vulnerable to la
Lupa's temptations. The proverb is presented initially (italicized) as
cultural knowledge. It is then repeated by Nanni himself, as an indication
of his inability to contend with the very force that he, too, has at last
come to recognize ("—No! non ne va in volta femmina buona . . . — *singhiozzava* Nanni"). By the third time, the elements of the proverb are
thoroughly melded to the narrative, originating no longer in village or
character perspectives, but in the supposedly objective and otherwise
unidentified narrator: "Quando tardava a venire anzi, *nell'ora fra vespero
e nona*, egli andava ad aspettarla."

This progressive repetition, leading from implicit warning to open
thralldom, is accompanied by another set of recurrent phrases. These
derive from Nanni himself and indicate not resolution but helplessness:
"—Andatevene! andatevene! non ci venite più nell'aia! . . . Andatevene!
andatevene! Non ci tornate più nell'aia!'" Again, the subjective presence
of the narrator is indicated only by the ironic juxtaposition of discursive
and diegetic elements and the apparently innocent but actually condemnatory notation, "e le ripeteva ogni volta." The terrific power of la Lupa is
reaffirmed by Maricchia's protests in the subsequent paragraph; these,
too, uselessly repeated "ogni volta." The entire movement is set against
the recurrent mockery of Nanni's early—and now so obviously mis-
placed—self-confidence: "—O che avete, gnà Pina?' . . . —Che volete,
gnà Pina?'" As a returned soldier, a man of the world, Nanni had thought
to be able to accomplish what no one else would or could have. He
intended to make a simple gain out of la Lupa's daughter, a gain that a
usual girl, and her attached responsibilities, would not have afforded.
But even Nanni's early victory appears short-lived. He secures the two
things that will work against him in his battle with la Lupa by binding
him to her; the dowry and the marriage to Maricchia: "—Ed io invece
voglio vostra figlia, che è zitella.'"

It should be clear, then, that the continued repetition of proverbial
elements and popular naming merely affirms and extends the text's symbolically unified presentation of la Lupa. At the same time, the emphasis
on these elements, in relation to Nanni's mistaken perception of his own
situation, gives rise not to the unity of unquestioned belief, but to the
disjunction of irony. During the middle portion of the story, the contrasts
between Nanni's perceptions and the narrative's descriptions, as well as
between Nanni's acts and his own words, indicate a basic incongruity
between the character's cognitive and pragmatic functions. In regard to
Nanni, the formal repetition of the proverbial material proceeds away
from identity into the irony of difference. This difference, which is

perceived by the reader only across the advancing barrier of what Lévi-Strauss terms irreversible narrative temporality, creates an essential and increasing disjunction in the category of belief. Each time the central proverb is presented, the narrative moves further from the assumptions implicit in Nanni's initial perceptions and thus reconfirms the reader's knowledge of la Lupa by establishing an informed skepticism in regard to her victim. Finally, it should be noted that even the apparent movement from identification to identity with respect to la Lupa carries, in relation to Nanni, the detachment of progressive difference, since the clause used to reaffirm the seemingly objective knowledge within the earlier proverb ("prima che il diavolo tornasse a tentarlo") is based not only on the proverb but also on elements of Nanni's own mechanically ineffectual protestations ("Non ci *tornate* più nall'aia! . . . e la *tentazione* dell' inferno!"). These same elements are again present as prelude to the final scene: "e poi, come *la Lupa tornava a tentarlo.*"

These progressive interactions of the characters, in the narrative "phrases" of diegetic organization, thus create fundamental textual attitudes through repetitions of identity and contrast. These attitudes are signaled on the superficial level of shifting narrative tones, or verbal attitudes, both by the regular recurrence of popular epithets (coupled with occasional expressions of guarded admiration for la Lupa: "Proprio come un uomo"; "trecce superbe") and by the subtle barbs turned against her victims ("un *vero* servo di Dio"; "—Andatevene! andatevene! non ci venite più nell'aia!' Ella se ne andava *infatti*"). Such notations give rise to the spontaneous effects of verbal irony even as they signal an underlying organization that is complex but not disunified, and to which they ultimately bear a relationship not of disjunction but of developing unity. It is around this seemingly infinite play of discursive and diegetic elements that the narrator constructs the coded system of attitudes making up the supposedly objective, impersonal narration. The exact understanding of this play will prove especially important in reading the story's concluding lines.

In terms of both the ideological underpinnings and the plotting of the novella, the effect of this unity of discursive and diegetic elements is to give the appearance of necessity, of destiny. The seemingly inevitable completion of la Lupa's designs is signaled not only by her naming and introductory description but also by the apparent innocence of her initial interaction with Nanni, presented as randomly realistic composition of place, but including significant proleptic details ("una volta *la Lupa* si innamorò di un bel giovane che era tornato da soldato, *e mieteva il fieno con lei* nelle chiuse del notaro"). Nanni's subsequent seduction, followed by his and Maricchia's inability to escape la Lupa even under the protection of the civil law, again reinforces the narrative's original perceptions of la Lupa's powers. This is especially true during the scene in front of the "brigadiere." Both the careful organization of la Lupa's response and the seemingly coincidental nature of her claim (Nanni had asked to be sent off himself, not to have her sent away) indicate the same preconceived series of events which Nanni has seen too late and still cannot escape, and which has now become the irony of his own destiny. In part, he creates this irony himself, in his attempts to resist his share of destiny, just as la Lupa avoids direct irony by actively accepting her s. It is important, however, that destiny effectively entangles them both, since la Lupa too is caught in the net of passion which holds Nanni. As is generally true in nineteenth-century realism, ironic elements thus cluster around certain characters at the expense of others, but the dominance of ironic recupera- tion is reserved for only one position within the text, that of the narrator himself (which is to say, the author implied *within* the dual narrative functions of diegetic and discursive organization).

The irony in Verga's text permits the narrator to know this destiny and even to continue his narration under its sentence, but not to escape it. Finally, he is implicated, along with the objects of narration, in the labyrinthine logic of desire. If this is the case, how can we, as readers involved in the logic of the realist text, hope to gain enough detachment to see that the irony governing Nanni's presentation is due not so much to his helplessness against external forces as to the continual misappre- hension of his own progressively internalized desire? How can we see that the powers that the moral ideology of the patriarchal community characterizes as external are internal phenomena, corrupting the social values underlying the perceptions not only of Nanni and the village but also of the narrator's realist discourse? Indeed, it is only through re- sistance to these uncontrolled powers that the moral code of the village is constructed. This same process of construction holds for the reader, who finds himself inscribed from the very beginning within the com- munal discourse of patriarchy not as impartial observer but as victim: "due occhi grandi così, e delle labbra fresche e rosse, che *vi* mangiavano."

The most efficient solution to this predicament of evaluation is provided by the text itself, in the elaborate and patently symbolic elements that combine with the elements of realism to form its discourse. Like other texts of classical realism, Verga's novella utilizes mythic components to organize the seemingly contingent aspects of the narrative. The coherence of naming, the simple syntactic organization that lends the text the appearance of adopting the logic of its characters while depicting their world from their own perspective, and the air of primordial superstition hanging over the entire text all contribute to the realistic portrayal of life in nineteenth-century rural Sicily. At the same time, however, they point to the primary, prenarrative oppositions that give rise to the narrative and that govern all of its aesthetic components, mythic and realistic alike. This is true both for the individual characters and for the special type of desire which drives them.

As is often the case in Verga's most dramatic fiction, the psychological development of the characters in "La Lupa" remains elementary. It is provided for the reader as much by external description and concise, illustrative action as by internal analysis. Even the interior phenomena of specifically named emotions are always correlated with externally verifiable sensual effects ("quello che si dice *innamorarsi*" = "*sentirsene ardere le carni* sotto al fustagno del corpetto, *e provare* . . . *la sete* che si ha nelle ore calde di giugno"). As in Condillac's fable of the sensitive statue, two codes are established and correlated in Verga's texts through a series of interrelations. One of these is for the faculties of sensual perception, the other for those of intellectual, or in Verga's major texts preeminently affective, response. The potentially complex psychological developments of emotion and intellect thus retain the coded comprehensibility of typically delimited external results. In this manner, the sensual perception of concrete particulars may seem to dominate in Verga's narrative. Such a conclusion is, however, too facile. Far from subordinating the combined powers of affect and intellect to that of the senses, this maneuver increases the force of all three through the economy of active metaphorical union. Indeed, the text provides the first full depiction of la Lupa's motivations not through internal analysis, but in the indirect reflection of the habitual behavior and "choral" discourse of the village, presented in the temporally expansive manner that Genette terms the iterative:[18]

> Al villaggio la chiamavano *la Lupa* perché non era *sazia* giammai—di nulla. Le donne *si facevano la croce* quando la vedevano passare, sola come una cagnaccia, *con quell'andare randagio e sospettoso della lupa affamata;* ella *si spolpava* i loro figliuoli e i loro mariti *in un batter d'occhio, con le sue labbra rosse, e se li tirava dietro alla gonnella* solamente a *guardarli con quegli occhi da satanasso,* fossero stati davanti all'altare di Santa Agrippina.

La Lupa's seemingly transcendent power is demonstrated by the defensive reflexivity of the women she passes ("*si* facevano la croce") and, more significantly, by the women's shared fears for their husbands and male children ("si spolpava i loro figliuoli e i loro mariti in un batter d'occhio"). Furthermore, once the symbolic order of cultural expectations has been established, a tone of knowledgeably subdued irony may be created by playing within that order's bounds ("fossero stati davanti all'altare di Santa Agrippina"). But what exactly does it mean to be la Lupa, never to attain satisfaction no matter how great or how frequent the attempts ("non era sazia giammai—di nulla")? Why is it that all the normal institutions of social control—marriage, the Church, the concerted actions of the villagers themselves—prove inadequate to contain this force that has appeared among them as the unnatural union of animality and humanity, wolf and woman? And, finally, why should la Lupa's passion always seem to arise from a lack that is neither derivative nor dependent but timeless and absolute ("giammai . . . nulla")?

To be in a position to answer these questions we must first confront two others, which in terms of the narrative precede them and which we have already begun to approach, what is lycanthropy in Verga's text, and what is passion? The *lyk/anthropos* is an ancient superstition, doubtless arising both from the material circumstances of primitive man's encounters with his especially skilled competitors and from fear's subsequently ritualized reverence. As we have seen, rather than putting the village's perceptions in question, Verga's text takes them over for its own with only the subtle reservation of irony. This procedure is evidenced by the development of the narrative's proverbs, the progression of la Lupa's relationship with Nanni, and the setting of her first verbal expression of desire ("una sera ella glielo disse"). The darkness of "la vasta campagna nera," the sounds of the dogs that "uggiolavano," and the separation of Nanni from the group of men sleeping "nell'aia" all indicate the contest between the male-dominated band and the external, man-eating threat. In the transitional time of evening, la Lupa wants one thing: "—Te voglio! Te che sei *bello come il sole*, e dolce come il miele. Voglio te!" The central phrase is the translation of a common Sicilian saying "beddu comu lu suli." Occurring within la Lupa's own discourse, it serves as a privileged textual reaffirmation of her symbolic function in the narrative. Driven by the demands of sexual appetite to consume everything that is not her, she seeks out all that is foreign—provided she can locate an accessible point of internal similarity such as the symbolic honey of concupiscence. As a creature of night and darkness ("aveva soltanto un seno fermo e vigoroso *da bruna* . . . era pallida"), she takes as her object the most vulnerable and literally the most brilliant prey, whose very enticement ("dolce come il miele") derives both from its role of wild sustenance and from its intimate relationship with the golden sun.[19] She seeks not just to attain but to conquer and repeatedly devour this solar brilliance, under whose countenance she alone may wander without fear, in "quell' ora fra vespero e nona."

As mentioned earlier, lycanthrophy is a superstition of possession. Whether gnà Pina had ever been a participant in village life, as her propagation of offspring would appear to indicate, is a problem posed but not openly resolved within the text ("Maricchia . . . [aveva] la sua bella roba nel cassettone, e la sua buona terra al sole, come ogni altra ragazza del villaggio"). By the immediate period of the narrative, however, it is clear that the power that has possessed gnà Pina will brook no counter, even to the point of savaging her own daughter ("Se non lo pigli, ti ammazzo!"). La Lupa's willful renunciation of the ties of blood between mother and child finds its complement in her violation of the social and moral order (canon law) with Nanni, whom even the supposedly objective text twice insists on calling "suo genero." On the level of character as well as social organization, this transgression of the incest taboo resides at the very core of the narrative. Although la Lupa desired Nanni prior to the marriage, she does not have him until afterward. Her only loss of vitality during the narrative is determined not exclusively by her overactivity, as might be assumed from the fears of "le donne," but also by her frustration at the inability to express the passion of this specifically barred desire (though not to satisfy it fully, since that would be impossible): "*La Lupa* era quasi malata.*"*

By describing la Lupa's sickness in the proverbial terms of the unclean recluse ("diavolo . . . eremita"), the villagers reemphasize the distance between her and them. As in the scene of la Lupa's early declaration of desire, the entire middle portion of the narrative organizes this simple opposition of nature and culture, with la Lupa and Nanni serving as transitional figures and the "aia," situated between the village and the burned stubble of the open countryside, serving as the transitional place, the "sanctified" spot for what is to become the profaned rite of sexual encounter. Although the eventual dispute over the house indicates the progressive weight that the narrative places on the village's socialization of Nanni (like the second confrontation in Grimm's version of "Little Red-cap"), the outcome of the contest is by no means clear until, or more precisely *through*, the concluding scene.

The motion indicated by the superstition of possession—or the active reversal of rationality and social control—permits the village to organize itself in opposition to la Lupa through insistence on the supernatural character of her power. In this way, the threatening forces are excluded from the sanctity of the "focolare" but not from village life, and their necessary anteriority to that order, constructed only in relation to them, may thus remain hidden. La Lupa had been gnà Pina, had lived in the village and produced offspring. Though that very offspring is now irreparably tainted by continuing connection with the offensive spirit, the legitimacy of Maricchia's birth as gnà Pina's child is indicated by the narrator's otherwise inexplicable sympathy for her present plight, which she, too, understands so well ("Maricchia, poveretta, buona e brava ragazza, piangeva di nascosto").

As in Lévi-Strauss's treatment of the transitional figure of the South American Jaguar, la Lupa is thus seen as a character that had possessed culture but lost it ("brutale *anche* se volete"). Again, this is parallel to Livy's second reading of the foundation legend (wife—>whore) and opposite the first (she-wolf—>surrogate mother). By suppressing the progressive temporality and difference of metaphor in favor of the repeated identity of unquestioned naming, both the village and the narrator are able to present la Lupa, the very incarnation of irrational passion, as having completely possessed the human figure. This maneuver permits them to name the essence as well as the body by first freezing the shifting arbitrariness of the proper noun and then connecting it in a necessary relationship with the fated power. Human culture, and specifically patriarchal Catholicism, is thus seen as either coexistent with or prior to the aberration of uncontrolled animality rather than proceeding from and in reactive opposition to it. The belief in lycanthropic possession is, indeed, concerned with origins. But it is about them only through the ideological effacement of their true nature. Within the village, gnà Pina exists no longer, except in the mistaken perceptions of Nanni. Even Nanni uses that appellation only prior to the confrontation amidst the gathering evening and the whining dogs.

By invoking the transcendent power of the cross and fearing for the menfolk despite the protection of "l'altare di Santa Agrippina," the women of the village affirm the oppositional nature of the supernatural power even as they effectively gloss over the temporality of gnà Pina's possession and the contingency of her corporeal existence. The fundamentality of the sacred/profane opposition is perhaps emphasized by the verbal interplay of naming (Agrippina/Pina), but this is not the only manner in which the lexical elements of narration are utilized to underscore the conflict's necessary and transcendent nature.[20] The spirit's eyes, and the will these eyes express, appear to transcend the bounds of time and place in precisely that communal figurative language that both the village and the narrator repeatedly adopt to portray them ("occhi grandi così . . . occhi da santanasso . . . occhi da spiritata . . . occhi neri come il carbone . . . mangiandoselo con gli occhi"). Furthermore, it is around these eyes, and the unified image of possession they present, that the narrator himself organizes two of the text's rare inventories of descriptive details: one at the novella's opening, the other at its conclusion. In terms of the perceptions of the narrative, then, la Lupa represents a singularly abhorrent figure, sexually active but nonproductive, possessed by a seemingly uncontrollable force, beyond domestication or socialization because neither truly natural nor fully human, offensive to nature and culture alike and therefore utterly alone, *supernatural*: in short, *lykanthropos*.

The narrative's recurrent description of the eyes of the possessed has an interesting postscript in Verga's letter to Rod, in which the agent of possession is described as a "passione *cieca*." Nonetheless, these same eyes, which express but do not see, filled not with the image of the outside world but with aggressive desire, are able to locate the object of that desire in a figure who is also subject to at least transitory blindness ("Nanni spalancò *gli occhi imbambolati, tra veglia e sonno* . . . e stese *brancolando* le mani"). It is clear, then, that la Lupa's seemingly blind passion is made up of two inextricable components, desire and will. It is important that, in connection with la Lupa, Verga's conception of will is somewhat closer to Nietzsche's than to Schopenhauer's, since la Lupa's violent power works not in conjunction with, but in direct opposition to, the entire social edifice of rational control.[21] In the terms of orthodox theology (following Bonaventure's system), her will derives all of its energy from affect rather than reason and finds its only outlet through the senses. She is thus cut off from the divine intellect and remains, in theological as well as popular discourse, "scellerata." Although she may demonstrate rational cunning, affect always precedes and follows. As a figure existing in time and place, la Lupa has not only the finally unappeasable "fame da lupo" but also the force and the means to attempt appeasement, no matter how illusory satisfaction might prove.

With respect to character configuration, la Lupa thus represents a realistic figure (gnà Pina), as well as the demonic force that has overtaken that figure. Although this power is insatiable and indestructable, it is cyclically strengthened and weakened ("Una volta *la Lupa* si innamorò. . . . *La Lupa* era quasi malata"), and, in the perceptions of the village and the narrator, the character has now become inseparably fused with it. In this light, the narrative can be said to depict la Lupa as the personification of libidinal energy, just as the established and only slightly less vigorous moral strictures of the Church and village represent the patriarchal superego. La Lupa's "masculine" and therefore unnatural aggressiveness indicates the polemical nature of patriarchy's depiction of her behavior; it also demonstrates Verga's ideologically motivated anticipation of Freud's claim that there is only one libido, which is masculine by nature.[22]

La Lupa's primitive unity is permitted in part by the symbolic merger of sexual desire with the constant need for sustenance, in the imagery of the ravenous wolf. For la Lupa, desire cannot remain unbound, but neither can it find its outlet in the liberating imagination, which could then give way to the fully human interaction of pity, admiration, and love. Instead, it both begins and ends in the necessary destruction of its own relentless need. La Lupa's imposingly inhuman unity of passion forbids imaginative creation, which would require control as well as energy. La Lupa's desire thus leads only to continual attempts at appeasement or to death; or, more properly, since "fulfillment" in this case can only represent the power's temporary and incomplete cancellation ("*quasi* fatale"), it should be said that such attempts lead both to appeasement *and* to death. Nonetheless, they do so in terms of the same cyclical logic that makes reaching these limits into an a priori impossibility—since gnà Pina can die, but the timeless spirit that is la Lupa cannot—and thus turns every approach toward death into inevitable rebirth.

It is especially significant, therefore, that the force possessing the body of gnà Pina has its origin in a forbidden realm ideologically depicted as beyond both nature and culture. Gnà Pina's desire has become the externalized desire of the Other, just as, through the transferring force of her passion, it also becomes Nanni's. But as long as it retains its locus within la Lupa—that is, within the supernatural and thus outside fully established social discourse—it can never be sanctified as truly human. On both the individual and social levels, then, la Lupa functions in the semantics of narrative content and the syntax of structure as the hypostatized recognition of desire or, in Jacques Lacan's terms, the discourse of the Other.

The village's motivated misapprehension of the prior force of passion, which is attributed to a realm that is profane yet barred only in a very precise sense (i.e., it may come here, we may not go there), corresponds to the village's denial of the contingency and temporality of naming itself ("gnà Pina" = "la Lupa"). In regard to social organization, this process parallels the village's depiction of the strictures of Christian truth and moral law as absolute and unquestionable rather than ideologically motivated. As Rousseau saw in the *Social Contract*, the social code arises only in response to the perception of a threatening force, which is then termed external and contemporary, but which is also internal and permanent.[23] The development of social convention gives rise to the accepted lie of metaphorical truth in the language of contractual law (as in the dowry, the battle for the house), which effaces worldly difference in favor of legal uniformity. Only as the language of this law is established do the categories of individual freedom (cutting across communal restraint) and epistemological identity (cutting across difference) come into being *as concepts*. True social liberty (civil and moral) is then seen as possible solely in conjunction with control itself.[24]

Although this control derives its initial energy from a source not its own and is therefore fully accessible to the shaping interpretations of ideology, its oppositional relation to the prior power of passion is seen not as capricious, but as essential if society itself is to survive. This is the reason for the extraordinary irony of la Lupa's legal acumen, since the very uniformity of the legal code may be used to protect her, as a nominal if negative member of society, even though all her power is directed against the fundamental values of that code. By utilizing the legally recognized title of *property* in relation to the house, she manages to retain the presocial "right" of aggressive *possession* ("la force ou le droit du premier occupant") in relation to Nanni.[25] Her battle is not against Nanni, but for Nanni against "il Signore." To borrow the terms of Rousseau's argument, she manipulates the lower order of the civil law and thereby overturns socialized man's highest achievement, creative moral liberty ("la liberté morale, qui seule rend l'homme *vraiment* maître de lui; car *l'impulsion du seul appetit est esclavage*, et *l'obéissance à la loi qu'on s'est prescritte est liberté*").[26] La Lupa thus represents a return to a quasi-natural state of compulsive expression. For both la Lupa and Nanni, however, this movement outside the bounds of society leads finally not to freedom but to slavery. This is true in the logic of Verga's analysis as well as in Rousseau's ("passione cieca"; "l'impulsion du seul appetit").

Within the social world of Verga's text, the basic oppositions of passion and control (irrational/rational, nature/culture, libido/superego) are pushed to a transcendent realm in terms of pure expression (the power possessing la Lupa) and absolute repression (the Catholic deity). The regular, day-to-day activity of society is established in the field of battle between these two opposing extremes. Though this maneuver effectively obscures the *source* of the fundamental opposition, which has its origins in the passion that is initially grounded in both desire *and* need, it cannot erase the effects in language. These effects take form as metaphors for the prior energy, which has been externalized as the ideologically interpreted discourse of the Other. These metaphors then combine in the forms of individual and social discourse, both of which have come into being only across the transforming barrier of misapprehension which effaces their origins. The complexly referential language of realist narrative then claims legitimacy by hiding the motivated perception of difference necessary to its origins, becoming, in Verga's term, "spassionato," or, as he says in the introduction to "L'amante di Gramigna," cleansed of all trace of the subjective "peccato d'origine."

Once again, the interaction of realistic and mythic elements in Verga's text leads to the predetermined logic of destiny. Even the irony that dissociates *verismo*'s narrator from the objects of his own supposedly impersonal discourse serves to permit this dual illusion to proceed, since the apparent disjunction in regard to Nanni leads not to rupture but finally to degrees of recuperation at every level. Just as the possessing agent of desire represents the Other for the possessed, so la Lupa *in toto* represents the personification of the Other, both for Nanni as an individual and for the village as a whole. What Nanni needs to do (and society through him) is to channel the seemingly external discourse of the Other into his/its own discourse. By means of this procedure, the ideological order of the patriarchal community is reaffirmed at the same time as the village's communal and otherwise "parentless" son situates himself fully within the code of its "timelessly" ordained law. The village thus conquers the lie at the conceptual origin of social freedom by momentarily subordinating the force of the threatening power to its own order. Human society severs its connection with the offending entity through programmatic misapprehension of the power's source, which, far from supernatural, is the self-regenerating taint of its own "original sin." Passion repels, then, but it also attracts, in the complex mixture of admiration and hatred which the narrative demonstrates for its Girardian scapegoat.

[handwritten margin notes: "molto importante Dark"; "Proust"; "destiny in verismo"; "oui"; "Girard, Luce"]

It is important to note that in Verga's texts, as in Dostoevsky's narratives or in Freud's early and middle works, the scapegoat is not just a figure but more fundamentally a function, not only Oedipus or even the Devil but also the unconscious itself. In Verga's novella, la Lupa's profane *form* is banished once more in society's endless struggle to authenticate its moral order, but her *energy*, masked and controlled by the illusion on which society absolutely depends, is again reinstalled as the driving force of life itself.

As a figure intervening between la Lupa and Nanni, Maricchia bears a unique relation to both of them and to the village. She is depicted initially as a victim of guilt by association and then as a pawn in her mother's designs. Since the narrative's economy admits internal analysis only in terms of external reactions, it may appear that Maricchia remains a static rather than a developing character; but close examination of the text shows this not to be the case. Although it is possible to read Maricchia's initial recalcitrance as either a meager attempt at independence, an expression of bitterness at continuing maltreatment, or both, it is clear that at first she wants nothing to do with her mother's schemes or with Nanni ("Nanni era tutto unto e sudicio dell'olio e delle olive messe a fermentare, e Maricchia non lo voleva a nessun patto"). As I have already argued from another perspective, it is precisely by succumbing to her mother's demands that Maricchia eventually gains her freedom, through the very socialization that permits her to channel the inherited strength of her will against her adversary. Once she has been ushered into the communal order, her early feelings of disgust with Nanni turn to love. This is true even though the physical markers associated with the object of her newfound passion do not change ("l'amava anche lei quel marito che le avevano dato per forza, *unto e sudicio delle olive messe a fermentare*").

Like Nanni, then, Maricchia moves across the symbolic space between the inexhaustible forces of individual passion and social control. As long as her emotional attachments and material circumstances restrict her to functioning merely as an appendage of her mother and her absent father ("la roba di suo padre"), sexuality evokes feelings of aversion and disgust. Although these feelings take the external characteristics of the object as their mask, they are actually connected with the threat of sexuality itself. Once the early attachments are broken, to be actively transformed in a sanctioned union with a socially appropriate object, disgust is able to give way to the fully mature expression of love, in a process generally similar to the one Freud described in the *Three Essays* of 1905.[27] Though only sketched, this progression in "La Lupa" is clear, and once again it leads to the observation that although the will to freedom begins in the natural drive of primitive affect, true liberty, and its moral fulfillment in Verga's text, is seen as possible solely within the established structure of the social law.

Even given the novella's extremely abbreviated form, Nanni remains a problematical figure. La Lupa takes possession of him by turning his initial vulnerability to her full advantage and subsuming the other within the orbit of the self. As we have seen, the aura of available affect associated with Nanni is appropriate to his social position as a young, unmarried male "tornato da soldato" as well as to the symbolic nature of his task with la Lupa in the Notary's fields. Verga's directions to the stage version (1896) reaffirm these points of similarity as well as Nanni's fundamental narcissism: "Nanni Lasca, bel giovane—tenero colle donne, ma più tenero ancora del suo interesse . . . *denti di lupo, e begli occhi di cane da caccia.*"[28] These introductory notations would seem to point to a contest between exclusively primitive emotions in which libido would indeed speak only to libido, as, for example, between nymphomania and satyriasis; but this is not the situation. As we have seen, the story gains its momentum not through equal oppositions, but through a series of contrasts which are necessarily uneven, just as the basic prediscursive confrontation libido/superego gains its generative power through temporally unequal and therefore progressive origins. The discursive resolutions of these mediated and constantly regenerated oppositions, on the level of theme as well as character interaction, build the novella's compact, though far from unambiguous, plot.

At the beginning of the narrative, Nanni is depicted as active but only secondarily productive; in the middle portion he is essentially passive; whereas by the end he is shown as both active and, in the hysteron proteron of the narrative's logic (first procreation of the children, then socialization of the parent), fully capable of social productivity. This development involves redirecting Nanni's active male energy to society's ends, in the reaffirmation of the incest taboo. Outside of the limits of this fundamental law, and the circulation of sexual partners which it regulates, society itself is seen to be impossible. At the same time, however, the violation of the law is *also* inevitable as soon as Nanni thinks he can have things both ways. This narcissistic inability to reconcile the rules of pleasure with those of reality gives rise to the violence of the denouement, in the forced conciliation of what is actually a permanent struggle.

The threat to Nanni's masculinity, which the incest transgression entails, is apparent in the text. The underlying fear of castration which the symbol of the wolf represents has been discussed in many contexts and was pointed out by Freud as early as his case history of the "Wolf Man" (1918).[29] The specific indications of the effects of succumbing to la Lupa's enticements recur throughout the narrative: "delle labbra fresche e rosse, *che vi mangiavano.* . . . Te voglio! Te che sei . . . *dolce come il miele . . . mangiandoselo* con gli occhi." It is during the period of Nanni's helpless passivity that la Lupa consummates her relationship with "suo genero," becoming, in deed as well as in wish, the sexually dominating phallic mother. Only by reclaiming the right to the phallus for himself can Nanni gain his freedom from la Lupa through voluntary submission to the patriarchal law.

The slavery of unrestrained passion is thus exchanged for the restrictions that are now seen as prerequisite to the true freedom of moral liberty. Nanni accomplishes this by first raising the ax, the symbol of his own phallic potency as well as the agent of destruction, and then turning that agency against the externalized embodiment of the prior sin of desire. The raised ax thus effaces the mark of Nanni's own transgression at the same time as his continuing expression indicates the true location of the supposedly cancelled drive: "—Ah! malanno all'anima vostra!— *balbettò* Nanni." La Lupa's energy, as well as the forces that work to redirect it, live on in the play of internal/external, retention/expression, which becomes the stutter of Nanni's own discourse.

La Lupa's prenarrative regression out of culture is matched *within* the narrative by the arc of Nanni's retreat into nature and his subsequent rebaptism into culture, now fully sanctified under the aegis of the social law. By defending both his own position and the communal health of "l'egoismo collettivo," Nanni restores what Vittorio Spinazzola terms "l'ordine del patriarcato."[30] This restoration is accomplished neither in the "aia" nor amidst the scorched stubble of the countryside, but in the place of work itself, in the vineyard bordering the now carefully tilled "seminati verdi." Through Nanni, the psychic energy of the outcast is once again bound within the social order, at least for the moment. As Lawrence perceived, Nanni finally "recoils" against the damage done to communal life "at its sexual root."[31] A measure of caution is necessary, however, in assessing the novella's conclusion, about which so many conflicting opinions have been ventured.

It is easy to concur in Fredi Chiappelli's statement that as long as Nanni stands alone he remains weak, even through the concluding scene, whereas within society he finds the communal strength of public penitence (among *il brigadiere, il parroco*, his fellow communicants, and even the participant souls in purgatory).[32] The final scene, with its violence of ritual slaughter, would thus represent not so much Nanni's individual renunciation as a reaffirmation of the strength of the communal law, seen as residing in the ax. This reading is undeniably correct as far as it goes. By the end, the depth of Nanni's feelings for Maricchia and his sense of shame are clear ("La povera Maricchia non fa che disperarsi. Ora tutto il paese lo sa!"), as is his understanding of the seriousness of his transgression. He has seen for himself that this particular law is not only social and temporal (*il brigadiere, il parroco*) but also absolute ("il Signore"). Yet his attempts to evoke pity or shame from la Lupa are useless. During the illness subsequent to his accident, he approaches death ("Io ho visto la morte cogli occhi"), and the memory adds a special urgency to his fears. This is the second mention of illness in the story, and it is as symbolically significant as the first. In part, Nanni's sickness represents the influence that his conscience is gaining in his socialization. The illness itself thus indicates the cure that is taking place. It would be tempting, therefore, to read the story's concluding lines as an affirmation that Nanni's restoration is at last complete, that he raises the ax, which Verga's stage directions openly term "la scure omicida," and destroys his tormentor without further delay.[33] It is impossible to agree with Guy Dumas that the opposite takes place, that this scene is merely a recapitulative confirmation of Nanni's continuing failure; but it would be equally rash to claim that the ax falls, since in both the narrative and the drama that is precisely what does not happen.[34]

It is significant that in the previously cited letter of January 1908 to Rod, which was written in response to the staging of the concluding scene by the Grasso Company in Paris, Verga did not suggest reworking the conclusion to clarify his intent.[35] He complained openly about Grasso's treatment, which presented Nanni falling into la Lupa's arms at the end ("figuratevi!"). Verga stopped short, however, of requesting reorganization of the movement to show that the ax actually falls, nor had he seen fit to alter a single word of the conclusion of the novella when he revised *Vita dei campi* for Treves's 1897 deluxe edition.[36]

Verga's decision can perhaps be explained by the surprisingly intricate symbolic interaction of the characters themselves. It must be remembered that, in terms of character configuration, Nanni's socialization entails not only his renunciation of la Lupa's form but also full internalization and redirection of her energy. Like Maricchia and all the other characters (even those only transitionally human, such as gnà Pina and the pointedly vulnerable priest), Nanni's movements are restricted within the bounds of the opposing powers of pure expression and total restraint. The narrative itself is an outgrowth of this prenarrative opposition, and it thus exists solely as the representation of the temporal compromises between these forces or, in psychological terms, as both the product and the depiction of the functional ego. La Lupa is, in her symbolic unity, a hapax even among the extraordinarily basic figures that populate Verga's Sicilian stories. Only the fully supernatural powers are permitted to demonstrate such purity in their imposing unity of attributes. Verga's text, as realism, is not primarily about them, but instead about the complexly human mediations of their struggle. In order to live and function in society, Nanni may not become, even for a moment, the symbolically pure and unified superego. It is true that for society to exist the ax must fall; but in order for the dialectic of life itself to continue, the purifying act has to occur "off stage." The energy represented by "il diavolo" can and *will* reappear.

At the same time, Nanni must be thoroughly implicated in the act's performance. In this way, he continues to be possessed by the will of the Other, but the affect behind that will is passed through the patriarchal social order rather than emanating uninhibitedly from its source. Through his rebirth out of physical and moral abomination into mature contrition, followed by the defeat of the phallic mother and participation in the communal law, Nanni shares symbolically in his own fatherhood. In order to complete this progression, Nanni depends on the support of the rest of the village, but to establish his masculinity within society, he must demonstrate, even though in ritual fashion, the ability to act on his own volition. Again, the basic opposition underlying the narrative remains unbalanced and therefore fully capable of generating the progressive relationships of renewed discourse, though by the end the weight has shifted within the ideologically organized text to the side of patriarchal control. The unity of presentation, which had been threatened both by the continuing power of the "wicked witch" over the village "children" and by the narrator's irony, is thus reestablished in the motion of the predestined act. Or, in the terms of Verga's texts, the plot concludes not with Nanni or even la Lupa, but with the symbolic expression of social enforcement, "la scure omicida" and the internalized Word's continuing stutter into only momentary silence.

Nanni's story, then, lies in the development of his ego in relation to the triad of forces—the libido, the superego, and the phenomenal world—among which it must arbitrate. It is important for the thoroughgoing verisimilitude of realism that these forces organize not only the formation and interaction of the characters and their society but also the production of the text itself, through the anthropomorphic agency of the narrative voice. Though Verga's text demonstrates pity for Maricchia and an ironically guarded sympathy for Nanni's predicament, there is only one character who evokes admiration, la Lupa ("Ella se ne andava infatti, la Lupa, riannodando le trecce superbe"). How can this be explained within the text that we have characterized as so thoroughly patriarchal? It is true that as a character la Lupa bears a fundamental similarity to the logical situation of the narrator, who establishes positions both inside and outside the parameters of village knowledge while remaining the sole master of his own narration. The basis of their similarity may be discovered, however, on a level that precedes even the logical organization of the narrative at hand, in the nature of discourse itself.

By the period of Vita dei campi, Verga's aesthetic theories had crystallized. For both Verga and Capuana, verismo provided a means of depicting material and psychological phenomena with scientific accuracy ("[il] fatto nudo e schietto"). To quote further from the introduction to "L'amante di Gramigna":

Il semplice fatto umano farà pensare sempre; avrà sempre l'efficacia dell'esser stato, delle lagrime vere, delle febbri e delle sensazioni che sono passate per la carne; il misterioso processo per cui le passioni si annodano . . . nel loro cammino sotterraneo . . . costituirà per lungo tempo ancora la possente attrattiva di quel fenomeno psicologico che forma l'argomento di un racconto, e che l'analisi moderna si studia di seguire con scrupolo scientifico.[37]

For Italian *verismo*, this "scientific" process did not entail the elimination of the intertwined passions giving rise to the entire history of human behavior. Rather, for Verga, as for Zola, realism meant describing the elements of human emotion and behavior so precisely as to permit interpolation of the hidden yet empirical causes that motivate action "in their subterranean journey." It was the process of depiction itself, not the represented behavior, which was to be dispassionate.

Even as Verga insisted on the appearance of analytical objectivity, he was able to see, nonetheless, that such a goal was illusory. Furthermore, this very pretense is seen to distinguish realistic art in its essential and finally ineradicable nature as a symbolic representation that claims truth by means of the meticulous obliteration of its own factitiousness. Only through the success of this maneuver can art, and specifically *verismo*, appear "to have made itself," without any trace of the "original sin" of authorial contact. This play of passion and control is regarded as shaping not only the artistic metaphors for character and society but also the very production of art itself:

> Quando nel romanzo l'affinità e la coesione di ogni sua parte sarà così completa, che il processo della creazione rimarrà un mistero, come lo svolgersi delle passioni umane, e l'armonia delle sue forme sarà così perfetta, la sincerità della sua realtà così evidente, il suo modo e la sua ragione di essere così necessarie, che la mano dell'artista rimarrà assolutamente invisibile, allora avrà l'impronta dell'avvenimento reale, l'opera d'arte sembrerà *essersi fatta da sé*, aver maturato ed esser sorta spontanea come un fatto naturale, senza serbare alcun punto di contatto col suo autore, alcuna macchia del peccato d'origine.[38]

Artistic creation, then, like all fruitful endeavor, is seen to derive from the "mystery" of initial passion, which is tempered at its very source by willful as well as rational control. The author thus situates himself within the subjective discourse of his text even across the theoretical barrier of objectivity.

The goal of objectivity remained only an ideal, but the ambition to achieve it, and the position of unchallenged dominance which it brings as its reward, continued to recur as figures for artistic creation in all of Verga's theoretical texts that were contemporary with *Vita dei campi*. Indeed, it was Verga's rigorous pursuit of *verismo*'s objective ideal which makes it necessary to look beyond the narratives themselves for clarification of his methods, to the prefaces and introductions that border the fictional texts and establish a dialogical relationship with them. In certain respects, these texts provide tentative theoretical models for reading the contiguous narratives. Although these texts are often confusing and at times contradictory, their complexity is due to the logical difficulties inherent in the theory and practice of realist illusionism, rather than to their indecision or artistic uncertainty, as has been suggested from time to time, perhaps most recently by Giacomo Debenedetti.[39] In all cases, passion is seen as the synthesizing force that cuts across and eliminates differences in favor of identity and that thus opens up the very possibility of artistic expression while providing the metaphors essential to all unified perception.

The intimate connection between ambition and artistic creation, along with the knowledgeable assessment of analytical objectivity, was made most concisely in the much discussed preface to *I Malavoglia* (1881), in which Verga described his master plan for the characters in the cycle of novels to be called *I vinti:*

> Ciascuno, dal più umile al più elevato, ha avuta la sua parte *nella lotta per l'esistenza, pel benessere, per l'ambizione*—dall'umile pescatore al nuovo arricchito—alla intrusa nelle alte classi—all'uomo dall'ingegno e dalle volontà robuste, il quale si sente la forza di dominare gli altri uomini; di prendersi da sé quella parte di considerazione pubblica che il pregiudizio sociale gli nega per la sua nascita illegale; di fare la legge, lui nato fuori della legge—*all'artista che crede di seguire il suo ideale seguendo un'altra forma dell'ambizione*. Chi osserva questo spettacolo non ha il diritto di giudicarlo; è già molto se riesce a trarsi *un istante* fuori del campo della lotta *per studiarla senza passione*, e rendere la scena nettamente, coi colori adatti, tale da dare la rappresentazione della realtà com'è stata, o come avrebbe dovuto essere.[40]

It should be noted that in this reduced version of the preface Verga devoted the greatest space to the discussion of one of the central characters of the project's last novels, which he eventually abandoned without having published a line. The description of this impressive figure crowns the presentation of the projected series: the man of willful intelligence who strives to dominate others not despite but because of the public's prejudice against his "unlawful" origins. This characterization then leads directly to the figure of the artist, who is seen to be caught on the same wheel of ambition. This "ambition" is made up of the very mixture of lack, desire, and will which links both the impressive character and the hypothetical creator to la Lupa. In each case, the driving passion gives rise to expression, for one in the realm of sexuality, for another in that of government, for the third in artistic creation.

Nevertheless, *verismo's* artist, as distinct from his characters, succumbs to his passion only at the expense of creation itself. The objective control of form is seen as absolutely necessary to artistic production; and without it truly realistic art cannot exist ("è già molto se riesce a trarsi un istante fuori del campo della lotta per studiarla senza passione"). Since his production remains individual, the creative artist must himself find the mechanisms for objective control, rather than depend on the social imposition of form. At the same time, even an artist's strategic withdrawal into objectivity is spurred by the passion possessing him, since the drive to produce *in* form is itself forged in the cauldron of desire ("all' artista che crede di seguire il suo ideale seguendo *un'altra forma dell'ambizione*").

For both Verga's narrator and his characters, then, control entails the passage of energy into form. Unlike the characters, however, *verismo's* artist is necessarily condemned to know this illusion. For la Lupa, trapped in her own need and therefore never free, the imposition of social control means form's end; whereas for *verismo's* artist, form is the key that permits imagination's liberation from need and thus represents the control that allows productive fulfillment of artistic desire. As in the synthetic creation of the metaphors for character and society, for Verga, writing embodied the true freedom that only analytic control could bring. This view of creation was not new. In its mingling of analysis and synthesis, rationality and affectivity, it derived from late Enlightenment and Romantic theories of language. *Verismo's* aesthetic, however, bears the seal of authenticity in the programmatic insistence on depicting the world as it is, since society, in the competitive post-Darwinian universe, is now viewed as constantly changing in a determined if imperfectly known fashion. The artist himself and all of his perceptions are also involved in those changes. At the same time, art's synthetic powers permit the freezing of change in formal illusion. Although the irony in "La Lupa" allows the narrator to know the temporal and representational illusions that form entails, just as it frees his imaginative faculties for pity and admiration, it cannot permit him to escape the fundamental logic of illusion itself. More than any of his characters, the narrator of realistic fiction—and through him, his objectively self-knowledgeable author—finds himself implicated in the semiwillful misapprehension of the falsehood at the conceptual origins of realistic art. It is this distinctive combination of willful desire and objective knowledge which allows the ordered discourse of representational fiction to begin. Once this clear awareness has been stated, however, it is only the continuing misapprehension of the interaction of knowledge and desire, in the constant regression into affectivity and return to control, which permits realist discourse to continue in the necessary *méconnaissance* of its own program ("tale da dare la rappresentazione della realtà com'è stato, o come *avrebbe dovuto essere*"). For the realist to borrow a formula from Nietzsche, only within the artistic expression of fantasy can the forces of Dionysus actively commingle with those of Apollo, and then only in art's inevitable deception. Once purified in form, however, and so raised to a higher order, this same child of illusion is rechristened truth ("allora avrà l'impronta dell'avvenimento reale").

For *verismo*'s artist, the objective withdrawal essential to artistic creation provides a privileged position straddling the boundaries of his own society. At the same time, sympathetic knowledge of the passion necessary to creation gives rise to the guarded and profoundly ambiguous admiration that Verga's texts repeatedly harbor for emotionally charged borderline figures and outcasts, such as the illegitimate "uomo dall'ingegno e dalle volontà robuste," la Lupa, and 'Ntoni Malavoglia. Verga's own behavior as a member of the lesser Sicilian aristocracy presents analogs of this same process. In his taste for existing at the edge of socially permissible affectivity, Verga consistently preferred active philandering to the bonds of marriage.

It should be clear, then, that "La Lupa"'s characters, their society, and the production of the text itself, as well as the novella's diegetic and thematic configurations, are all generated by the complex struggles between passion and control. The narrative creates a logical universe developing out of these struggles. Both the fundamental oppositions and the contrasts they generate can be schematically represented in an adaptation of the Greimas-Rastier diagram[41] (see Figure 2).

The idealized unity of la Lupa as both possessed and possessor permits her identity with passion; whereas the negative strictures of the Church and State may be located within the position of control. The functional ego, the daily activity of free society, the productive pairing of Nanni and Maricchia, and artistic creation itself arise in the struggle between these forces. Although rational culture and irrational nature are portrayed in necessary opposition, actual society exists only in the battle of mediations between them, with one force victorious at one moment, the other at the next. In this way, Verga's text retains the driving energy of passion even as it espouses control. Ideological valuation may therefore be traced on the most basic level of textual generation as well as in the full development of character and plot.

The lower points of Figure 2 are determined by their relation of contradictory disjunction with the separate poles of the dominant, generative opposition (formed by contrary disjunction). Renunciation represents the denial of passion; bondage is the forced relinquishment of all control. The social evaluations of the four primary forms of sexual relationships in the story correspond to the corner positions in the grid—ceremonial marriage (profitable: prescribed), incest (harmful: forbidden), bondage (not profitable: not prescribed), and renunciation (not harmful: not forbidden). Theoretically, many other relationships could fill in the two lower positions (as A. J. Greimas and François Rastier note, extrapolation of certain of Lévi-Strauss's works would place male adultery in the lower right as not prescribed, which, in terms of the diagram for "La Lupa," could then be ideologically interpreted as the renunciation of marital responsibility by the male and the continuing bondage to extramarital

Figure 2.

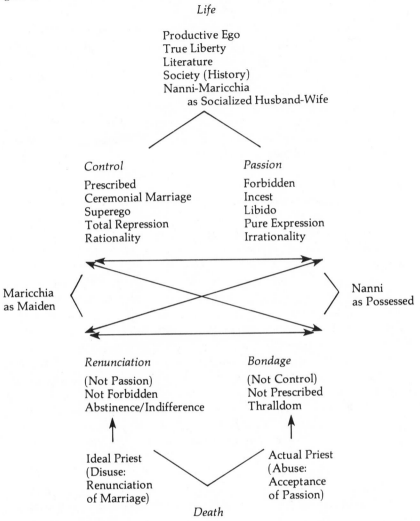

Life

Productive Ego
True Liberty
Literature
Society (History)
Nanni-Maricchia
     as Socialized Husband-Wife

Control

Prescribed
Ceremonial Marriage
Superego
Total Repression
Rationality

Passion

Forbidden
Incest
Libido
Pure Expression
Irrationality

Maricchia
as Maiden

Nanni
as Possessed

Renunciation

(Not Passion)
Not Forbidden
Abstinence/Indifference

Bondage

(Not Control)
Not Prescribed
Thralldom

Ideal Priest
(Disuse:
Renunciation
of Marriage)

Actual Priest
(Abuse:
Acceptance
of Passion)

Death

desire by the female). Although such phenomena are central to many of Verga's works before and after "La Lupa"—*Eva,* "Cavalleria rusticana," "Jeli," *Mastro-don Gesualdo,* to mention only a few—these relationships are not really operative within this novella.

The remaining characters represent various combinations of the other positions in the diagram. While in passive subjugation to la Lupa, Nanni embodies passion turned to bondage, since the very force of his being is dominated by the profane will of the Other. As a maiden, Maricchia exists between the repression represented by social prejudice and her own willful renunciation of marriage. The village priest, in his ideal state of abstinence, would logically remain within the confines of renunciation, though his acceptance of la Lupa's passion places him at least momentarily under bondage. Perhaps because of the extraordinarily primitive nature of Verga's oppositions, true productive life is seen to exist unchallenged only at the upper point in Figure 2. The entire movement of the narrative dialectic is ultimately directed toward resolution in this position. Although the death of society most clearly resides between the negative poles of renunciation and bondage, it should be noted that within Verga's ideologically ordered text *all* the mediations outside the primary one lead either to disuse or abuse of life's force, and so to death.

Beyond the features of the novella discussed so far, there is another distinctive set of mythic elements operating in Verga's narrative. These are remnants of Mediterranean and European myth proper. Although these subordinate configurations share the basic attributes of mythic components outlined earlier in terms of repetition, idealization, and unquestioning belief, they differ in that they are only partially realized within the narrative. Rather than being fully re-created within the text, the configurations are incorporated into "La Lupa" at midpoint in their development from prenarrative oppositions to articulated fiction. This does not mean, however, that they function merely as repeated thematic references or as secondary materials utilized to buttress the narrative edifice. Because these vestigial configurations, too, find their way into the narrative only through interaction with the elements of realism, they may be shown to function on both mimetic and diegetic levels with the force of verisimilitude. Since these particular mythic elements can usually be traced back through Mediterranean culture to pre-Roman and indeed pre-Hellenic origins, it may be said that in their fashion they help establish the depth of Verga's text as an authentically "Sicilian" narrative. As we shall see, this authenticity is also demonstrated by the system within which these elements are ultimately subsumed, specifically that of Catholicism.

Because Verga's novella is so economical, it is important that these elements of myth proper serve as narrative shorthand creating *ranges of reference*, or analogy, rather than establishing specific denominations, or synonymy. In other words, Verga's text, as realism, proceeds by suggesting symbolic correspondences, not by founding absolute identities. The realist text thus adopts elements from the genre of myth proper and subordinates them within its own mode of discourse. The principal pairing of Aphrodite with Adonis should be clear, especially since this mythological couple became, with progressive social change, an active opposition. Because this opposition is central to the novella's subtext, it must eventually be treated in detail. First, however, it is necessary to clear up what appear to be interfering analogies with other deities. Through this procedure it should be possible to pass beyond the overt methods of organization in Verga's text to the ideological implications underlying its discourse as a historical product. In this way, "La Lupa" may be evaluated in terms of the criteria of intentionality which it shares with all poetic artifacts: perfectly sufficient unto itself and imperfect by all other standards, every one of which, nevertheless, must remain available for critical adoption.

In certain respects, it would be tempting to associate la Lupa with Demeter (Ceres), and her daughter with Persephone/Kore (Proserpina). This reading would explain la Lupa's intimate relationship with the harvest ("affastellava manipoli su manipoli, e covoni su covoni") as well as the poppies she holds at the story's conclusion. It would also offer a second, mythological explanation for la Lupa's sickness. Such an association would also furnish a solution to one of the story's principal dilemmas, the presence of Maricchia as la Lupa's offspring; but this is not the only solution to the problem of the two generations. Moreover, the ties between la Lupa and Demeter are especially tenuous due to one irresolvable difficulty: in symbolic terms, la Lupa strives to occupy, and until the narrative's conclusion does occupy, the roles of both Demeter *and* Persephone. Or, more precisely, she embodies the entire constellation of dominant female attributes of which these two deities are only secondary representatives.

The distinctive features of Persephone, the "seno fermo e vigoroso *da bruna*," along with the continual pallor, therefore accrue not to the daughter but to the mother (though it should be noted that both Persephone and Aphrodite, as Melaenis or Scotia, may be associated with death and darkness). Once again, the stage directions for the drama are even more explicit: "La gnà Pina, detta la *Lupa*, ancora bella e provocante, malgrado i suoi trentacinque anni suonati, col seno fermo da *vergine*."[42] There is, however, a third aspect of la Lupa's age and social status indicated by the text's initial proverb, "il diavolo quando *invecchia* si fa eremita." La Lupa thus embodies the pre-Olympian triad of the apotheosis of womanhood, the Great Goddess: maiden, nymph, and crone, ruler of the underworld, the earth, and, through her offspring-consort ("bello come il sole"), the sky.[43] Although she remains "scellerata," the earth's matriarchal she-wolf thus repeatedly ingests, but does not destroy, the solar power that she herself has created. Even the progression of the novella's descriptive imagery emphasizes the all-encompassing nature of this role, with its special sexual energies, in the shift from the "seno fermo e vigoroso" to the openly dominant "petto *prepotente*."

At first there is a strong temptation to link Nanni, too, with a god of ecstasy and fruition, Dionysus or perhaps his tamer Roman avatar,

Bacchus. Nanni's activity in the "vigna" would support this suggestion. The olives that Nanni treats, and with which he becomes so soiled, are subject, like grapes, to a process of fermentation. Nanni is, like such deities, a figure intimately connected with women and fully capable of being given over to passion.

It is important, however, to recall that Nanni's passion is not self-generating. In his intimate and subordinate relation with la Lupa, Nanni therefore corresponds more completely to the initially dependent half of the mythological pairings of goddess and consort, of which perhaps the best known are Aphrodite/Adonis and Cybele/Attis.[44] These pairings regularly combine gods of vegetation, and therefore of death and resurrection, though of different qualities. Whereas the original female component represents fruition in its wildest and most mysterious aspect, the male consort introduces a secondary element of order. As in many fertility myths, these couples are incestuous, the male generated by the female then coupling with her, though rationalized versions occasionally change this basic relationship to one of goddess/mortal. For Verga's novella, an important variant of this relationship is contained in the story of Anchises, king of the Dardanians, who was seduced by Aphrodite one evening in the hut of his herdsmen on Mount Ida. In the account in the Homeric *Hymn to Aphrodite*, the goddess' overwhelming desire, the evening scene, the animals moving through the darkness, and Anchises' separation from the group of men sleeping below are all evocative of la Lupa's initial evening encounter with her future victim:

> [She] went straight to the homestead
>   across the mountains.
> After her came grey
> wolves, fawning on her. . . .
> But she herself came to the neat-built
>   shelters,
> and him she found quite alone in the
>   homestead—
> the hero Anchises, who was comely as
> the gods.[45]

Once consummated, these relationships are usually portrayed as lasting; however, in the later Hellenic (and purposefully demystifying) versions, this is not always the case. Aphrodite eventually tires of Anchises, and even her relationship with the youthful Adonis is challenged by Persephone, with whom, in alternate seasons, she is supposed to share him, as Maricchia and la Lupa share Nanni. Although these later developments provide reconfirmation of the basic thrust of the myth, at least for the moment their ideologically motivated revisions and extensions are not so central to our investigation as the original opposition. In each of these mythological couples, the male is ultimately crippled or slain with a wound (a thunderbolt, a boar's tusk) to the body. This provides another organizing factor in Nanni's illness: "Poco dopo, Nanni s'ebbe nel petto un calcio dal mulo." Nonetheless, even though the gods then descend into death ("Io ho visto la morte cogli occhi!"), they revive with the new season (Adonis's revival was symbolized by the anemone), just as Nanni returns to life in time to tend the new crops ("seminati verdi . . . la vigna"). In the most profound sense, then, the poppies of the story's conclusion (realistic in themselves but clearly overdetermined as "papaveri *rossi*") represent the shared property of the goddess and her consort, the soporific leading to sleep as well as the blood of symbolic resurrection.[46]

For Nanni, then, la Lupa symbolizes three aspects of femininity, the roles that Freud described as "the woman who bears him, the woman who is his mate and the woman who destroys him."[47] La Lupa's extraordinary quality as a character lies in her ability to sustain the unified position of all three roles. La Lupa embodies, for the patriarchal community, more than just individual womanhood. Depicted as a supernatural power of either masculine, feminine, or neutral form ("occhi da satanasso . . . occhi da spiritata . . . il diavolo"), she is fully able to participate with males and indeed to outstrip them:

> [*La Lupa*] andava nei campi, a lavorare cogli uomini, *proprio come un uomo*, a sarchiare, a zappare, a governare le bestie, a potare le viti, fosse stato greco e levante di gennaio, oppure scirocco di agosto, allorquando i muli lasciavano cader la testa penzoloni, *e gli uomini dormivano bocconi a ridosso del muro a tramontana*.

The hunger of the she-wolf wandering "affamata" is traditionally linked with the drive to procure sustenance not only for the she-wolf but also for her cubs. Although within the immediate period of the narrative la Lupa is portrayed as solitary and nonproductive ("Maricchia stava in casa ad allattare i figliuoli"), the fears of the socialized village women hinge on this very threat, that she might steal their sons and husbands for herself even from the sanctified bosom of the communal order, "davanti all'altare di Santa Agrippina."

In terms of the symbolic organization of the story, then, la Lupa incarnates the greatest threat patriarchal society can confront, the overturning of its order in favor of matriarchy. Although this threat is ideologically depicted as an obscene aberration, the symbolic organization of the novella clearly demonstrates that it represents a regression to a state that is feared but only dimly perceived. Nonetheless, this earlier order has not been eliminated; it has instead been subsumed within the patriarchal code. Verga's text thus manifests the residual fears of this order, not the system itself. In common with the mythological opposition of Aphrodite and Adonis, the novella continues to harbor remnants of this order in Vichian fashion within the continually recoded metaphorical components of narrative. It is therefore uncertain in the text whether this society would have been one of pastoral barbarism, as la Lupa's command of the open countryside might indicate, or of early agrarianism, when women still retained the "mysteries" of agriculture ("a sarchiare, a zappare, a governare le bestie, a potare le viti"). The movement of Verga's text as a whole is nonetheless clear. La Lupa's interest narrows to one partner alone, instead of the promiscuity of multiple partners, in a symbolic movement toward monogamy ("Voglio te!"; "senza di te non voglio starci"). At the same time, the text's agricultural references indicate a fairly consistent state of development throughout, with special emphasis on order at the conclusion (the ax resting in the elm tree, the vineyard, the green rows). The overall progression would thus be from J. J. Bach-ofen's speculative first stage of nomadic polygamy, in which Aphrodite, as the divine bitch ("cagnaccia"), represents the goddess of wild vegetation, to the second stage of "Mutterrecht," in which the Demetrian principles of monogamy and agricultural order prevail.[48]

Although Bachofen's scheme was caught up in the deterministic notions of nineteenth-century evolutionism, his ideas are suggestive for the evaluation of Verga's text. Verga would not have had direct knowledge of Bachofen's work, but Bachofen does represent a tendency in the study of mythology and folklore which Verga knew and used. Bachofen's hypothesized passage from "haeterism" to social control parallels la Lupa's apparent progression toward monogamy. But it runs precisely counter both to la Lupa's prenarrative regression into irrationality and her symbolic motion within the fields, since she begins with the harvest and moves through the work of agriculture only to end wandering in the midday heat over the stubble of the immense fields "che si perdevano nell'afa," toward the suggestively Vulcanian home of that other mythological companion, "lontan lontano, verso l'Etna nebbioso." Viewed from this perspective, la Lupa's agricultural activities with the men, like her claims in relation to the house, are obviously only a feint, a means of remaining close to Nanni, or of keeping him close to her, rather than a true submission to another order. The text concludes with the union and momentary completion of these two basic movements, la Lupa's ultimate regression into death and Nanni's rebirth into the mature law of patriarchy. From this perspective, too, the dispute over the house is central, since in terms of both property ("la roba di suo padre") and domicile, la Lupa will submit to patriarchy's laws only if she can retain the ultimate "right" of matrilineal control: "La casa è mia. Non voglio andarmene." For the time being, the results of her otherwise inexplicable response to Nanni's request ("—Per carità, signor brigadiere, levatemi da questo inferno!") are not only the retention of the house but also her son-in-law's continued presence in it. As in the mythic subtexts, the question of matriarchy thus appears concretely on the level of the individual characters, while only *symbolically* on that of full society.

Nanni's role in relation to this matriarchal power is crucial. In symbolic terms, the text entwines the relationship between mother and child and that between two lovers. Though Nanni is subservient to la Lupa, she is in turn reliant on his responses once he has been singled out as the object of her desire. He thus possesses a measure of masculine, even "soldierly" power, though it is circumscribed by la Lupa's actions and needs. During the middle portion of the narrative, Nanni functions as the male king installed within feminine rule, the figurehead enthroned by the dominant female power and permitted to serve only at her pleasure. As in the social customs underlying the mythical oppositions and, through them, Verga's text, Nanni waits in his appointed spot, watching "in cima alla viottola bianca e deserta" above the "aia," trapped in the role of thralldom/kingship from which all the powers of patriarchy are at least temporarily unable to rescue him.

According to the custom, insofar as its outlines are traceable through the myths, the reign of matriarchy's king appears to have been terminated in a very special way. In the words of Robert Graves, at the determined end of the king's sexual office, in the ritual spot atop the mountain, he was destroyed "as a queen-bee destroys the drone."[49] Again, not only perceptions of natural phenomena but also social customs give rise to myth, forming the metaphors that gain constantly renewed and recoded life in narrative discourse. Within Verga's text, as we have seen, the threat of castration is openly thematized through the descriptive imagery. Nanni's illness is similar to the symbolic fate of Attis and Adonis and is also followed by communal lamentation at his apparent death ("[Nanni] fu per morire . . . tutti i vicini e i curiosi piangevano davanti al letto del moribondo"); yet Nanni, unlike the gods and, perhaps, their natural/historical models, does not yet have death as his destiny at the narrative's close. On the level of myth proper as well as in psychological symbolism, Nanni turns what was to be the instrument of his own destruction against his adversary/partner and puts an end to the previous progression by establishing a new order. In doing so, he moves from the transitional (second) position of tearful, androgynous passivity into active male dominance. Within the narrative, his actions thus enforce the order that he himself has re-created. The incest taboo, and with it the momentarily threatened code of patriarchal monogamy, is again reaffirmed. As suggested by Bettelheim's definition, the body of symbolic components making up the narrative coheres to form the one fully mythic command of the superego, "Thou shalt not."[50] In terms of the moral values underlying the novella, la Lupa and her daughter may therefore be seen not only as representatives of different generations but also as symbols of two different and radically opposed means of organizing social life.

Along with the tension between matriarchy and patriarchy, or, more exactly, the symbolic reaffirmation of patriarchy's established order, there is another mythic opposition within the narrative which remains to be discussed, that between paganism and Catholicism. This, too, is an uneven contrast between two opposing bodies of coded material. This apparent opposition is actually a progression. The relations between Adonis, Attis, and Christ (as well as the shadowy cult figure Mithras) were outlined by Freud in *Totem and Taboo*.[51] It is not necessary to accept all the hypotheses of that study in order to understand the fundamental similarities between these figures. In Verga's text, the symbolic link between the principal male figure and the olives and grapes may thus be read in Christian as well as in pagan terms. It should be noted that Nanni and Maricchia are diminutives of Giovanni and Maria. Society's initial perception of Maricchia as a tainted figure, along with her battle against the profane force of "il diavolo" and the narrator's constant and knowledgeable sympathy for her plight, makes the analogy of naming more than circumstantial. Though Catholicism's Maria is not a full deity herself, she comes to represent the primal image of bountiful Christian motherhood. Again, this entails not the destruction of feminine power but redomestication of its functions (Lupa→lupacchiotta). Moreover, the symbolic connection in Christian naming is emphasized through a pair of contiguous clauses, each generated in opposition to la Lupa: "[Nanni] cavava fuori l'abitino della *Madonna* per segnarsi. *Maricchia* stava in casa ad allattare i figliuoli, e sua madre andava nei campi."

In the sense of the mythic oppositions taken over by Catholicism for its own, Nanni→Giovanni (John) serves as a type of Christ ("il Signore"). This relationship is clarified beyond doubt in the play.[52] Like Christ and the male fertility gods, Nanni is wounded (*cf.* the thorns, the soldier's spear), descends into death, and arises.[53] It is important that Nanni's worldly resurrection occurs not only in the spring but specifically at "Pasqua." This notation picks up the seemingly realistic thread of Catholic temporality running through the narrative ("a Natale"; "fra vespero e nona"), and it provides a ritual time for symbolic revival, just as the "sacrato innanzi alla chiesa" provides a sanctified place. Both of these effects testify to the capacities of Christianity to subsume totemic symbolism and pagan ritual within its own order, and so does the assumption of Mary as a major yet beneficent figure within the code of Catholic patriarchy. It is nonetheless important that Nanni finally meets the opposing spirit in more or less neutral territory, neither in the churchyard nor the wild country, but amidst the symbols of organized work and ordered fruition. Like Nanni's illness, his raising of the ax is a sign of the Christian restoration already in progress. The question of whether legal society is initially formed with the death of the Father and the penitent rebirth of the son(s), as in Freud's analysis, remains outside Verga's text.

For Nanni, however, acting in the distinctively Freudian mixture of defiance, hesitancy, and guilt, it is clear that patriarchal society is re-created on the individual level with the male's active self-liberation, through purification of the Mother's all-embracing power. Myth and realism combine, then, to form both the red poppies and the ax "che lucciava *al sole*" above the terrible Gorgon's head.[54] Nanni refuses his role in a profaned matriarchy. He returns to a different "wife and mother," and she, too, is now subservient to the familial order of patriarchy. With the support of Maricchia and the village, Nanni takes his place as the Christan sun/son of his true Father and restores the patriarchate through his own violent rite of passage. Nonetheless, admiration remains for the devil's energy even as la Lupa herself is momentarily overcome: the conciliation is always forced, and the struggle must continue.

It is especially significant for the patriarchal text that Nanni resembles a type of Christ. In Verga's narrative, even the mythological models represent mediating figures. As the union of man and god, Christ, too, suffered passion. At the opposite extreme, the devil is a figure capable not only of passion but also of reason (diabolical cleverness, devilish treachery). Through these symbolic associations (Nanni→Christ; la Lupa→Devil), the various oppositions of passion and control are not only mediated but also reintegrated into a system of values which is seen to exist as the ordained reflection of a transcendental order. Post-Darwinian man may err, but the timeless law of Providence remains in force. For the ideology of Verga's text, patriarchy triumphs not only because it is established and stronger but also because, in both worldly and absolute terms, it is morally superior.

At this point, designation of the symbolic oppositions utilized to focus the narrative's depiction of social life permits us to expand the earlier logical rectangle in a manner originally outlined by Fredric Jameson.[55] Verga's fundamental themes may be conceptualized as generating a series of negatives which are both cumulative and discursive, retaining the unity of their contents even as they are projected onto the next successive level. The movement from the narrative's base to its surface thus becomes increasingly accessible to the reader as the story proceeds, even though the basic generative mechanism remains suppressed until, or again through, the novella's conclusion (see Figure 3).

As may be seen by reviewing the vertical columns, Verga's text moves from individual psychological attributes to broader systems of moral value and social organization. This does not mean, however, that the realist text actually constructs its characters and society from the ground up as much as it re-presents a prior perception of their existence. In other words, the text's progression is really the discovering and filling out of a picture of life which it claims is already given. In this way, on the level of both individual character and full plot, Verga's text retains the apparent

Figure 3.

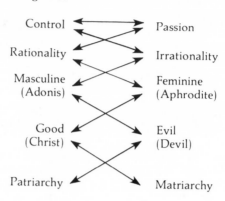

unity of a destiny decreed and accomplished. For this text of classical realism, time does move forward, but only within a closed system, the fulfillment of which is already past. Once again this closure demonstrates the subtle but pervasive superiority of the knowledgeable narrator with respect to his characters. In its detachment from the narrative world, this knowledge represents both the crisis of realism and the function that permits its discourse to continue, through escape from the randomness of material existence. The aesthetic need for at least tentative closure pushes the realist text past this randomness in the ideological search for an hypostatized unity that may then take the name of society as such, pre-determined fate, or even the text itself in its quality as a finished artifact.

The social appraisals inherent in the organization of the text and opera-tive in both naming and description should be apparent. Femininity is re-garded as irrational and destructive unless subordinated to patriarchy's dominion, in which case it is permitted to retain its basic animal/material power while becoming both productive and nurturing ("coi figli *in collo*"). The matriarchal order is allowed to function as long as it remains a method of organizing the early interpersonal development of Catholic patriarchy's offspring rather than an opposing system with its own set of priorities, such as open female dominance. Outside this framework, ag-gressive femininity is seen not as natural but as unnatural. One may sur-mise that this pitiless perception of the social dangers of woman and of their victims derives from a deeply instilled patriarchal polemic.[56] On both deep and surface levels, then, Verga's text demonstrates a profound knowledge of Sicilian and generally southern Italian Ottocento culture, in which women were permitted a powerful formative role as long as they adhered exactly to patriarchy's rigid conception of their responsibili-ties.

Although Verga's narrative forms and directs meaning through the interaction of realistic and mythic elements, there is a generating principle that underlies even this basic combinatory process. As is distinctively apparent in the realist text, this principle lies in the motivated perception of human history itself, that is, in ideology. Assuming this is so, however, how can we account for Verga's consistent suppression of Italian national history throughout *Vita dei campi*, written during the very period when the debate over Italy's future as a fledgling nation was so animated?

It is not easy to justify the text's studied avoidance of the political and economic turbulence of post-Risorgimento Italian life. Nor does it suffice to say that this agitation was felt not so much in the South as in the North (with the general strike of 1872 in Milan, the anarchist risings in Bologna, Bakunin's activities in Florence, where Verga had met him, and the irredentist demonstrations of 1879). Depretis's "trasformismo" affected the *entire* country in the gradual movement of the new and cumbrous machinery of state from right to left. Moreover, the Franchetti-Sonnino inquest of 1876 was directed at the very region Verga took for his subject. And in other texts, written not long after *Vita dei campi*, Verga did turn *verismo*'s camera to focus on the social plight of a people caught in the sudden and confusing transformation from feudal clans to a heterodox, family-based agricultural capitalism.

One explanation for this historical lacuna may be found within the symbolic organization we have already described. For Verga, as the later novella "Libertà" amply demonstrates, the Italian Risorgimento represented a communal outbreak of passion, necessary to overthrow the established reactionary order, but extreme in its irrationality and in its inability to direct its energies toward lasting benefits.[57] In his youth, Verga had been a comparatively liberal Republican (in Sicily, the faction opposing the Bourbon monarchy). After the Unification of 1861, however, he became progressively conservative. It is true that he was sympathetic to the lower classes and genuinely knowledgeable about their hardships, but despite suggestive reinterpretations by Luchino Visconti and others, Verga's position did not make him receptive to socialism.[58] He continually refused the type of economic and political analysis which would have permitted him to see the causes that generated oppression in Italy and that, by institutionalizing it, kept it respectable and active. This refusal put him in the self-conscious position of helping to create a revolution in realistic style and subject matter (precisely, "anti-letterato") while becoming increasingly skeptical of all social change. In other words, Verga believed in the reality of historical change, but *not* in the future of social progress. Although he remained a loyal nationalist deeply interested in Italian affairs and was named a senator near the end of his life, his idealist skepticism kept him from espousing any far-reaching economic or political solutions to Italy's urgent internal problems. As he said in a letter to the Sicilian deputy Napoleone Colajanni in November of 1891, "io, tenuto per rivoluzionario in arte, sono inesorabilmente codino in politica."[59]

Verga's response to political and social turbulence, evident throughout *Vita dei campi* and in the very organization of "La Lupa," was the redirection of passion through the individual validation of formal control. His position was more than a Romantic belief in the primacy of individual action or, at the opposite extreme, a promulgation of universal brotherhood under the shadow of an irremediable "human condition." Instead, his attitude represented a motivated misapprehension of the factors of class and nation precisely because these were perceived to be the most vulnerable points in passionate confrontation. Verga managed to describe the hopes and ambitions of his "vinti" from their own perspective, in the curious mixture of individual desire and universal truth; yet he did this without seeing that their perspectives, and his as well, were determined not by the inescapable coincidences of humanity and fate, but by the very factors so strikingly absent from his depiction. Both Verga's narrator and his characters remain caught in this web of misapprehension. The order of patriarchy itself is reified as the primary referent of Verga's novella, on surface and deep levels, in its depiction of communal life and its qualified acceptance of the masculine bourgeois valuations of rational objectivity and restraint. This is true with respect to style as well as theme, since the creating subject situates himself within the form of his product even across the theoretical barrier of *verismo*'s objectivity. At the same time, however, *verismo*'s objectivist aesthetic prevents the artist from *explicitly* taking account of his presence within the text and thus traps him, too, in the illusion of its program. As in the introduction to "L'amante di Gramigna," the subterranean network of passion is seen to constitute the one fundamental ground of history's truth, but only as it is objectified, defused, and so rendered technically and morally presentable. The frozen moment in the history of social life is described accurately, but not fully, through the text's establishment of a negative relationship with the passions of the very historical struggle in which it, too, figures as observer and participant. History functions, therefore, as a privileged subtext thoroughly enmeshed in the oppositions giving rise to the narrative. This is so even though history's effects are at first apparent only as the traces left on village life by the disinterested passage of the outside world.

Viewed in this way, "La Lupa" takes its place as a fully post-Risorgimento product with a genuine historical perspective residing at its base, embodying passion yet finally espousing the absolute need for control. Verga could see, as did Rousseau, that true liberty is only possible within restraints, but he regularly refused to see that society's conception of truth is neither transcendent nor timeless, but is itself shaped by the very form that social repression takes. Or, as Engels pointed out in *The Origin of the Family, Private Property, and the State* (1884), published midway between *Vita dei campi* and *Mastro-don Gesualdo* — which revealed Verga's increasing uneasiness — the development of the State under rising capitalism represented not only organized control but also institutionalized oppression by class. Though Verga's texts testify to the action of history, his subtexts repeatedly support historical regression. Even as Verga viewed the effects of historical conflict, this insuperable pessimism kept him from taking the one logical step that might have permitted him to see the redirection of that conflict's course.

By infusing his depiction of the empirical world with the radiance of timeless truth, Verga added an aura of destiny to the subject-object relationship even as he effectively concealed the subtle yet pervasively influential role of material life in human consciousness;[60] however, Verga's distinctive mixture of Plato and Rousseau, Dante and Vico, went only as far as Darwin and no further. Darwinian transformism was accepted as a principle, even though regretfully and even though its mechanisms remained subordinated to the transcendent law of destiny. But the pan-European disputes of the First International, and the dynamic class analysis dialectical materialism had made possible, were never permitted to wield a positive influence in Verga's analysis. Verga's novella, in its thoroughgoing illusion of objective verisimilitude, its interplay of passion and control, and its distinctive adoption of an apparently open but symbolically closed plot, represented the fulfillment of a new and consummately dramatic narrative program. In the resolution of its most basic oppositions as well as in its description of the phenomenal world, however, the novella embodied a wish for the future as seen solely with the eyes of the past.

What does it mean, then, to say that Verga's text is about the ideological organization of patriarchal society and the rebirth of the individual into the temporal and moral world of matter and sense? One thing it clearly does not mean is that Verga had conscious grasp of all the implications of his material. However, it does mean that, a generation before Frazer and two before Freud, Verga had already sensed the psychological and social issues that modern realist literature — in its unique epistemological relationship with the world it both grows out of and claims to represent — has continually attempted to approach.[61] This is true even though that approach, like the motion of a cat across new ground, may be constituted most fundamentally by circumvention and/or retreat. In adopting literary *and* social models as its basic texts, Verga's narrative established a mode of intertextuality giving rise to a discourse at once contemporary and timeless, authentically new yet adapted and recoded from the past. It is only through a semiotics of perception and expression, literary and worldly, that we can give his texts the reading they not only deserve, but so urgently require. By examining these narratives both inside and outside the limits of their own language, literary criticism may free itself to serve its necessary and valuable functions, to unlock the methods and assumptions of the fictional text and, at the same time, those underlying our own perception as a community of readers and critics.

5

Verga, Lawrence, Faulkner, Pavese

I Malavoglia: *Signs of Desire and Sins of Exchange*

Even with the appearance of *Vita dei campi,* Italian *verismo* had only established a beachhead on a literary terrain that, with the single exception of the northern *Scapigliatura,* had remained traditionally romanticized, elegant, and highly conservative. To Capuana's great chagrin, when Francesco De Sanctis, the dean of nineteenth-century Italian critics, finally lectured on contemporary realism in the late 1870s and early 1880s, he looked outside Italy for his subjects, first to Zola and then to Darwin. Nor was Verga's first full novel in the realist mode an instant success with the critics or the public. Verga's disappointment at *I Malavoglia*'s reception is evident in a letter of April 1881 to Capuana: "*I Malavoglia* hanno fatto fiasco, fiasco pieno e completo."[1]

Since its publication, Verga's masterpiece has had an uneven fortune in Italian letters. When the empiricist-idealist polemics hardened around *verismo* in the 1880s and 1890s, *I Malavoglia* continued to inspire positive and negative treatments; but as the dominant narrative mode began to change at the close of the century, and as D'Annunzio abandoned his youthful realism for the lush, florid prose of his mature novels, the excitement once generated by *verismo* and its entrenched opposition faded. First Benedetto Croce, then Renato Serra and Luigi Pirandello found ways to underscore the philosophical and literary limitations of *verismo* even while retaining respect for Verga's major works and for *verismo*'s "spinta liberatrice" which had permitted their conception.[2] The few Italian materialist critics who could have confronted the assumptions and strategies of Verga's narratives during this period were either silent or were notably unsuccessful in coming to terms with the works themselves.[3]

Verga lived until 1922, but the years following 1906—the year that Treves published the narrative version of *Dal tuo al mio*—were filled with Verga's now famous silence. During the rule of the Fascists, to whom the very idea of Italian "vinti" was subversive, Verga's critics were so quiet that by 1941 Massimo Bontempelli seemed to have forgotten all of the old debates and went so far as to assert: "Intorno a Giovanni Verga le acque sono sempre state tranquille. Gran novatore e distruttore di consuetudini letterarie, non ha mai fatto polemica, e nessuna o poca se n'è fatta su lui."[4]

With Italy's liberation from Fascist censorship, and the concomitant outburst of Italian "neorealism," interest in Verga's work resumed. Although Verga became a literary hero for a generation of writers as diverse as Cesare Pavese and Italo Calvino, his narratives received very little criticism that was really new or that diverged significantly from the original positions staked out by Croce, Luigi Russo, and post-DeSanctian critics. (The single exception to this was the intensive investigation, which has recently been revised and expanded, of Verga's innovations in the *style indirect libre*.)[5] The postwar biographies and critical anthologies merely confirmed and extended earlier critical biases. Indeed, the continued torpor of critical activity in the 1950s and 1960s led Gaetano Ragonese, with regrettable accuracy, to characterize contemporary approaches to Verga's work as having reached the end of a "blind alley."[6]

With the cultural shock of 1968, all this changed. Because of the historical significance of Verga's work, and because Verga shared French Naturalism's interest in the day-to-day experiences of the lower classes, his narratives have held a special attraction for the generation of leftist critics who came of age in the sixties and early seventies. Critiques by polemically Crocean and Catholic writers have also continued to appear, and, for the first time, there has been serious interest in Verga's work outside of Europe, though Verga's special combination of mythic and realistic effects has remained a stumbling block for many writers.[7] It is not surprising, then, that what has come to be known as "il caso Verga" continues to represent the "banco di prova" for the current generation of Italian critics.[8]

Following the novel's Naturalistic preface, the story of the Malavoglias of Aci Trezza opens very much as an authentic, nineteenth-century family chronicle. Block introductions are provided for the principal family members, and notations of region (Sicily) and date (1863) are unobtrusively inserted in the text. The *style indirect libre* is in evidence from the beginning, as is the subtle irony used to distinguish the perspective of the knowledgeably sympathetic but carefully distanced narrator. The lupin deal, which embodies the economic, social, and moral tensions of the novel's first section, and which eventually results in the family's decline in the village, introduces the action of the story. The transaction is presented initially as a perfectly normal occurrence in the life of the village, but the compact for the lupins, along with the economic desires it represents, leads not only to the death of the male heir, Bastianazzo, but also to the disruption of the entire family, including the patriarch Padron

'Ntoni, the widowed la Longa, 'Ntoni and his sister Mena, and even the younger children. The deal itself is sketched in a few deft strokes:

> Padron 'Ntoni adunque, per menare avanti la barca, aveva combinato con lo zio Crocifisso *Campana di legno* un negozio di certi lupini da comprare a credenza per venderli a Riposto, dove compare Cinghialenta aveva detto che c'era un bastimento di Trieste a pigliar carico. Veramente i lupini erano un po' avariati; ma non ce n'erano altri a Trezza, e quel furbaccio di Campana di legno sapea pure che la *Provvidenza* se la mangiava inutilmente il sole e l'acqua, dov'era ammarrata sotto il lavatoio, senza far nulla; perciò si ostinava a fare il minchione. —Eh? non vi conviene? lasciateli! Ma un centesimo di meno non posso, in coscienza! che l'anima ho da darla a Dio!— e dimenava il capo che pareva una campana senza batacchio davvero.[9]

Only in retrospect is this "discussion" filled out as a scene through the specification of time and place: "Questo discorso avveniva sulla porta della chiesa dell'Ognina, la prima domenica di settembre, che era stata la festa della Madonna, con gran concorso di tutti i paesi vicini."[10] By reversing the elements of narrative temporality (first the details, then the frame) Verga's narrator retains both the impressionistic fluidity of the story's presentation and his own position of special knowledge in relation to his characters and his reader. This is true even though the overall plotting of Verga's two major novels follows the standard linear development of classical nineteenth-century realist texts, in which significant events give birth to others in the metaphorical "genealogy" of family and social life.[11] As we shall see, however, in Verga's texts *both* of these types of narrative advancement are subsumed in a larger frame, which is predetermined rather than truly progressive and which shapes the reader's perceptions of character and plot.

The irony separating the narrator from his characters is typical of the procedures of *Vita dei campi* and later of *Mastro-don Gesualdo*. Verga's distancing devices depend both on knowledge and evaluation, or narratorial perspective: "*veramente* i lupini erano un po' avariati; ma non ce n'erano altri a Trezza, e quel *furbaccio* di Campana di legno *sapea pure*." At times this style appears to be straightforward third-person narration, but the mixture of description, snatches of dialogue, and evaluative commentary ("che pareva una campana senza batacchio davvero") creates the effect of the repetitive speech-and-response of communal discourse's choral organization. Indeed, at times it is difficult to determine the precise origins of perspective ("veramente . . . furbaccio . . . sapea pure . . . pareva"), since such commentary could originate in either a single character (Padron 'Ntoni or another member of the community), the specially knowledgeable narrator, the common discussions of the village, or any combination of these.

As in "La Lupa," the function of naming in *I Malavoglia* proceeds from the simple representation of village discourse (*"Campana di legno,"* initially italicized) through incremental repetitions involving both irony and allegory. Later on, the reason for the name "Dumbbell" or, more literally, the useless "Wooden Bell," is attributed to Crocifisso's habitual feint of deafness in response to his debtors' excuses and pleas for pity. In this opening chapter, however, the nickname appears to be motivated by Crocifisso's needy clients' envy and thus seems to indicate not his cleverness but his stupidity: "che pareva una campana senza batacchio davvero" (one is reminded of Boccaccio's "zucca al vento"). In the daily life of Aci Trezza the economic underpinnings of such motivation are clear. As everyone agrees and reaffirms with the nickname itself, "Dumbbell" is rich not so much *because* he is clever but, ironically, *despite* his stupidity. Nonetheless, the narrator, as well as the village, must at the same time find a way to account for "Dumbbell's" undeniable success ("quel furbaccio"), which may then be turned *against* him in moral terms, as the narrative's nonproductive yet wealthy capitalist ("minchione").

The complexity of this chain of reference (communal desire→village jealousy→"Campana di legno") is characteristic of the metaphorization of naming in Verga's narratives. *I Malavoglia* is singularly important in Verga's development as a realist because of the frankness with which the mechanisms of naming and reference are discussed from the opening paragraphs. The narrative begins by explaining that "Malavoglia" is not the clan's official surname: "Veramente nel libro della parrocchia si chiamavano Toscano."[12] Such confusion of naming, which is standard procedure in fables and tales, might appear to be merely a grace note included to fill out the fairy-tale motif of the story's opening ("Un tempo *I Malavoglia* erano stati numerosi come i sassi della strada vecchia di Trezza"; *cf.* "C'era una volta").[13] The metaphorical equivalence people = stones could then be read as typical of the mythic quest for origins (as in the story of Deucalion and Pyrrha). This theme is reinforced by the second sentence, which seems to offer the text's explanation for the confusion Malavoglia/Toscano, but which turns out to be merely a ruse, a means of broaching the question of origins and then momentarily dodging its implications: "ma questo non voleva dir nulla, *poiché da che il mondo era mondo* all'Ognina, a Trezza e ad Aci Castello, li avevano *sempre* conosciuti per Malavoglia, di padre in figlio, che avevano *sempre* avuto delle barche sull'acqua, e delle tegole al sole."[14]

For Verga, the question of origins does lie at the heart of man's investigations concerning the nature of the real world and his place in it. A rigorous critique of the social and moral implications of such questioning, based on an underlying view of desire and temporality, runs throughout Verga's novel, beginning with the preface. The important point to be made about the narrative's opening is, however, that such questions are raised specifically in relation to naming, that is, in relation to the rhetorical functions and the referential validity of language itself. In this way, the conventions of the village tale come under constant scrutiny in the narrative. The combination of simple, direct narration and ironic distancing is again typical of Verga's major novels, but by posing the problem of referential transparency in terms of language itself, *I Malavoglia* takes a skewed view of its own materials and becomes, as Russo has noted, an "epica ironizzata."[15] The novel thus utilizes the conventions of the village tale even as its own discourse breaks their unity in seemingly realistic fashion.

The problem of referentiality was a favorite topic of late nineteenth- and early twentieth-century novels. (The examples of Joyce and Proust come readily to mind, but there are many others.) Verga's narrator argues from tradition ("da che il mondo era mondo") to assert both the conventionality of naming and the impossibility of connecting signifier with signified in any *necessary* fashion in the real world of everyday reference. Indeed, the name "Malavoglia," which should mean "ill will," indicating both ill humor and reluctance, seems not to be an accurate description of the family at all. Such a disjunction would appear to be realistic, since there is no worldly reason why a name passed on for generations should accurately characterize each and every family unit. The narrator first reports this inaccuracy and then reaffirms it with his own evaluative commentary: "tutti buona e brava gente di mare, proprio all'opposto di quel che sembrava dal nomignolo, *come dev'essere.*"[16]

However, once Verga's narrator has clearly established the realistic conventionality of linguistic signs, his text then proceeds to utilize what appear to be the *necessary* relations of naming and named. The utilization of such relations becomes a strategy that is subordinate but nonetheless essential to the narrative's discourse. There is an allegory of familial naming at work in the novel, but it is created and exploited by the text itself, not by the world that the text is supposedly representing. It is ironic, therefore, that the allegorical relationship between "bad will" and the family is reaffirmed not as stubborness but, through the lupin deal, as the predetermined sin of desire itself ("mala voglia" or, literally, "bad desire"). In the development of the plot, the name functions as the emblematic representation of the "vaga bramosìa" of the preface's opening. The two most obvious martyrs of the piece are also appropriately named. It is true that Mena's nickname, Saint Agatha, has been bestowed by the family; however, "Bastiano"→"Bastianazzo" (evocative of the martyred Saint Sebastian) is the character's *actual* name. In this way, like Henry James and other turn-of-the-century realists, Verga manages to incorporate the allegorical naming of Romantic fiction into his seemingly realistic text.

Again, in Verga's novel this procedure is not, strictly speaking, allegorical, since both the irony and the occasional randomness of realistic naming prevent any allegorical reading from turning into an authentic key for interpreting the text. For Verga, naming is a mixture of allegory, irony, and chance. This mixture is demonstrated by the text's ironic introduction of Maruzza as "la *Longa*, una piccina," by the openly contradictory indications that "la Locca" and her sons are or are not weak-minded, and by the continual punning on the name *Provvidenza*. At one time or another, all of these questions of naming are implied in the speech or in the thoughts of the characters, but the overall arrangement of ironic and allegorical indicators is controlled by one figure alone, the supposedly objective narrator. This play of allegory and irony spreads throughout the discursive *and* diegetic aspects of the text to establish the two poles of the narrative's range of attitudes, which, as Spinazzola has shown, are those of pathos and satire.[17]

The narrative's treatment of Padron 'Ntoni's proverbs also demonstrates the pervasiveness of these ironic and allegorical effects. Like the narrator, Padron 'Ntoni argues from tradition to assert that "il motto degli antichi mai mentì,"[18] but, unlike the narrator, Padron 'Ntoni is unwilling or unable to distinguish between necessity and chance. He is therefore forced by the "logic" of his own feelings to assert that the *conventional* wisdom of the "ancients" is *necessarily* true. The text then provides examples of this proverbial wisdom:

> —"Senza pilota barca non cammina" —"Per far da papa bisogna saper far da sagrestano"— oppure —"Fa il mestiere che sai, che se non arricchisci camperai" —"Contentati di quel che t'ha fatto tuo padre; se non altro non sarai un birbante"— ed altre sentenze giudiziose.[19]

As is appropriate to Padron 'Ntoni's character, and as is generally true of common sayings, many of these proverbs are negative and all are conservative. They counsel caution, restraint, and obeisance to the established order. These and Padron 'Ntoni's other "sentenze guidiziose" consistently demonstrate a concern for the traditional roles of work and familial leadership and a fear of change in either of them. It is true that the distribution of the labor force and the organization of the family unit were both subject to important change in late nineteenth-century Italian life. Although the realist text is not required to concur in the value of such changes, it *is* obligated to represent the real world's onslaught on Padron 'Ntoni's models of traditional wisdom. Because of this obligation, Padron 'Ntoni's proverbs end up in the later chapters as jumbled phrases in a world that holds no place for them, as signifiers that have been severed from their original meanings and now exist without rhyme or reason ("senza capo e senza coda," p. 386).

It is nonetheless important to bear in mind that the lupin deal is Padron 'Ntoni's idea, and that in this instance the *Provvidenza* is not being used for fishing ("Stick to your trade"), but as transport for the objects of commercial exchange. Padron 'Ntoni himself thus goes against the traditional wisdom he so ardently defends. Bastianazzo is martyred as a result of the family's sin of desire against a "providence" that is both proverbial and divine. From this perspective, too, the allegories of proverbial wisdom combine with the irony of the Malavoglias' desire for change and create the narrative's sense of destiny in its depiction of the family's fall.

In certain respects, this mixture of Christian morality and everyday economics is a realistic aspect of the text's representation of life in mid nineteenth-century Sicily. Even "Campana di legno" invokes this combination during the bargaining with Padron 'Ntoni ("Ma un centesimo di meno non posso, in coscienza! che l'anima ho da darla a Dio!"). Once the lines of Christian references have been established, the narrative is free to move back and forth inside them, as in the punning on "providence" and in the irony of Campana di legno's other name, "Crocifisso" (this appellation for the one character who has neither Christian love nor charity). The text's framing of the lupin deal in terms of transgression and punishment does more than merely establish the narrative's validity as realism, since the frame itself indicates not only the pessimistic world view of Verga's characters but also the ideological slant of the text as a whole.

At first it seems that the entire matter is a simple one of credit and exchange ("un negozio di certi lupini da comprare a credenza per venderli a Riposto"); but as the news gets out that thè beans are spoiled, the deal has to be renegotiated with the mediation of Piedipapera (pp. 188-89). What had appeared to be a scheme to exchange produce that did have clear use value now becomes a matter of exchange that would be manipulated to *conceal* the values of use (which in this instance are obviously curtailed). The *form* of exchange remains, but its *content* has become irredeemably corrupt. True, exchange is never transparent. Like the act of representation itself, any exchange entails a metaphorical similarity that actively hides difference and that therefore depends on an *agreed upon* falsehood ("A = B"). Nonetheless, the added element of deceit colors the Malavoglias' part in the lupin deal from the moment the bargain is sealed ("Là! pagateli a Natale, invece di pagarli a tanto al mese, e ci avrete un risparmio di un tarì a salma!'. . . . E [Piedipapera] cominciò ad insaccare: —In nome di Dio, e uno!'").[20]

It might seem, then, that the family is being punished for their complicity in what would have become duplicity at the moment of reselling the lupins; however, the heavy-handedness of the narrator's foreshadowing at the end of the first chapter ("e questa fu *l'ultima* sua parola che *si udì*") and the coincidence of the "festa de' Morti" discussed throughout the second chapter make Bastianazzo's death seem something more than punishment for simple capitalistic deception.[21] Maruzza's death from cholera, contracted while she was earning "qualche soldo" by making rounds selling eggs and fresh bread (pp. 327-28), appears to be a retribution not for deception but for *any* desire for commercial profit outside the traditional channels of the family's activities as fishermen ("tutti buona e brava gente *di mare* . . . di padre in figlio, che avevano sempre avuto *delle barche sull'acqua,* e delle tegole al sole").

The question therefore arises, why is Verga's text so steadfastly opposed to the "vaga bramosìa" to change one's position in society by means of economic advancement ("per menare avanti la barca")? This question is not an easy one, but it is worth investigating, since it is central to the narrative's presentation of characters and events. Initially, the lupin deal represents this very type of "vague desire," but in the diegetic progression of the narrative, the lupins come to represent the house as well, since their loss eventually leads to the loss of the home and the eviction of the family. As we have seen, the fact that the lupins are rotten determines not only the practicalities of the exchange but also the text's moral judgment of the desire that inspired the deal. The corruption of nature ("lupini . . . avariati") entails the loss of pure and supposedly *natural* family life ("la casa *del nespolo*"). This corruption begins with the desire to change one's state in society, continues with the process of risk and potential gain or loss, and ends in disaster. The economic system of capitalist exchange is thus seen as the destroyer of the *focolare* and of the emotions of love and pity which the family engenders and on which it thrives. Bastianazzo is sacrificed on the altar of this new system of desires. Eventually, so is Mena, since she is denied the opportunity to beget her own family with the simple but good-hearted carter, Alfio. This occurs because of a series of reasons, most of which either feed into or stem from the lupin deal: first, the cupidity of Padron 'Ntoni as paterfamilias; second, the failure of the deal and the subsequent impoverishment of the family; and, finally, the dishonor caused by Lia's unfortunate reputation as a "fallen woman."[22]

Although Verga's narrative portrays the family's desire for change as a transgression, the text does not simply oppose desire to reason and then see the former as bad and the latter as good. Indeed, one problem with the system of capitalist exchange is that it is too coldly rational and thus sacrifices those very emotions and desires that, when combined with reason, make man human. Still, no sustained combination of reason and emotion is seen as possible within the text. This is because of Verga's extraordinarily pessimistic view of history's path, which is described in the preface as "il cammino fatale, incessante . . . per raggiungere la conquista del progresso."[23] For Verga, as for many writers since the Renaissance, the golden age of unity and contentment is past and the world is irrevocably fallen; there is no hope in heaven or on earth. Time does go forward, but only within a system of relations which is spurred by desire and which leads to predetermined doom. At best, all one can hope is to "ingannare il tempo" (p. 399). This is why the question of origins is broached but deliberately confused in Verga's texts. The origins *are* authentic and "timeless" (the "antichi"). But with the entry of desire for advancement and thus of capitalist time and its fiction of "progress," they are also barred. Once this desire has been set in motion, the only results seen as possible in this new world are negative and destructive: the suffering of la Longa, the sacrifices of Bastianazzo and Mena, the alienation and sickness of Padron 'Ntoni, and the walking "anomie" of young 'Ntoni. Even the note of hope sounded by the future union of Alessi and Nunziata is quickly silenced by the similarities between Alessi and Padron 'Ntoni and the example of the inevitable failures that that type of character is seen to experience in the new world.

In contrast to competitive economic advancement, Verga's text implies that work itself, and the old familial order on which it depends, are the true goals of life. In reward for the suffering involved in labor, mankind is compensated by a full affective life and by a traditional sense of honor. In reward for the attempts at economic advancement, one receives either an increase in property and a reciprocal loss in affectivity (as do "Dumbbell," Mazzarò of "La roba," and even Mastro-don Gesualdo) or outright misery (as do the Malavoglias). Because of Verga's view of worldly temporality, any respite from this chain of events is construed as either ephemeral or doomed. In Verga's reading of Italian history, in which the rise of capitalist competition and the specious linking of human with economic worth meant the destruction of the old familial codes of both work and honor, the attainment of life's true goals became increasingly difficult and finally impossible. To Verga, as distinct from Marx, it appeared not so much that labor produced value, but that labor, and the order it implies, like Padron 'Ntoni's "five-finger" metaphor for family life, *is* life's value. Outside of this frame, constructed from elements of both positivism and vitalism and then superimposed on Sicily's feudal heritage, all desire is seen as fetishistic and therefore tainted from its inception. The rotting lupins are simply the emblem of this desire's primal sin. Once again, as in Verga's other major texts, the signs of desire both represent and become the family's destiny.

The family's downfall is determined, then, by its attempt to retain the old codes of work and honor while espousing the new values of profit and capitalist exchange. The friction that this attempted conciliation causes is painfully evident in the scene of the family's pathetically confused rehash of the lawyer Scipioni's initial counsels (pp. 236-38). The lupin deal, however, is not the most violent transgression in the narrative, nor is its subsequent conciliation the most obviously forced. Young 'Ntoni, by attempting to retain the code of honor *and* turn a profit even as he renounces the values of work, becomes the text's true outcast, the prodigal son who returns home but does not reform.

'Ntoni's comings and goings contribute to the plot of the entire narrative, and especially the second half. When 'Ntoni returns from the navy, with all his experiences of the outside world and his confidence in his own knowledge and abilities, he has strong doubts about the importance and the practicality of the family's ventures, but even so he stays home and continues to perform as part of the unit. In the beginning of chapter 10, which later includes the tempest, the narrator describes 'Ntoni's familial labors as "traveling" on the sea; however, 'Ntoni is discontented and disconsolate ("'Ntoni andava a spasso sul mare tutti i santi giorni, e gli toccava camminare coi remi, logorandosi la schiena").[24] Nonetheless, when the work is most challenging and nature most reluctant to yield her bounty, 'Ntoni is at his best as a true family member ("quel ragazzo aveva il cuore più grande del mare. . . . —Il sangue dei Malavoglia!— diceva il nonno").[25]

As the family's economic difficulties become more pressing, however, and as 'Ntoni continues to wander aimlessly about the village like the race of "new men," going "girelloni pel paese" (pp. 318-19 passim), his alienation from village life is increasingly apparent. With the examples of the passing sailors to whet his appetite despite the emotional ties that would keep him home, 'Ntoni desires more ardently than ever to go off "a farmi ricco!" His second departure further damages the unity of the home ("Casa mia, madre mia," p. 246, or, as Mena says with Padron 'Ntoni's approval prior to 'Ntoni's leaving "—Il peggio . . . è spatriare dal proprio paese, dove fino i sassi vi conoscono, e dev'essere una cosa da rompere il cuore il lasciarseli dietro per la strada. 'Beato quell'uccello, che fa il nido al suo paesello,'" p. 321).[26] As is typical of the associative spread of Verga's prose, Mena's comments reintroduce both the imagery of mythic origins ("dove fino *i sassi vi conoscono*") and the serious use of proverbial wisdom ("Beato quell'uccello"). Mena's language thus condemns 'Ntoni for breaking the familial unity, yet it is not really 'Ntoni's intention to break this unity or even to move up in social status. He has no wish to become a member of the bourgeoisie (or to become "a lawyer," a profession that his grandfather associates with not working, because it is cut off from labor itself, p. 321). 'Ntoni simply wants to be rich, to live the fairy-tale life that others live in the cities far away and that he imagines to be "without work and worries" (p. 322). This indicates his real sin within the text, the desire to be both content and idle.

When he returns home after his long absence, his shame and his failure to achieve what was an impossible dream are obvious. He doesn't even have proper shoes ("Ma per fortuna delle donnicciuole, tutt'a un tratto si venne a sapere che era tornato 'Ntoni di padron 'Ntoni, di notte, con un bastimento catanese, e che si vergognava di farsi vedere senza scarpe," p. 341).[27] It is important for the subtlety of Verga's effects that at this point, rather than presenting an outright condemnation of 'Ntoni's actions and desires, the narrator plays on the family's spontaneous greeting of the errant son and on the emotional warmth and support portrayed as both natural and beneficial: "Ma il nonno e i fratelli gli fecero festa egualmente, come se fosse venuto carico di denari, e le sorelle gli si appesero al collo, ridendo e piangendo . . . e gli dicevano: —Ora non ci lascerai più, non è vero?"[28]

Of course, 'Ntoni does leave again, breaking the order of his return to family life and reversing the conclusion of the prodigal son motif. Because of the mechanisms already touched upon—'Ntoni's inability to reconcile the rules of work and honor with those of pleasure, and his desire for profit without labor—his ultimate exclusion from the social order is inevitable. Even the village's supposed sympathy for his difficulties becomes the insincere "carità pelosa" (p. 363) evocative of Manzoni's novel. The violence of 'Ntoni's exclusion is evident both in terms of individual action (in 'Ntoni's stabbing of Don Michele) and institutional condemnation (in the elaborately orchestrated trial scene, and the defense lawyer's disastrous failure to reconcile the legal code of the fledgling nation with the moral code of the village in relation to the gossip about Don Michele and Lia). This violence indicates 'Ntoni's true role in the narrative; he is not the hero but the scapegoat.

The presentation of 'Ntoni and the contraband incident, like the description of Padron 'Ntoni and the lupin deal in the first part of the novel, reaffirms the deep-seated ambivalence of Verga's text. Transgression against the given social order is seen as both disruptive and dangerous, but the institutions upholding that order (the judiciary, the police, the military, the hospitals, the economic system itself) are seen to be equally dangerous to the future of Italian social life. Like Hegel, Verga sees that the relation between master and slave severs the master's connection with the products and activity of labor and therefore alienates him from his humanity in a way that can never be assuaged (as in Campana di legno's trading, or in Don Michele's incapacity to love anything but his own official "braids," chaps. 13-14). At the same time, the solution of turning everyone into masters would cut all men off from labor and ruin humanity; whereas turning everyone into equal laborers is seen as historically impossible, since the development of capitalism means the end of both the family and the working unit (hence Padron 'Ntoni's particular bitterness at going "a giornata"). In other words, Verga can see and even sympathize with 'Ntoni's continued anomie—his estrangement from society as well as his violent reactions and his inability to understand the nature of his own plight. No solution except continued estrangement appears possible, however, given Verga's view of history and 'Ntoni's continuing sins of idleness *and* desire. 'Ntoni must suffer and pay; but, unlike Achilles or the prodigal son, he is permitted neither momentary success in battle nor any redeeming knowledge of his own state.

It is important to see that Verga's attitude is not merely a middle-class celebration of the joys of work and the stability of the family (a perspective that is so apparent in Mazzini's influential nineteenth-century treatise, "The Duties of Man"), and that Verga's attitude does not represent a materialist polemic against the destruction of family life by an economic system that effectively turns the subordinate members of the family unit into slaves (as in *Capital* 1.4.15). Verga's position is fundamentally different from both nineteenth-century idealism and materialism, since no solution to these social problems is seen as possible in his texts. By locating the primal moment of family unity *outside* the time of the narrative itself, and by portraying the family's decline in the modes of both myth and realism, Verga's text judges the present and the future of social life in late nineteenth-century Sicily. Suffering remains, as in the text's other archetypal figure, the "mater dolorosa" ("la madre addolorata," pp. 280 passim).[29] No worldly solution can be found, as is evidenced by the text's constant criticisms of both capitalism and socialism.

'Ntoni's ultimate exclusion is required, then, both by the moral valuation and the diegetic progression of the text. There is simply no place for him in Aci Trezza. "—Addio— ripeté 'Ntoni. —Vedi che avevo ragione d'andarmene! qui non posso starci. Addio, *perdonatemi* tutti" (p. 403).[30] As he leaves once again, 'Ntoni finally acknowledges the voice of that other transitional figure, the sea, who literally "devoured" the voice of his father Bastianazzo (p. 189) and would have eaten 'Ntoni too (p. 295). The sea is the figure who has no fixed home except as the mediation between Aci Trezza and the wide world, the figure in whom all who labor as fishermen are mirrored, but in whom no one can trust, as the choral spread of proverbial commentary repeatedly indicates throughout the text: "Il mare è amaro e il marinaro muore in mare" (pp. 203, 222, 230); "Chi ha roba in mare non ha nulla" (p. 300).[31]

The motif of 'Ntoni's sea "travels" and "battles" in chapter 10 is extended and revised in chapter 15 by the sea's "voice," which is at once that of an adversary and a friend. This voice represents the authentically individual *genius loci* ("ad Aci Trezza ha un modo tutto suo di brontolare") as well as the universal outcast ("perché il mare non ha paese nemmen lui, ed è di tutti quelli che lo stanno ad ascoltare, di qua e di là dove nasce e muore il sole").[32] The sea's story belongs as an integral part of 'Ntoni's story ("ed è di tutti quelli . . . e par le voce di *un amico*") because, like 'Ntoni, the sea represents the first and last outcast, finally rootless, constant and undying, yet condemned to know the endless sorrow of desire and infinite exchange.

At the novel's conclusion, as at its beginning, the interaction of realism and myth thus creates a mythologized image of human history, in which desire and hope do exist, but in which there is finally no room for hope's fulfillment. As the 1880s progressed and Verga saw the continuing development of Italian capitalism and Sicily's increasing dependence on, and subservience to, the official powers in the North, the last vestiges of lyrical hope disappeared from his writing. In "La roba," the destructiveness of Mazzaro's fetish for things appears to taint not only the *forms* of exchange but also the *essence* of things themselves ("Roba mia, vientene con me!"); nor does the possession of land, as an authentic part of nature, afford any escape or solace in this new world, as is so apparent in the plight of Mastro-don Gesualdo.

The impersonality of these later narratives indicates Verga's growing bitterness. At the same time, the narratives establish what will continue as the cornerstones of the standard mythology of the dependent South: the corruption of the Garden world and the culpability of the powers in the North. Even as his narratives provided the elements for a careful analysis of this mythology, Verga himself shared in the skewed perceptions of the solitary Sicilian. His texts thus arise as the reaction to, and simultaneously the embodiment of, his subjects' perceptions of their own predicament. The complexity of economic and cultural dependency's effects on the myths buttressing Verga's narratives are uncannily evocative of the clashes of perspective in many of William Faulkner's novels, in Faulkner's equally mythologized depictions of the postbellum American South. Before turning to Faulkner's works, however, it is instructive to trace the remarkably different combinations of myth and realism in the narratives of Verga's English translator, that other poet of passion and continual exchange, D. H. Lawrence.

Women in Love *and* The Man Who Died:
From Realism to the Mythopoeia of Passion and Rebirth

It would be perverse to confine *Women in Love* to the category of realism, but it would be equally misleading to depict the novel solely as symbolist. This is because both these strains of nineteenth-century literature feed so strongly into Lawrence's narratives. Indeed, they mingle in such eccentric and unpredictable ways as to have frustrated generations of literary critics and historians, not to mention the broader reading public. There exists a consensus among the multitude of Lawrence's partisans and antagonists that his work is difficult, but the crux of the difficulty, the peculiar interaction of realism and myth designed to explain and validate his developing philosophical system, has probably perplexed more readers than it has convinced. Having recognized the abiding and very real nature of this difficulty, we might hope to venture where more luminous angels have at times feared to tread.

Like the great family sagas of nineteenth-century realism, *The Rainbow* and *Women in Love* trace the genealogical, social, and moral development of a principal family, the Brangwens of Nottinghamshire. *Women in Love* breaks with the saga tradition, however, in the radical limitation of its psychological focus, which centers on the romances of the Brangwen sisters with Rupert Birkin and Gerald Crich. In *Women in Love*, the progress and conflicts of these paired romances furnish the matter and the plot of the narrative.

Since the Crich family history as mine owners figures with some prominence in the early and middle sections of the novel, it might appear that Lawrence retained the nineteenth-century realists' interest in the historical development of labor and of familial and social relations in industrial England. Long before the novel's conclusion, however, it is clear that Lawrence is using these notations of social history as yet another symbolic prop for his own moral system, which claims historical validity even as it subordinates the facts of history by giving them a secondary and merely supportive role. As in Verga and later in Faulkner and Pavese, the ideological interpretation of history does play an important part in Lawrence's texts, but in indirect and often obscure ways.

Lawrence's drive to rejuvenate, reconstruct, and *openly* recode and reverse older symbols in a new, all-encompassing system eventually gave him his reputation as a visionary writer rather than a merely diagnostic one. As this drive grew, Lawrence began to leave behind the type of realist frame he had built for the series of narratives published in the early twenties. By the end of his career, he was often using myth as the predominant organizing principle and realism as its ungainly handmaiden, as a reading of *The Plumed Serpent* or *The Man Who Died* shows.[33] In a way, Lawrence's end as a full-fledged prophet underscores his beginnings in the classical realist tradition of the nineteenth century, followed by his development as a mature novelist in the crisis years of World War I. The times cried out for answers to the West's problems, and Lawrence thought he had caught at least a glimmer of a solution. After a careful examination of two central chapters in *Women in Love,* "Excurse" and "Death and Love," we should be in a position to account for the striking organizational and stylistic differences in one of the most successful works in his patently mythic mode, *The Man Who Died.*

"Excurse," like the earlier wrestling chapter "Gladatorial" and the later "Snowed Up," is organized as a battle,[34] but unlike the struggle between Birkin and Gerald, or that between Gerald and Gudrun, the one between Birkin and Ursula is ultimately and happily resolved. The chapter's three major sections—the gift of the jeweled rings, the argument and the rejection of the rings, and the long, two-phased reconciliation and sexual coda—clarify the nature of the opponents as well as the questions at issue. As the chapter progresses, the battle motif is emphasized by the narrator, who openly establishes an evaluative, slightly ironic distance in reporting more than his characters can apprehend ("It was a crisis of war between them, so they did not see the ridiculousness of their situation," p. 349). As in the narrator's occasional use of humor, this ironic distancing permits the narrative both to present and to qualify the characters' often overstated positions and their deeply passionate encounters.

At first, when Birkin appears with the motorcar at the grammar school where Ursula teaches, there is hardly a hint of the battle to come. If anything, the important struggle seems to be the one going on *within* Birkin, in his initial disappointment at Ursula's coolness ("her face was closed and unresponding, and his heart sank"). This is followed by his despair at ever establishing any "serious connections" (p. 345). By shifting from the straightforward, distanced narration of the opening paragraph into the *style indirect libre*, the narrator reproduces Birkin's thoughts with a semblance of immediacy:

> At moments it seemed to him he did not care a straw whether Ursula or Hermione or anybody else existed or did not exist. Why bother! Why strive for a coherent, satisfied life? Why not drift on in a series of accidents—like a picaresque novel? Why not? Why bother about human relationships? Why take them seriously—male or female? . . . And yet, still, he was damned and doomed to the old effort at serious living.

The mingling of narrator and character consciousnesses in this passage permits the articulate if repetitive reproduction of Birkin's often confused and excited mental processes ("Why bother! . . . Why not? . . . And yet, still, he was damned and doomed"). Though Lawrence uses the *style indirect libre* sparingly, its effects help to reflect the psychological processes of his characters and thus to create the psychological realism that is a principle attribute of his middle work, as his narratives move back and forth between description and the give and take of narrated dialogue.

Since Lawrence uses so much conversation between individuals, his approach in *Women in Love* is often more direct and, in this respect, more fully representational than other writers' use of occasional, illustrative snatches of speech, or Verga's "choral" voices.[35] Nonetheless, both the dialogues themselves and the narrator's interspersed summaries of action and speech contribute directly to the chapter's underlying motifs: battle, death, and rebirth. Lawrence's conversational and descriptive technique is incrementally repetitive, as he admits in the 1919 preface, but even though these repetitions create the appearance of individual expression and self-discovery through speech, they are not random:

> He smiled, slightly, He wanted her to come to him. . . . He had taken her at the roots of her darkness and shame—like a demon, laughing over the fountain of mystic corruption which was one of the sources of her being. . . . As for her, when would she so much go beyond herself as to accept him at the quick of death? . . . He was not very much interested any more in personalities and in people—people were all different, but they were all enclosed in a definite limitation, *he said*. . . . They acted and reacted involuntarily according to a few great laws, and once the laws, the great principles, were known, people were no longer mystically interesting. . . . Ursula *did not agree*. (P. 348; my italics)

This summary and the subsequent discussion lead directly to Birkin's mention of Hermione, providing the psychologically realistic motivation of jealousy for the ensuing argument and for Ursula's violent rejection of the rings. The argument, too, is replete with the imagery of death, which is now presented directly in the characters' dramatic language. There is only brief narratorial commentary to indicate the rising emotional tensions, and it is always keyed to the characters' seemingly visible physical reactions:

> "Won't it be lovely to go home in the dark?" she said. "We might have tea rather late. . . ."
> "I promised to be at Shortlands for dinner," he said. . . . "Hermione is there. . . . I suppose I ought to say goodbye to her. . . ."
> Ursula drew away, closed in a violent silence. He knitted his brows, and his eyes began to sparkle again in anger.
> "You don't mind do you?" he asked irritably.
> "No, I don't care. . . . Why should I mind?" Her tone was jeering and offensive. . . . "I *assure* you I don't. . . . Go where you belong—it's what I want you to do."
> "Ah, you fool! . . . For you can only revolt in pure reaction from her—and to be her opposite is to be her counterpart."
> "Ah, opposite!" cried Ursula. "I know your dodges . . . [and] your word-twisting. You belong to Hermione and her dead show. . . ."
> "If you weren't a fool . . ," he cried in bitter despair, "you'd see that one could be decent, even when one has been wrong. I *was* wrong to go on all those years with Hermione—it was a deathly process. . . . But no, you would tear my soul out with your jealousy. . . ."
> "I jealous! I—jealous! . . ." And Ursula snapped her fingers. "No, it's you who are a liar. It's you who must return, like a dog to his vomit. . . . It is lies, it is false, it is death. . . . You belong to that old deathly way of living—then go back to it. . . ."
> And in the stress of her violent emotion, she got down from the car and went to the hedgerow, picking unconsciously some flesh-pink spindleberries, some of which were burst, showing their orange seeds. (Pp. 349–50; emphasis in the original)

Throughout this encounter, Birkin is associated with darkness, corruption, and death. In the heat of confrontation, the accusations themselves appear realistic, but Ursula's "unconscious" actions at the end of this segment indicate the framework of mythic associations: Ursula with Persephone (the hedgerow and the picking of the spindle berries; the orange seeds, similar to pomegranate seeds), and Birkin with Pluto, the "demon" of darkness through whose power comes life. This is one of Lawrence's favorite myths. It remained important throughout his writings and provided the subject matter for one of his last and finest poems, "Bavarian Gentians" (originally entitled "Glory of Darkness").[36] He had used the myth earlier in *Twilight in Italy* by associating Pluto with the "dark-skinned Italians ecstatic in the night and the moon" and then polemically contrasting them with the "blue-eyed old woman ecstatic in the busy sunshine."[37] In *Twilight in Italy*, the crucial problem of union—precisely the one that Lawrence strove to solve in "Excurse"—remained without solution. By itself, Christianity (represented in the travel book by the dispassionately "neutral" and "average" monks working in the garden below) is inadequate for this "twilight" task of joyous mediation:

> Where, then, is the meeting point: where in mankind is the ecstasy of light and dark together, the supreme transcendence of the afterglow, day hovering in the embrace of the coming night like two angels embracing in the heavens, like Eurydice in the arms of Orpheus, or Persephone embraced by Pluto?
>
> Where is the supreme ecstasy in mankind, which makes day a delight and night a delight, purpose an ecstasy and a concourse in ecstasy, and single abandon of the single body and soul also an ecstasy under the moon? Where is the transcendent knowledge in our hearts, uniting sun and darkness, day and night, spirit and senses? Why do we not know that the two in consummation are one; that each is only part; partial and alone for ever; but that the two in consummation are perfect, beyond the range of loneliness or solitude? (P. 31)

In *Twilight in Italy*, as in several of Lawrence's last narratives, the myth precedes and openly frames the presentation of the philosophical system. This type of allegorical procedure does occur in *Women in Love*, in the text's open and often treated use of Germanic and Eastern myth to pair the narrative's central characters with a variety of mythic correspondents, such as Pan, Cain, the Nibelungs, Norse gods and tricksters, Cybele, and Aphrodite, many of which may have been adopted from Frazer or from other turn-of-the-century anthropologists.[38] The most scintillating aspect of the novel is, however, the extraordinary subtlety with which Lawrence uses mythic counterparts not to allegorize but to shade and fulfill his characters in a seemingly real world. Birkin does correspond both to Pluto and to Pan ("like a demon laughing over the fountain of mystic corruption which was one of the sources of her [Ursula's] being"), but at this point in Lawrence's development, the myths do not openly lead the narrative. Rather, they provide depth for the psychological realism that then feeds back into his complex moral system. The struggle between darkness and light continuing throughout "Excurse" is resolved in the "star-equilibrium which alone is freedom" (p. 365), but the resolution occurs first on the realistic plane of sexual, psychological, and cultural motivation, and only second on that of myth. Lawrence's creation, use, and reuse of mythic signs thus becomes an active process of symbol *formation* rather than the mere *repetition* of a prior set of allegorical emblems (such as occurs in D'Annunzio's *Il fuoco*, for example, or in part 1 of Goethe's *Faust*). Oddly enough, the dynamic mixture of allegory and symbol actually distinguishes Lawrence's brand of psychological *realism*. This combination is one reason why Lawrence's writing at this point was not only highly original but also extremely demanding of its audience.

The openly allegorical elements of myth in "Excurse" derive from two primary sources, the cult of the Great Mother and Genesis. The first of these occurs in Birkin's thoughts ("Ursula was the perfect Womb, the bath of birth, to which all men must come!", p. 353). The image extends the earlier textual references to Cybele, Aphrodite, and other avatars of the Great Goddess (pp. 196, 281). For Lawrence, if this female power remains separate, either apart from, or strictly opposed to, maleness (as the initial reflection of the moon in "Moony"), it is both frightening and destructive, a "hateful tyranny." At the same time, however, Lawrence thought he saw a way to resolve this male-female opposition in a developing system of relations culminating in equilibrium. This vision gives Lawrence's work its sense of hopefulness even amidst despair.

The second openly mythic reference occurs in Ursula's consciousness five times, first just before the "dazzle" of revelation at the inn:

> She saw a strange creature from another world, in him. It was as if she were enchanted, and everything were metamorphosed. She recalled again the old magic of the Book of Genesis, where the sons of God saw the daughters of men, that they were fair. And he was one of these, one of these strange creatures from the beyond, looking down at her, and seeing she was fair. (P. 357)

The indication that Ursula "recalled *again*" and also the paratactic biblical style ("that they were fair") point up the origin of this imagery in Ursula's developing religious sentiments in chapter 10 of *The Rainbow*. In this way, the image serves to tie *Women in Love* and *The Rainbow* together as a complete picture of her moral progression into womanhood. At the same time, it is important that whereas the imagery had initially been used in service of the psychological individuation of an adolescent mind, in *Women in Love* it becomes part of a full system of values and beliefs, which extends past the isolated ego of the single character to include not only Birkin but eventually all of humankind. The image is repeated as Ursula discovers the "heavenful of riches" at the back of Birkin's thighs ("It was the daughters of men coming back to the sons of God"). The subsequent imagery infuses Ursula's "paradisal . . . flower of luminousness" with Birkin's Miltonic "dark fire" of electricity. As Ursula discovers and releases this "source of the deepest life-force, the darkest, deepest, strangest life-source of the human body, at the back and base of the loins," she and Birkin become one, yet remain integral beings emanating from that communal source, each an "essential new being . . . quite free." The "sons of God" imagery is repeated again and again as Ursula finds this source, "deeper, further in mystery than the phallic source," and from which come "the floods of ineffable darkness and ineffable riches" (p. 359).

The obvious anality of this and other passages is more than simple perversity. Lawrence felt he had found a way to pass beyond the rational, male-dominant (and thus strictly oppositional) aspects of phallic love by propounding an unseen source of the human spirit deeper than the externally verifiable effects of the phallus.[39] This is why the source must remain mysterious even though its existence is definite, since its essence can only by divined from its sensual effects.[40] In Lawrence's system, this internalized source is common to both men and women. Its discovery and utilization lead to emotional and spiritual fulfillment. At the same time, neither Ursula's "emotion" nor Hermione's "spirituality" can be permitted to remain separate traits: if permitted dominance, either will lead to destruction and death. Death remains necessary because of the world's "fall" into mechanical rationality (exemplified in the novel by Gerald as the new type of mine owner, succeeding his now outmoded, benevolent father), but in Lawrence's overall system, this death is seen as only preliminary to rebirth into knowledge of the corrupt yet fecund source of the human spirit, the "source of darkness" (p. 362).

This is why Birkin and Ursula, upon reawakening out of their "pure swoon" at the inn, decide "then and there" to write their formal resignations from "the world of work." From *Women in Love* on, Lawrence's system always pushed him past the individual subject into a theory of social relations and so into history, although history itself, like the pre-Christian "sons of God" motif or another of his favorites, that of the phoenix, is made to fit into the patterned cycles of birth, corruption, death, and rebirth. This indicates a central difference between Lawrence and several of his more pessimistic nineteenth-century models, such as Verga, since Verga had seen the world as irredeemably fallen, whereas Lawrence saw the fall itself as pointing toward resurrection and renewal.[41] As opposed to any linear and pessimistic view of history, Lawrence's cyclical vision thus permitted him to develop the theme of rebirth in relation not only to individual characters but also to mankind generally. This is true even though in *Women in Love*, and indeed during the entire period of World War I, both for Lawrence and the West itself, the central question remained suspended and finally unanswered: rebirth into what?

After the scene at the inn, Ursula and Birkin drive off again, now thoroughly intertwined in the dual imagery of light and dark, death and life, rational understanding and mystic revelation, knowing and not knowing: "Darkness and silence must fall perfectly on her, then she could know mystically, in unrevealed touch. She must *lightly, mindlessly connect with him*, have the *knowledge which is death of knowledge*, the reality of surety in not-knowing" (p. 365; my italics). As they enter Sherwood Forest, with its literary overlay of Romantic battle as well as its darkness and "spirit of place," they are still struggling, but they are struggling together rather than one against the other: "They would *give each other* this star equilibrium which alone is *freedom*" (my italics).[42] Like Birkin's gift of the rings and then Ursula's gift of the flower ("a piece of purple-red bell-heather"), this gift is both symbolic and palpably real, in the physical exchange of intercourse. Again, the ultimate scene of union reflects and extends the psychological processes of the characters; moreover, it completes the gradual internalization that has made the phases of their mutual rebirth possible.

At first Birkin had remained outside of Ursula's power, "like a demon, laughing over the fountain of mystic corruption," afraid of the "perfect Womb." After the initial reconciliation on the road, he, too, had felt reborn: "His mind was sweetly at ease, the life flowed through him as from some new fountain, he was as if born out of the cramp of a womb" (p. 356). The images of the fountain and the womb are thus blended and internalized *before* the mutual play of revelations at the inn. The image of the gift is not completed, however, until the union is actively reaffirmed in the full night of darkness, "the night masculine and feminine, never to be seen with the eye, or known with the mind, only known as a palpable revelation of mystic otherness."

Both of them have their desire "fulfilled" as the three topoi that organize the chapter—the gift, the night journey, and the rebirth into knowledge—are brought together in tentative conclusion: "She had her desire of him, she touched, she received the maximum of unspeakable communication in touch, dark, subtle, positively silent, *a magnificent gift and give again*" (my italics). They awake into the new day, full of remembrance of the primal, "secret" knowledge that has continued to exist, even amidst the mechanically rational contemporary world, and that they have now inherited as their ultimate gift. But the problem of the real world and their return to it remains: "It was already high day when he awoke. . . . Then they kissed and remembered the magnificence of the night. It was so magnificent, such an inheritance of a universe of dark reality, that they were afraid to seem to remember. They hid away the remembrance and the knowledge." For Lawrence, passion is therefore necessary to spiritual and emotional rebirth, but mere sexual groping is never enough. Knowledge of passion's rites, and the ability to conceal these if need be, must both precede and follow.

Like "the gift and give again," rebirth is never final; it must be continually affirmed in repetition. This is why the motif recurs with such frequency throughout the remainder of the novel, and especially in chapter 29, "Continental." There, as elsewhere in the final chapters, Ursula and Birkin are reborn together, along with the world itself (during the sea journey, pp. 443-44, or the trip south at the end of "Snowed Up"), whereas Gerald and Gudrun are reborn separately, one apart from the other (pp. 451, 453). These separate rebirths merely underscore Gerald's and Gudrun's inability to come together to form a whole couple as

Ursula and Birkin had done previously. Though this inability becomes increasingly apparent in "Snowed Up," it is clear as early as "Death and Love," the chapter that follows "Excurse" and with which in certain respects it forms a tandem. Lawrence's text is, however, proceeding by opposition rather than by complement, as may be seen on both the realistic and the mythic levels.

In part, the imagery of the two chapters links them together. As in "Excurse," equilibrium is once again a key term in "Death and Love," but here, rather than occurring in the narrator's depiction of the two characters together, the term occurs as a function of Gerald's individual will ("He would have to find something to make good the equilibrium," pp. 368-69; "he would equilibriate himself," pp. 375-76). This separateness also appears in the chapter's allusion to Genesis ("She reached up, like Eve reaching to the apples in the tree of knowledge," p. 379), since here Gerald remains an object of fear and an "unutterable enemy."

As in the previous chapter, the play of light and dark recurs in the text's imagery, and Gerald, like Birkin, appears as a creature from another realm, "a supernatural being" (p. 391), but now, rather than biblical, the allusion is Gnostic. Gerald is the Light ("His face was strong and luminous"), but, unlike Ursula's light, Gerald's cannot mingle with darkness. As "Hermes" (p. 393), "the enemy," or the luminous angels in Gnostic creation myths, he is trapped in the darkness of matter and uses his will not to mix with it but to battle against it. When Gerald comes to Gudrun's room in the night, the battle is joined:

> He had come for vindication. She let him hold her in his arms, clasp her close against him. He found in her an infinite relief. Into her he poured all his pent-up darkness and corrosive death, and he was whole again. . . . This was the ever-recurrent miracle of his life. . . . And she, subject, received him as a vessel filled with his bitter potion of death. . . . The terrible frictional violence of death filled her, and she received it in an ecstasy of subjection, in the throes of acute violent sensation. . . . All his veins, that were murdered and lacerated, healed softly as life came pulsing in, stealing invisibly in to him as if it were the all-powerful effluence of the sun. His blood, which seemed to have been drawn back into death, came ebbing on the return, surely, beautifully, powerfully. (Pp. 393-94)

Gerald is permitted momentarily to purify himself of darkness by subjugating Gudrun, but the "good immediate darkness" of "Excurse" (p. 363) has now become the "poison" Gerald expels into his opponent. Even after this violent union, they remain irremediably separated and, therefore, unfulfilled:

> She wanted to look at him, to see him.
> *But she dared not make a light,* because she knew he would wake, and she did not want to break his perfect sleep, that she know *he had got of her.*

> She *disengaged* herself, softly, and rose up a little to look at him. There was a faint light, it seemed to her, in the room. . . . In this darkness, she seemed to see him so distinctly. But he was far off, in another world. Ah, she could shriek with torment, he was so far off, and perfected, in another world. She seemed to look at him as at a pebble far away under clear dark water. And here was she, left with all and anguish of consciousness, whilst he was sunk deep into the other element of mindlessness, remote, living shadow-gleem. He was beautiful, far-off, and perfected. *They would never be together.* Ah, this awful, inhuman distance which would always be interposed between her and the other being! (P. 395; my italics)

Unlike "Excurse," in which the imagery of the fountain and Birkin's view from without is eventually internalized within the couple's relationship, here Gudrun remains to the end looking in from the outside ("She seemed to look at him as at a pebble far away under clear dark water"). Although Gudrun "makes a light" at the beginning and end of this segment (pp. 391, 397), now she is unwilling to disturb Gerald's "perfect" sleep, in which the only light seems to come from his own "living shadow-gleem." As in the myth of Cupid and Psyche which underlies this segment, Gudrun is never permitted to join with Gerald in total knowledge of him. Even as lovers they only come together in opposition and torment, as light versus dark, consciousness versus unconsciousness. This type of relationship is merely reaffirmed in the struggles and tragic conclusion of "Snowed Up." As Gerald awakes and leaves Gudrun in order to return in solitude to his own home, he has once again become the "dutiful," coolly rational yet "unconscious" avatar of twentieth-century industrial man: "Ah, the insensitiveness of that firm tread!" Gudrun's unspoken lament is echoed in the final comments of the narrator, who once again has become distanced and evaluative: Gerald "went quickly along towards Short-lands, in a grateful self-sufficiency." It is clear that Gerald's gratitude is due not so much to Gudrun as to his own untroubled feeling of solitary adequacy, but far from representing his strength, his very illusion of the perfect "self-sufficiency" of the individual ego turns out, ironically, to be his greatest weakness.

Another of the myths organizing Gerald's struggle with Gudrun, the story of Faust, serves to underscore this same basic weakness. Gerald is not self-sufficient, even though at times he might appear to be. The figure of Faust, of the single man who desires to know and therefore to control all, points up the fundamental ambiguity of Gerald's situation, in which he cannot unite blood passion with intellect and therefore fails both emotionally and spiritually. He *wants* Gudrun, yet he is as unable to mingle with her as she is with him. In "Death and Love," Gerald says, "I'd sell my soul a hundred times—but I couldn't bear not to have you here. I couldn't bear to be alone" (p. 377), yet Gudrun instinctively withdraws from the power of his will: "He drew her closer to him, with definite movement. . . . 'No,' she murmured, *afraid"* (my italics). The economically colored Faustian image recurs just before the final scene of battle, as Gerald stalks his prey like a wild beast, yet decides with cool rationality to invade Gudrun's home and dominate her: "But he could get at her—he would get at her. He would not go back tonight till he had come to her, if it cost him his life. *He staked his all on this throw"* (p. 387; my italics).

Like the myth of the Gnostic angels, the Faust myth again demonstrates Gerald's inability to form personally meaningful and lasting "connections." The repetitively emphasized snow myth and the fable of the failed *Übermensch* at the novel's conclusion also reaffirm this inability. These are not, of course, the only allegorical procedures at work in the narrative (the social allegory of the *roman à clef* as well as the open intertextuality with George Eliot's novels, especially *Adam Bede*, are two others). The combined effect of all these diverse elements creates an aura of symbolic destiny for the struggle between Gerald and Gudrun; moreover, the final outcome is openly prophesied in "Water-Party," after the escape from the "mad" cattle, when Gudrun strikes Gerald: "And she felt in her soul an unconquerable lust for deep brutality against him. . . . He recoiled from the heavy blow across his face. . . . 'You have struck the first blow,' he said at last. . . . '*And I shall strike the last*,' she retorted involuntarily, with confident assurance. He was silent, *he did not contradict her"* (p. 194; my italics).

Through repetition of the battle, and prophecies of its outcome on both realistic and mythic levels, Gerald's death, like the battle itself, comes to appear "inevitable" (p. 391). The repetition of phrases used to describe different characters' psychological reactions at crucial moments also creates this aura of inevitability and foreknowledge: "*Something froze Birkin's heart*, seeing them standing there in the isolation of the snow, growing smaller and more isolated" (p. 502, at the conclusion of "Continental"); "But [Gerald] *felt something icy gathering at his heart"* (p. 525; my italics). In the end, Gerald's initial mark of Cain (p. 28) is thus fulfilled in the narrative as he becomes the ritually self-destroyed scapegoat. The willful violence of Gerald's destruction is the fitting conclusion to a battle that, ironically, both he and Gudrun had to fight even though neither could finally win.

Returning for a moment to the two chapters "Excurse" and "Death and Love," we should note that these, too, are opened and closed with a key phrase. Again, the phrase is a common literary description of emotional response and may therefore appear simply as part of the novel's psychological realism. At the same time, however, it is used to introduce and conclude the two mythic battles and thus enters Lawrence's narrative scheme on the levels of both realism and myth. The phrase is used first to describe Birkin's reactions to Ursula's initial coolness: "She consented. But her face was closed and unresponding, and *his heart sank*." The second occurs in the narrative's description of Gudrun *after* Gerald's union with her. At this point he has finally awakened and she wants him to leave, so much so that she is "sick with terror" that he will stay. "'You must go, my love'. . . . He put his arms round her. *Her heart sank"* (p. 397). The initial disappointment in "Excurse" leads to the joys of union and of secret knowledge, whereas the concluding repetition of the phrase in "Death and Love" reaffirms the failure of both and thereby serves as yet another textual prophecy of what has been inscribed as Gudrun and Gerald's ultimate and now seemingly inevitable doom.[43] Their union has tied them together, but in the last chapter, the battle, rather than ending, is to become total war.

If *Women in Love*, in reflecting the world's uncertainties and failures during the years of the novel's creation, takes as its subject "things gone dead," then its most fitting companion piece, the narrative of man's resurrection, is *The Man Who Died*.[44] This is not to say that the two narratives share the same mode. All of the myths that both support and complicate the realism of *Women in Love*, as well as other myths, do recur in the later narrative, but now in a dominant rather than a subordinate role. This dominance represents Lawrence's break with the techniques and strategies of nineteenth-century realism. Lawrence began *The Man Who Died* in 1927 and completed it in 1928. Two years later he himself lay dead in Vence. The narrative was published in Paris by Harry and Caresse Crosby under its original title, *The Escaped Cock*. This title was a bit too suggestive for Lawrence's English and American publishers, who later brought the book out under a less obviously phallic one. Though it is occasionally referred to as a novel, the term long story is more accurate, since the whole work comprises no more than 20,000 words, or roughly fifty to sixty pages.[45]

This brevity is an important factor in the narrative's overall effect, because the story thus avoids the tediousness of much of Lawrence's other writing in a similar mode, such as *The Plumed Serpent* or even *St. Mawr*. Still, no amount of concision can save the text from occasional lapses into the comical sententiousness of B-grade dialogue:

> "Master!" said the slave, "Our lady would speak with you at the house of Isis."
> "It is well," said the wanderer. (P. 193)

Fortunately, this type of strained formality is not too common, and it passes quickly enough not to mar the rest of the narrative's language, which at times equals the finest passages of lyrical prose in Lawrence's canon.

The story describes the resurrection of a figure who at first appears to be Christ. He rises from the tomb as a disillusioned and embittered "saviour" and renounces his mission and his earlier preachings. Later, but as the dismembered Osiris rather than Christ, he becomes fully healed through the internalization of the powers of the sun in conjunction with the ministrations of a priestess of Isis. Like a romantic version of Apuleius's *Golden Ass, The Man Who Died* treats Lawrence's two great themes of passion and death within this framework of resurrection. Again, the mythic nature of Lawrence's apocryphal morality play is immediately apparent on the surface of the text (the initial "awakening" in the tomb, the references to the Roman soldiers, and the encounter with Mary Magdalene are only a few examples of the openness of Lawrence's technique here). It is clear that by the end of his career, Lawrence had become impatient with merely restating the formulas of realism in order to support the now openly mythic and totalizing pattern of his moral systems. In this narrative, his impatience led him to a procedure that went far beyond realism's general tendency toward symbolism and that finally ended in the open re-creation of myth itself.[46]

The tale is introduced by a parable, the story of the cock that tries to escape. In reverse order, the introduction thus "reads" as the legend for the emblem that is the remainder of the narrative. The parable begins: "There was a peasant near Jerusalem who acquired a young gamecock which looked a shabby little thing, but which put on brave feathers as spring advanced, and was resplendent with arched and orange neck by the time the fig-trees were letting out leaves from their end-tips." This seems a standard opening for a popular tale, replete with the "There was [once]" opening and the informal ellipsis of common speech ("which looked [like] a shabby little thing"), but it is important to point out the control and, at the same time, the suggestiveness of Lawrence's prose in this and similar passages. The metamorphosis of the "shabby little thing" into the "resplendent" cock is matched by the seasonal rebirth of nature herself. The metaphorical association of psychological attributes with the details of physical description (*"brave* feathers") subtly provides a "personality" for the animal in the fabulist tradition. The hint of sexual potency ("resplendent with arched orange neck") is furthered by the choice of fig trees as nature's symbol of fruition. This suggestion is then openly affirmed in the following paragraphs:

> By some freak of destiny, he was a dandy rooster, in that dirty little yard with three patchy hens. He learned to crane his neck and give shrill answers to the crowing of other cocks, beyond the walls, in a world he knew nothing of. But there was a special fiery colour to his crow, and the distant calling of the other cocks roused him to unexpected outbursts.
>
> "How he sings," said the peasant. . . .
> "He is good for twenty hens," said the wife.

The associative richness as well as the synesthesia of the passage ("there was a special fiery colour to his crow") are typical of much of the text;

moreover, these paragraphs are important not only for their evidence of technical mastery but also for the open functioning of their symbols within Lawrence's now thoroughly allegorized system. The linking of sunny brightness and sexuality recurs with regularity throughout the narrative, in the thoughts of the central figure and in dialogue as well as in descriptive passages. The image of the cock confined within the walls and then betrayed and tethered by his "masters" parallels the situation of the entombed Christ. Indeed, as the cock's crows of protest and defiance wake the peasant, they also coincide with the awakening of the "man who died" ("At the same time, at the same hour before dawn, on the same morning, a man awoke from a long sleep in which he was tied up"). This coincidence, stressed through the clause's initial trebling, links the two figures together and ends the parable of defiant potency as it introduces the narrative's central figure.

Lawrence's open allegorization of the symbols of his *own* system now gives way to the full recasting of *standard* mythology. Lawrence uses Christian and Egyptian frameworks, and he also makes open references to the "all-tolerant Pan" (p. 197) and mentions the purple anemones of Adonis's rebirth (pp. 166, 209); moreover, Lawrence is probably following Frazer's work and intending the cock itself as a symbol for Attis.

By playing these different kinds of symbols against one another, Lawrence's text occasionally creates a mild form of irony, as when the peasant's wife mistakes the "gleam" of money for true brightness (p. 181), but this type of ironic distance is utilized only in relation to minor characters who have not understood the narrative's system of values. Far from creating a disturbance within the overall allegory, these effects merely serve to reinforce its unity. This result is therefore opposite the use of irony in Lawrence's more realistic and less dogmatic texts.

It is also worth noting that the irony in *The Man Who Died* serves not to glorify the all-knowing position of the narrator, as would have been standard in realism, but instead to emphasize the allegorical system itself. Though this system is manifest within the text, it exists apart from the narrative as the unified, generative source of meaning. In realism, this source of meaning would be the author's perception of the world, but in Lawrence's openly mythic narratives, he had stopped trying merely to describe the world he saw around him. Again, the allegorical system leads rather than follows in these narratives, and the presentation of realistic place, character, or event remains thoroughly subordinate.

It is still necessary, having said this, to remember that Lawrence did not simply abandon the human world for that of his visionary dream. He wanted desperately for the world to change in accordance with his emotional and spiritual values, and he hoped that his writings would provide the public with the knowledge necessary for that change. This is true despite the obvious social skepticism of the text (pp. 183-84 passim), the recurrent disdain for people whose only values lie in their material possessions and who therefore can have "no rebirth," and the overt antipathy toward slaves and servants. Although by 1928 Lawrence claimed to have given up his "mission" and to have decided to leave mankind to its own blindness (like his alter-ego within the narrative), the very creation of these mythic texts demonstrates the continuation of his hopes for the way the world should and *could* become.[47]

If I have described Lawrence's system at this point in his career as fixed, that does not mean that the narrative to which it gives rise is devoid of movement. Once again, the movement in Lawrence's narrative is the motion of desire itself. Although the "man who died" awakens in part 1, his complete rebirth and the healing process it entails are not accomplished until the end of part 2. His primary lack—the fulfillment of which gives rise to the narrative progression—is the capacity for desire. His mind functions, and he can experience and recall physical sensation, but in part 1 he is not yet whole:

> But the sun had grown stronger. . . . He opened his eyes, and saw the world again bright as glass. It was life, in which he had no share any more. But it shone *outside him*, blue sky, and a bare fig-tree with little jets of green leaf. *Bright as glass, and he was not of it, for desire had failed.* . . . Yet he was there, *and not extinguished.* (P. 170; my italics)

The gradual awakening of the "man who died" is shaded, as is the initial metamorphosis of the "shabby little" cock, by the play of light and dark and is ultimately accomplished through sexual union. The "man who died" has known darkness, and now, in the night, must learn the power of light. This knowledge is provided by his experience with the priestess of Isis. Women are essential to this process of rejuvenation, although Lawrence's misogyny and his basic fear of women required that even the most powerful of female characters remain supportive rather than dominant (in which case they regularly appear destructive). In an openly symbolic rather than realistic frame, the union between the priestess and the "man who died" recalls that of Birkin and Ursula in the chapter "Excurse." As the priestess ministers to his wounds, he feels himself come alive:

> Then slowly, slowly, in the perfect darkness of his inner man, he felt the stir of something coming. A dawn, a new sun. A new sun was coming up in him, in the perfect inner darkness of himself. He waited for it breathless, quivering with a fearful hope. . . . "Now I am not myself. I am something new. . . ."
> He crouched to her, and he felt the blaze of his manhood and his power rise up in his loins, magnificent.
> "I am risen!"
> Magnificent, blazing, indomitable in the depths of his loins, his *own sun dawned*, and sent its fire running along his limbs, so that his face *shone unconsciously.* (Pp. 206-7; my italics)[48]

Although in certain respects this scene may appear perversely comic, its organization is important for understanding the narrative's system. The dawning of the suns *inside* the "man who died" completes his rebirth. Again, as in "Excurse," the mutuality of this fulfillment is essential. The priestess had waited alone for seven years, since she was twenty, for the "re-born man" whose sun would be neither the ephemeral sun of an Anthony nor the cold "winter" sun of a Caesar (pp. 188-90). She had served the "mystery" of Isis in Search, who looks "for the fragments of the dead Osiris, dead and scattered asunder." The "last reality" of his return is again described in terms of the sexuality of the "inward" sun, which represented, for Lawrence, the move past ascetic Christianity that he had been hoping to make as early as *Twilight in Italy:* "For she was Isis of the subtle lotus, the womb which waits submerged in bud, waits for the touch of that other inward sun that streams its rays from the loins of the male Osiris" (p. 188). The priestess' thoughts after her fulfillment echo the cry of joy of the "man who died": "I am full of Osiris. I am full of the risen Osiris!" (p. 208).

Through the ritual of healing, even the wounds of the "man who died" have become suns: "'They are suns!' he said. 'They shine from *your* touch. They are my *atonement* with you'" (p. 207; my italics). He now knows of the departure that "destiny" has decreed for him, and he prepares to leave the priestess and the child conceived within her. As he does so, the text again emphasizes the exchange of the sensual touch and the mutual connections of the internalized suns that begin within but then extend past the single character: "So he knew the time was come again for him to depart. He would go alone, with his destiny. Yet not alone, for the touch would be upon him, even as he left his touch on her. And invisible suns would go with him" (p. 209). Despite the serpent imagery concluding the narrative and the doom it implies, the "man who died" knows he will endure and return: "And I shall come again; all is good between us, near or apart. The suns come back in their seasons: and I shall come again" (p. 210). For Lawrence, unlike Freud, repression was a contingent and avoidable rather than an inevitable phenomenon. This position frames the ending of *The Man Who Died* by providing a Reichian "escape" for the intended scapegoat (pp. 210-11) and thus turning the violently repressive death of Christ into the passionate rebirth of Osiris. Christian repression is replaced with full sexual expression ("I am risen!"; "I shall come again"). This "blood-knowledge" of the sexual power ablaze within each individual is made to appear as naturally prior to the mechanistic repression of Western society. The scapegoating, which appeared necessary in *Women in Love*, is avoided in *The Man Who Died* by Lawrence's creation of a character who admits the powers of both passion and intellect in human relationships. Whereas the realism of *Women in Love* poses these psychological and moral questions as problems, *The Man Who Died*, through its open manipulation of myth and symbol to create new meaning, attempts to provide solutions.

This completes the mythopoeia of passion and rebirth in the story. The concluding imagery of the sun and its cyclical return are appropriate to the text, but their significance extends beyond its limits. At the time of the story's creation, Lawrence was ill, as the "man who died" had been ill and as the world itself seemed ill. It is impossible to ignore the public nature of the scandals surrounding Lawrence's works and his own feelings of intimate association with many of his central characters. There is perhaps no real answer to Mark Schorer's provocative question: "what, up to the bitter black end, impelled him?"[49] But Lawrence's hopes for cyclical and passionate rebirth, as through his creation the artist *himself* publicly became the reincarnated dying and reviving "man/god," might provide a clue.[50]

It is undeniably true that Lawrence's system led him to a dogmatic and thus distorted view of the individual psyche, of the relations between the sexes, and of human history itself; however, the desire that drove Lawrence to set forth and develop that view remains as valid and intriguing today as it was when he wrote. It impelled his life and his art, and it gave us the one great visionary writer of English narrative, in both realistic and mythic modes, of the period between the two world wars. Today it is obvious that the vital force Lawrence saw as potential in every human being cannot by itself provide a solution to social alienation in the fallen world of the little man, yet Lawrence's attempts to glorify that force, and to free vitalism from its positivist restraints, did inspire his readers and his critics to review the vision of the world which we inherited from the nineteenth century. It is perhaps not only his fault, but also ours, if his vision and the hope for human revitalization it represents have remained unfulfilled.

Southern Literature/Southern History: Flem in Hell, or The Trickster Tricked

In Faulkner's literary version of the history of the American South, realism at times leads myth and at other times follows it. Whereas Lawrence adopted these two different techniques in different narratives, again and again Faulkner used them both within the *same* narrative. This mixing of techniques helped to create the extraordinary depth of Faulkner's major novels and stories as well as the intricate ironies in perspective and attitude for which these works are so well known.

The Snopes trilogy is neither the most mythic nor the most realistic of Faulkner's narratives. The saga of the Snopeses' conquest of Yoknapatawpha County lacks the constant aura of allegory and symbolism so apparent in *Absalom, Absalom!* and *A Fable.* Even its most realistic effects are not as clearly set in the narrative's historical frame as those in *Intruder in the Dust,* or in some of the early works heavily influenced by Faulkner's relationship with Sherwood Anderson. It is, however, precisely this establishment of a mid-range between realism and myth which makes the trilogy so fascinating.

The boundaries of this range are clearest in *The Hamlet* (1940), the trilogy's first volume, composed some twenty years before Faulkner continued the story of the Snopeses in *The Town* (1957) and *The Mansion* (1959). *The Hamlet* describes the arrival and ascendance of the Snopes clan in Frenchman's Bend, a country town situated twenty miles southeast of Jefferson. The narrator summarizes, in the opening paragraphs, the hamlet's history and its succession of leading families, beginning with the holder of the original land grant, the aristocratic "Frenchman" with his tremendous pre-Civil War plantation, or, as the narrator puts it, "his family and his slaves and his magnificence."[51] By the period of the narrative's opening in the early 1900s, however, the plantation has been in ruins for many years and the land has been bought up by Will Varner. Varner, the current power in town, is a farmer, a businessman, and seemingly a master of all trades and professions.

It is during Varner's dominion that the Snopeses, first Ab and then his son Flem, arrive in Frenchman's Bend. They are sharecroppers, a far cry from the "aristocracy" of the Old Frenchman or even from the middle-class respectability of Yoknapatawpha's current elite of bankers and businessmen; however, whatever Ab and Flem lack in social credentials they more than make up for in shrewdness. Flem's rise from farming to clerking in Varner's store and eventually to the presidency of the bank in Jefferson, with Eula Varner as his wife, provides the subject matter for the rest of the trilogy. Faulkner's depiction of the clan's advancement in social status is similar to certain aspects of Zola's Rougon-Macquart series. However, to a far greater extent than Italian, French, or even American Naturalism, Faulkner's work creates strong doubts about the new social order in the American South and about the morality of capitalist exchange underlying it.

The realism of *The Hamlet* is not difficult to trace. Within the saga format, the social, political, judicial, and economic institutions of the rural South are portrayed in the novel's early twentieth-century setting.[52] Country humor, snatches of dialect, and precise description of nature and of the man-made environment are staples of the text. There is some use of the *style indirect libre,* but the prose is more straightforward and far less impressionistic than that of *The Sound and the Fury* or *Absalom, Absalom!* The mainspring of the story—the battle of wits between the itinerant sewing machine salesman, V. K. Ratliff, and Flem Snopes—also appears typical of the post-Civil War shift from an agricultural to a mixed economy, in which the predominant objects of exchange were not only land, crops, livestock, and sex but also currency and commodities.[53] In terms of realistic psychological motivation, it is especially significant that this battle begins as a seemingly rational, everyday contest between two skillful traders, Ratliff and Flem. It ends, however, in an almost heroic struggle, replete with mythic allusions and colored by a Balzacian obsession for the hoard of money which the narrative initially suggests may have been buried somewhere on the Old Frenchman place "when Grant overran the country on his way to Vicksburg" (p. 4). It is true that the person most obsessed with the fetish for the treasure is Henry Armstid, who was hardly stable to begin with; but the original idea to buy the Old Frenchman place from Flem and the elaborate strategy conceived to clinch the final deal both stem from Ratliff, the supposedly calm, unflappable defender of Frenchman's Bend's moral order. It was also Ratliff's idea to enlist the eccentric diviner, Uncle Dick Bolivar, in the search for the money. By the climax of the search, both Ratliff and Bookwright have become infected as well.

The overtly mythic elements of the trilogy come from a variety of sources.[54] Some stem from classical and preclassical Greek, Eastern, and Germanic mythology, such as the mythologizing of nature, the direct references to Eula as Helen, Earth Mother, and Brunhilde, and the Vulcan/ Venus/Mars triangle in *The Town*. Still others come from fabulist traditions. These include elements adapted from Aesop (especially the animal imagery), American Indian tales, European fables, and Southern folklore. As has often been noted in Faulkner criticism, this last source of material feeds into Faulkner's narrative by way of both oral and authentically literary examples. The work of George Washington Harris, A. B. Longstreet, Mark Twain, and others provided Faulkner with anecdotes and tall tales. At the same time, folklore enlivened his narration with the irony of rustic and particularly Southwestern humor; moreover, Faulkner was perfectly willing to go outside this group of writers to adapt whatever he needed, as in the ironic use of Washington Irving's "Headless Horseman" in the Labove-Eula Varner incident ("'Stop pawing me,' she said. 'You old headless horseman Ichabod Crane,'" p. 122).

The ironic tone of this type of humor mitigates the most Romantic elements of Faulkner's mythologizing of Southern history. The result, in *The Hamlet* as well as in parts of *The Sound and the Fury*, *Go Down, Moses*, and several other works, is the recasting of the battle cycles of myth and chivalric Romance in the light of ironic introspection and skepticism. In this way, the fictional *history* of the battle of wits between the traders of "Yoknapatawpha" serves as the *metaphor* that brings together the elements of realism and myth.

The tempering of myth with irony is especially evident in several of the most obviously mythic portions of the narrative's contest, including

Ratliff's tale of Ab's heroic horse swap with the legendary Pat Stamper; the scene of Flem in hell, with its Faustian overtones and the twist at the end when Flem and not the Devil is victorious; and finally, the legend of the treasure hidden in the land on the Old Frenchman place, which both opens and concludes the narration.[55] The battle between Ratliff and Flem is predicted by Ratliff himself in his early conversation with Will Varner about Jody Varner's vulnerability to the Snopeses:

> "I think the same as you do," Ratliff said quietly. "That there aint but two men I know can risk fooling with them folks. And just one of them is named Varner and his front name aint Jody."
> "And who's the other one?" Varner said.
> "That aint been proved yet neither," Ratliff said pleasantly. (P. 28)

Later, in the midst of his dealings with the Snopes clan, Ratliff reiterates his intention to best Flem. He gives Mrs. Littlejohn a message for Will Varner: "But if you happen to think of it. Just tell him Ratliff says it aint been proved yet neither. He'll know what it means" (p. 87). Finally, just before his calamitous defeat in the deal for the Old Frenchman place, Ratliff tells Bookwright that he intends to keep fighting "them Snopeses," though he cannot know that what is now a battle will, in *The Town* and *The Mansion*, turn into a full "crusade." Ratliff depicts his defense of the helpless idiot Ike and his continuing struggle against Flem in terms of simple moral determination:

> "I was protecting something that wasn't even a people [i.e., Ike Snopes], that wasn't nothing but something that dont want nothing but to walk and feel the sun and wouldn't know how to hurt no man even if it would and wouldn't want to even if it could. . . . I never made them Snopeses and I never made the folks that cant wait to bare their backsides to them. I could do more, but I wont. I wont, I tell you!" (P. 321)

But by the end of the narrative, it is clear that Ratliff is merely fighting a rear-guard action against the Snopes invasion. Like Ab Snopes in Ratliff's own narration of the horse swap with Pat Stamper, and like Jody Varner in Jody's early dealings with Ab, Ratliff is not to be the victor in this battle but the vanquished: the trickster tricked.

Flem is similar to Ratliff and Varner in that he will trade any item on which he can turn a profit; but, unlike them, Flem will trade not only in things but also in people. The narrative makes this point in the course of the elaborate ploy Ratliff devises in the combination sewing-machine-and-goat-farm deal. This transaction also involves Mink Snopes, to whom Ratliff sells the machine. The threat of barn burning, which earlier had proved the bane of Jody Varner, recurs in this section. It is now used by Mink, and Ratliff is free to repeat it in his dealings with Flem:

> "Then you give him a message from me [Mink]. Say 'From one cousin that's still scratching dirt to keep alive, to another cousin that's risen from scratching

dirt to owning a herd of cattle and a hay barn. To owning cattle and a hay barn.' Just say that to him." (P. 76)

The transaction is far too elaborate to summarize here, but the result is a moral victory for Ratliff, who does protect Ike and provide him with his $10 inheritance, plus $6.80 in profit. In order to do this, however, Ratliff has to "dig into his own pocket," as Cleanth Brooks has pointed out in his description of the deal.[56] Flem's "loss" is not nearly so clear-cut as Ratliff would have liked. The entire deal seems psychologically and culturally realistic, down to Ratliff's stratagem of the goat farm and his reliance on the domestic desires of Mink's wife. At the same time, the story of the inheritance and the traded and retraded notes grows out of a series of mythic precedents, one of them Ovid's version of the story of Erysicthon, the monarch who attacked a sacred grove of Ceres and was punished for his sacrilege with an insatiable hunger (*Metamorphoses* 8). To appease this hunger, Erysichthon sold and resold his daughter, who had the power to change her form and could return to him after each sale.

Erysichthon's original sin against nature was thus compounded by his breaking of the bonds of blood ties, in a steady progression of desacrilization. This moral failing resembles Mink's threat against Flem and Flem's eventual betrayal of Mink (as "blood kin," p. 320). More importantly, the story recalls Flem's use of Ike and his inheritance. Flem has an insatiable desire for profit, but he is not capable either of passion or satisfaction. His sexual impotence, revealed later in the trilogy, is emblematic of this lack as a human being and of the tragedy of waste represented by his marriage to the "earth-goddess" Eula, the "supreme primal uterus" (p. 114). Ratliff perceives Flem's shortcomings early in the story. He also sees that they have made Flem what he is: inhumanly rational and calculating and therefore ideally fitted to the cold and pitiless world of competitive capitalism and endless exchange.

Both Ratliff's understanding of Flem and Ratliff's all-too-human weakness in the battle against him are especially apparent in one of *The Hamlet's* most striking pieces, the mock-mythic anecdote of "Flem in hell." Initially, the presentation of the anecdote creates some confusion, since it is difficult to determine the perspective from which the anecdote is narrated. It seems to occur in Ratliff's imagination as he drives his buckboard along the road to Frenchman's Bend. Both the humorous tone of the piece and the language of rural trading would support this assumption ("He says a bargain is a bargain. That he swapped in good faith and honor," p. 149). It is true that Ratliff had been thinking about Flem as he rode along ("and there remained only the straw bag, the minute tie, the constant jaw"). The presence of the "straw bag" seems to tie the segments of narration together (pp. 147, 149, 150), but the bag has also been noted by the objective narrator (p. 145). The completeness of the anecdote and its italicized presentation as a set piece make it appear as something more than just a tale Ratliff would think up while driving along. Indeed, it seems like a literary version of a story told among a group of men swapping yarns; in fact, it is an avatar of a typical country yarn about the fellow who traded with the Devil and beat him, and ended up owning hell in return for the effort.[57]

Perhaps it is thus best to say that the story occurs in Ratliff's consciousness, with the text's omniscient third-person narrator intervening only in subtle ways to organize its presentation. Since the anecdote concludes book 2, there is no immediate reintroduction to clarify its perspective. This type of confusion, based on the often unexplained sharing of knowledge between the characters and the narrator, and on at least momentarily unclear perspective, is standard in Faulkner's more obviously modernist texts, but it is extremely rare in *The Hamlet*.[58] Ratliff and others do tell yarns that are presented as such in the text. (The tale of Ab Snopes defending the local honor in the horse trade is an early example.) But, except for the story of Flem in hell, the perspective is always clearly established.

The disturbance of the otherwise unified presentation is not accidental. The reader is jolted by the uniqueness of the sudden shift, and this momentary disjunction creates a critical distance. This distance is utilized by the text to alert the reader's critical faculties to the presence of an overriding irony within the story. The anecdote appears to be a simple version of the trickster tricked, in which Flem outwits the Devil. At this point in the narrative, such a reading would indicate Ratliff's knowledge of his opponent's cunning. It would also emphasize Ratliff's understanding of Flem's skills, since forewarned is forearmed. In the overall organization of the novel, however, the real victor is Flem, and the loser is not the Devil but Ratliff. Ironically, the figure of the trickster tricked is ultimately redoubled in the very person in whose consciousness the tale of Flem in hell seems to originate. The sudden disturbance of perspective introducing the tale is thus one of the narrative's formal methods of alerting the reader to what at this point is only an ironic possibility.

The outlines of the anecdote are simple. Flem has traded his soul to the Devil. We are not told what he received in return, but the natural assumption—as in the Faust myth underlying the anecdote—is that it was knowledge. This would be the knowledge of trading itself, of how to get along in the economics of the new postwar world. The entire deal is represented as a financial transaction, in which Flem did not actually "swap" his soul, but only offered it as security for his note (p. 152). When Flem comes to redeem the note, however, the Devil's underlings cannot find the soul. The humor in the description of their search and their bafflement in reporting its failure to their ruler is typical of Ratliff's style of narration:

'We done looked everywhere. It wasn't no big one to begin with nohow, and we was specially careful in handling it. We sealed it up in an asbestos matchbox and put the box in a separate compartment to itself. But when we opened the compartment, it was gone. The matchbox was there and the seal wasn't broke. But there wasn't nothing in the matchbox but a little kind of dried-up smear under one edge. And now he has come to redeem it. But how can we redeem him into eternal torment without his soul?' (Pp. 149-50)

At first the Devil is merely annoyed by his subordinates' incompetence and Flem's persistence:

> 'Tell him he can go. . . . Tell him we had a flood, even a freeze. . . . Turn him out. Eject him.'
> 'How?' they says. 'He's got the law.'
> 'Oho,' the Prince says. 'A sawmill advocate. I see. All right,' he says, 'Fix it. Why bother me?' And he set back and raised his glass and blowed the flames offen it like he thought they was already gone. Except they wasn't gone.'

The humor, the use of dialect, and the depiction of the Devil as a decadent Southern oligarch all contribute to the irony that tempers the myth and makes it resemble an authentic yarn; moreover, the reference to "the law" and the subsequent depiction of the Devil as a judge disputing a defendant's claim (pp. 152-53) demonstrate the narrative's evaluation of the very real limitations of the legal system in dealing with ethical and social problems. Here as elsewhere for Faulkner, the law is not adequate in and of itself to treat specific questions of morality. These limitations are later made explicit in the scene of the country trial in the "Spotted Horse" episode (pp. 322-32), in which Flem, even though absent, is again victorious.

Since Flem refuses to leave, the Devil first suggests tempting him, like Marlowe's Faust ("'the gratifications . . . the vanities'"), but as for "the gratifications," Flem has no interest in that type of passion or satisfaction ("He says that for a man that only chews, any spittoon will do"). "The vanities" turn out to be what he had in his suitcase all along. These possessions, too, are depicted in commercial terminology ("He brought a gross with him"). The suitcase itself has been "specially made up for him outen asbestos, with unmeltable straps.'" In other words, he has come with confidence and is prepared for a long stay.

In the last scene of the tale, Flem beats the Devil at his own game. Flem simply outargues his opponent by sticking to the terms of the original note and insisting on payment. More like Jody Varner than Will, the Devil still appears confident he can handle Flem and even threatens him with "criminal action," as Jody had implicitly threatened Flem's father. Again like Jody, the Prince ignores his elder counselor's advice and goes ahead with his dealing, but since the soul is gone, the Prince can't pay. "Who are you?" he screams, realizing at last that he is beaten. Flem now takes his place on the throne, "with that straw suitcase . . . among the bright crown-shaped flames." The Devil looks up in panic, "his eyes a-popping," and then tries to scramble off: "And the wind roars up and the dark roars down and the Prince scrabbling across the floor, clawing and scrabbling at that locked door, screaming."

Flem has got what he came for. He has taken over hell itself. Rather than hacking his kingdom out of nature, as Thomas Sutpen and even the Old Frenchman had done, Flem simply outwits the present owner. Ratliff imagines Flem sitting on "the Throne," just as before he had heard of Flem sitting in Will Varner's specially made flour barrel on the Old Frenchman place ("It was Flem Snopes that was setting in the flour barrel," p. 91). The text also notes another parallel between this Prince and the Varners: like the Varners in relation to the Old Frenchman, the Prince is not the original Devil, not the initiator of the line, but only the inheritor (as the Devil's counselor reminds him: "*Your father* made, unreproved, a greater failure. Though maybe a greater man tempted a greater man," p. 151; my italics).

This similarity between the mythic anecdote and Flem's actual situation as the new owner of the Old Frenchman place is, of course, intended by the text. It is made clear in the beginning of book 3, when the reader discovers exactly where Ratliff has been heading all along. He shows up at Will Varner's lot looking "neat, decorous, and grave like a caller in a house of death." He says to Varner, "You must have been desperate." It is true that Eula Varner was pregnant by McCarron, but her shame is not what Ratliff means. The narrator says: "He meant no insult. He was not even thinking of Varner's daughter's shame or of his daughter at all. He meant the land, the Old Frenchman place. He had never for one moment believed that it had no value. . . . And when he considered who Varner had relinquished possession to, he believed that the price had been necessity and not cash."

The parallels between the anecdote and Flem's conquest of the Varners's domain are emphasized not only by Ratliff's own words ("'You must have been desperate'") but also by the narrator's description ("like a caller in a house of death"). This accumulation of mythic associations is continued by the narrator at the close of book 3, when Eula is openly depicted as Persephone, the "wife" of Hades: "in the back seat with her mother, Mrs. Snopes sat. The beautiful face did not even turn as the surrey drew abreast of the store. It passed in profile. . . . It was not a tragic face: *it was just damned*" (p. 265; my italics). Again, Ratliff is part of the group Eula passes, but the perspective is not his alone. This mix of perspective permits the narrative to create the redoubled irony of the trickster tricked even as it appears to proceed by means of straightforward third-person description. In other words, the *ironic* disjunction of the incidents creates the distance between Ratliff and the all-knowledgeable narrator even as Ratliff's own discourse appears to be an *allegorical* reflection both of his own understanding and of Flem's situation. Flem's acquisition of the Old Frenchman place leads to the next exchange of the property, in which Ratliff, Bookwright, and Armstid are all duped by Flem's artifice. By the end of the novel, therefore, it is clear that Ratliff has not understood as much as his own words seemed to indicate.

At the same time, this distinction between Ratliff and the narrator should not be exaggerated. There are also important similarities between them, as there are between Ratliff and another major character, Will Varner. These latter similarities are apparent early in the novel and are openly emphasized by the text. Both Ratliff and Varner enjoy activity for its own sake and associate it with health ("'So you got well, hah,' [Varner] said. . . . 'I got busy,' Ratliff said. . . . 'Maybe that's the same thing,'" p. 77). Activity thus creates not only value but also the enjoyment of both use and exchange. Both Ratliff and Varner, moreover, share a certain amount of sympathy for their fellows. This sympathy springs from the faculty of imagination and from a sense of morality. However, there is also an important difference between Ratliff and Varner. Ratliff is unmarried and "itinerant," whereas Varner is rooted. Because of this, Ratliff can afford to view the situation in Frenchman's Bend with greater detachment than Varner can. Indeed, it is only when his detachment leaves him, in the obsessive search for the gold which concludes the novel, that Ratliff falls prey to Flem Snopes.

As long as his detachment and humor remain in force, Ratliff shares, to some extent, the logical position of the narrator: ironic yet sympathetic, knowledgeable yet only subtly condemnatory. This similarity is especially obvious, since Ratliff delights in storytelling and actually narrates portions of the narrative in his own voice. Like the narrator, Ratliff indulges in puns, wordplay, and in occasional commentary on the oddities of the Snopeses' practices of naming and of I. O.'s senseless proverbs. At the opposite extreme from Ratliff, the figure furthest from the narrator is Flem, whose thoughts are never presented with the technical closeness of the *style indirect libre*. So even though Ratliff is bested in the struggle with Flem, and even though Ratliff has some obvious limitations (his lack of roots and of feminine companionship), the narrative's sympathy for him as a character is never destroyed.

The implications of this continuing sympathy are important for the text and for the view of the world which it fosters. There are two major tricksters struggling in the novel, but they are not of the same stripe. Each exists at the boundaries of the moral and social institutions of village life (as Ratliff says at one point to Mrs. Littlejohn: "I aint never disputed I'm a pharisee," p. 198). In moral terms, one is good, the other bad. Indeed, Flem is so effective *because* he is evil, which, in the Faulknerian view of the world, means both inhuman and unnatural. For this reason, even Ratliff comes to regard Flem not just with distaste or even active animosity, but with "something very like terror" (a notation that is stressed through the narrator's suspended description of Ratliff's, and then the

Justice's, similar reactions, pp. 320-21, 329). By dissociating human sympathy from the faculty of imagination, and then negating the first and thoroughly rationalizing the second, the narrative creates the most dangerous threat to continuing human existence in the new South: the Faustian version of *homo oeconomicus*, Flem Snopes.

The power and effectiveness of Flem's role are the reasons why Ratliff, like the rest of the people in town, really "'cant beat him'" (p. 317), and why only the violence of a ritually purified Mink Snopes can rid Jefferson of the scapegoat at the trilogy's conclusion. Faulkner sees and freely admits the existence of evil in the world, but he is unable to offer any solution to the problems it creates except in terms of individual perseverance (like Ratliff's) or in seemingly transcendentally ordained violence (like Mink's).

The complexity of this situation again redoubles the irony of Ratliff's initial whimsy of "Flem in hell," followed by his own ultimate defeat in *The Hamlet*, since, through Ratliff, the figure of the narrator shares in the moral implications of the defeat. Ironically, it is *good* that Ratliff loses, because his loss demonstrates his human susceptibility to passionate desire, which permits him to experience both joy and sorrow. By openly turning the mythic underpinnings of the text against its most realistic psychological aspects, Faulkner's narrative creates a set of distancing devices which are more complex than those of the earlier examples of realism we have considered. These devices control the reader's reactions by forcing him to sympathize with certain characters and, at the same time, to evaluate their actions in a critical manner. Faulkner's irony is thus the opposite of any straightforward allegorical procedure. In becoming the trickster tricked, Ratliff ironically reaffirms his own humanity, along with that of the narrator, his author, and the participating reader. As the villagers say at the novel's end while discussing Armstid's mad obsession:

> "That Flem Snopes."
> "That's a fact. Wouldn't no other man have done it."
> "Couldn't no other man have done it. Anybody might have fooled Henry Armstid. But couldn't nobody but Flem Snopes have fooled Ratliff." (P. 365)

Because of the strange web of oppositions and similarities among the narrator, Ratliff, Varner, and Flem, and because of the extreme and seemingly arbitrary nature of the debasement of the last victim (Armstid) at the novel's conclusion, it should be clear that there is more involved in the text's depiction of the contest between Ratliff and Flem than just economic gain or the affirmation of moral virtue. Indeed, at question here is the very theory of desire and imitation which is implicit in the text's representation of the Ratliff-Flem rivalry. As I have suggested, in certain respects the actions and strategies of both Ratliff and Snopes mime those of the other. These two characters form a doubled pair and appear to desire a series of third objects, but they desire these objects only because of and through the desire of the other.

As the novel proceeds, this contest *for* something else becomes more and more a contest *against* the other. The obsessive nature of this type of relationship is manifest in Ratliff's gradual loss of his prudence and judgment. That such obsession leads not only to Ratliff's downfall but also to a momentary disruption of the broader social fabric is evident in Armstid's madness and in his family's hardship, which are both caused in part by the horse auction (as a result of which Armstid loses his money and very nearly his life) and by the special type of desire on which the auction depends: cupidity, or, in this instance, the hope of getting something in exchange for little or nothing.

Seen in this way, the horse trading in the "Spotted Horses" episode serves as an appropriate backdrop for the search for the treasure and the final deal involving the Old Frenchman place. Within Faulkner's narrative, as capitalistic desire fuses with mimetic desire, representation as such gives way to appropriation. In other words, imitation gives way to both personal and social violence. The resultant instability is manifest in the *real* dissolution of the public order, in the wild scene of the ponies' stampede. In certain respects, the visible effects of this disorder are humorous (the horses in Mrs. Littlejohn's boarding house, the chase through the streets), but the underlying disruption should not be taken lightly. The inability of the normal social institutions to restore order in and of themselves is emphasized by the scenes of irrepressible rage in both the rural and the city courts. Finally, the reestablishment of order is effected by the designation of the now totally insane victim ("the gaunt unshaven face which was now completely that of a madman," p. 366). Ratliff and Bookwright become "sane" again, and Flem becomes clearly victorious, in part because the differences between all of them and Armstid are now so apparent. Though Armstid cannot be saved, his public victimage permits the chaos of nondifferentiation (man↔beast, owner↔owned, sanity↔madness) to be replaced with the publicly acknowledged and carefully differentiated hierarchy: "Anybody might have fooled *Henry Armstid*. But couldn't *nobody but Flem Snopes* have fooled Ratliff."

This type of rivalry and ritual victimage, with its displacements and continually failed mediations, is a major component in many of Faulkner's works. It is especially obvious in the incest (potential and purely imaginary) and in the violent intrafamilial rivalries of *Absalom, Absalom!* and *The Sound and the Fury*, but the important distinction in *The Hamlet* is that these Girardian rivalries are only secondarily sexual. Their primary source here is monetary. Whereas in many of his theory of desire and imitation which is implicit in the text's representation of the Ratliff-Flem rivalry. As I have suggested, in certain respects the actions and strategies of both in the new South's competitive capitalism and in the economic and social desires it fosters. As becomes increasingly clear in the trilogy, the South's adoption of capitalism—its importation of a socioeconomic system that in many ways was not its own and in which it remained dependent on external models and funds—seemed almost as dangerous in Faulkner's view of twentieth-century America as it had in Verga's view of nineteenth-century Sicily.[59] To put this in other terms, Ratliff imagines Flem taking over hell by confounding the devil and establishing himself on the throne. In the overall progress of the trilogy, however, it is not hell that Flem Snopes takes over but Yoknapatawpha itself.

Faulkner's regionalism in *The Hamlet* re-created a fictional Southern county as well as a full system of moral and social values which strove to transcend the historical limits of the region. This mythologized portrayal of the heroic traders of the post-Civil War South offers no practical, far-reaching solution to the problems it depicts, no suggestion of how mankind might not only "endure" but also "prevail."[60] Faulkner's humanism did, however, locate those problems with striking accuracy in the momentarily victorious figure of Flem Snopes, the one character who knows only coldly rational exchange, experiencing neither the joys nor the sorrows of use. Although by the completion of the trilogy Flem's alienation from humanity is seen as a part rather than as the cause of these problems, at the end of *The Hamlet* there is no sympathy for him as he passes Armstid and moves on, headed for Jefferson and further diabolical "success": "Snopes turned his head and spat over the wagon wheel. He jerked the reins slightly. 'Come up,' he said." By deceiving Ratliff, Flem has won for the time being, but his victory will not last forever. Ratliff and the values he embodies eventually succeed in the trilogy not because of trickery or even cunning but because of moral superiority. In Faulkner's world, Ratliff thus represents a durable and uniquely engaging figure: the "trickster tricked" for the sake of good.[61]

Cesare Pavese and the Crisis of Realism

Cesare Pavese, along with his friend Elio Vittorini, was one of the grand masters of early Italian neorealism. His work as editor, translator, critic, novelist, and poet directly influenced a generation of Italian writers. From a historical perspective, his narratives provided the central link between Verga's *verismo* and the postwar neorealism of Italian novels and films. This is especially true of the early narratives (*Paese tuoi*, 1941, and the first *racconti*), in which the focus on the lower classes is most consistent and the adaptation of local *piemontese* dialect is most apparent. Pavese's importance as a novelist, however, rests not so much on these early works as on the narratives published in the forties and in the early fifties, which exhibit with increasing clarity realism's strategic dependence on myth.

Pavese saw, as did Verga, Lawrence, and Faulkner, the continuing desacralization and the progressive disruption of the human community in the modern world. But he perceived no direct solutions to these problems, either in his life or in his art. This lack, at once existential and epistemological, gives rise to the sense of uncertainty and despair which is fundamental to his mature narratives and which is never completely absent, even in the midst of their most elegiac passages.

Throughout his career, Pavese's work was influenced by his reading and translating of English and American novelists. He translated Sinclair Lewis, Melville, Anderson, Joyce (*Portrait of the Artist as a Young Man*), Dos Passos, Stein, Defoe, Steinbeck, Dickens, and Faulkner (*The Hamlet*, 1942), among others. The mixture of symbolism and realism represented by this list shows up repeatedly in Pavese's own narratives, and his particular interest in American writers is evident in his adoption of bits of American slang and witticisms in his novels.[62]

The movement of Pavese's career was generally from realism toward myth. This is evident in his prose and also in his poetry (from *Lavorare stanca*, 1936/1943, to the later poems, many published posthumously in the fifties, now collected in *Poesie del disamore*). His increasing interest in the timelessness of myth and in its validity for modern fiction was evident in 1950, when he chose Plato and Herodotus over Homer and Sophocles as writers who were able to move past the limits of the single, time-bound character and to concentrate on the mythic "rhythm of events" or the "intellectual-symbolical construction of the scene."[63] This preference for the aura of symbolicity and timelessness over the limitations of time and space was also apparent in his repeated championing of Vico and Melville as narrators. As Pavese's interests turned toward more openly mythic subjects and modes of presentation in his theoretical essays and in his fiction (i.e., in *Dialoghi con Leucò*, 1947), he seemed at times to discredit realism as a viable mode of narrative in the contemporary world,[64] but this appearance of refutation was only partially true. As in Lawrence, this is not a simple, straightforward progression from realism to myth. Indeed, Pavese's last and most impressive novel, *La luna e i falò* (1950), succeeds as narrative because of its constant utilization of both modes.

La luna e i falò is the first-person narration of a confused, searching, and thoroughly alienated man. The narrative is framed as the narrator's return to the land of his childhood, as a quest for roots. Initially, this approach might seem realistic, since the narrator is clearly interested in questions of historical "data" and in regional culture. Like other, more typically modernist works, however, Pavese's narrative abandons the traditional genealogies and seemingly linear action of the realist family chronicle. Indeed, the narrator is a foundling, and the very question of the validity of family relationships in the modern world is openly raised again and again in the text. Pavese also uses flashbacks and passages of lyrical reminiscence to break up the sequence of narrated events, and the novel thus appears to abandon the standard plotting of earlier realist fiction.

The effects of psychological realism, nevertheless, are not discarded. Instead they are limited to the consciousness of the narrator himself as he reviews the events of his own past and of his friends' lives in a realistically disjointed and even random fashion. The narrative voice thus reinstitutes the effects of a psychologically realistic presentation, even though the narrated events are difficult to follow and the narrative's language is an obviously literary mixture of formal Italian, *piemontese*, and, on occasion, American slang. At the same time, the division of the text into brief, almost uniform chapters of four to five pages keeps the narrative from becoming totally confusing at any one moment.[65]

The centering of the psychologically realistic aspects of the narrative in the persona of a speaker reviewing the often confusing data of his past reflects two presuppositions of Pavese's works. The first of these is that true knowledge comes from the past—and only from there. Even the insight gained by sudden revelation is in some way colored by prior perception. This is apparent in a notation in Pavese's diary in 1944: "La ricchezza della vita è fatta di ricordi, dimenticati."[66] But Pavese's position is not simply that humanity goes forward while looking forever backward. Reflection itself—as thought occurring in the present—influences an individual's perception of his or her past in the very moment that the past is influencing the present. The past and the present therefore intermingle, each modifying the other. The narrative image for this process of self-discovery in *La luna e i falò* occurs at the end of chapter 3, when the narrator, at loose ends in a foreign land, makes the crucial decision to return home: "Ma dove andare? Ero arrivato in capo al mondo, sull' ultima costa [i.e., America], e ne avevo abbastanza. Allora cominciai a pensare che potevo ripassare le montagne."[67] Once again, this theory of discovery through reflection and return occurs in the diary in 1944: "Chi sa quante cose mi sono accadute. . . . Vuoi dire: chi sa in quanti modi diversi vedrò ancora il mio passato, e cioè vi scoprirò avvenimenti insospettati."[68]

The other presupposition underlying Pavese's technique of self-discovery is that learning comes *in* and *through* language, through the act of narration. In other words, events do not precede narration as a set of givens which are then mirrored in the signs of speech. Rather, speech itself modifies and, in some fashion, creates the validity of our knowledge of events. In the novel, this lesson had been learned by the narrator while a boy through his discussions with his mentor, Nuto:

Fu così che cominciai a capire che non si parla solamente per parlare, per dire "ho fatto questo" "ho fatto quello" "ho mangiato e bevuto", ma si parla per farsi un'idea, per capire come va questo mondo. Non ci avevo mai pensato prima. E Nuto la sapeva lunga, era come uno grande. (P. 70)[69]

Here and elsewhere in the works of the middle and late forties, Pavese attempted to avoid both linguistic and materialistic determinism. He did this by grounding the meaning of human existence in an active combination of both the material and the linguistic aspects of life. The stress of this combination creates the conflicts that give rise to the narration of *La luna e i falò*. The book thus takes form as an attempted reconciliation between art and life, or, more accurately, between action in the everyday world and action in the world of narrative, or fictional creation. The fundamental nature of this opposition, reflected in the persona of the narrator, is what makes the book so challenging. It was also what made Pavese's personal life so troubled and his work so vulnerable to polemical critiques.[70]

Despite the disruptions in chronological time (caused by the active mixture of present and past), it is not difficult to re-create the plot underlying the narrative.[71] The narrator/protagonist is a native of the Langhe, a region in the foothills of the Alps south of Turin. He had left Italy to go to America and seek his fortune. The bleakness and the rootlessness of American life oppress him and make him long for his homeland, so that he decides to repatriate ("Allora cominciai a pensare che potevo ripassare le montagne"). He is a businessman constantly involved in exchange and has settled in Genoa, but he returns to the Edenic world of the Langhe regularly, and from time to time he considers buying some property there and settling down for good. The reader is told very little else about the narrator: he is forty years old, he was raised by foster parents, Padrino and la Virgilia, who took him in as a foundling from the hospital at Alessandria. Although the foster family received a monthly payment for taking him, the narrator makes it clear that he was accepted as part of the family and not merely as a servant. The family lived on a farm in Gaminella in modest circumstances and hoped that their communal labor would result in better days: "la Virgilia volle me perché di figlie ne aveva già due, e quando fossi un po' cresciuto speravano di aggiustarsi in una grossa cascina e *lavorare tutti quanti e star bene*."[72]

This type of idealized reminiscence runs through a great deal of the narrator's thoughts about his childhood. It gives rise to the obvious question of whether one can go home again, or indeed, whether such a return is a valid action or merely an escape. The narrator's return is rendered especially ambiguous because of his lack of knowledge of his true origins. The barred past of his childhood is idealized, but the "true" facts of his origin remain a nagging problem, mentioned again and again in his narration. In other words, as a foundling he is finally condemned to ignorance of his true roots even as he delights in memories of his childhood in the hills. The outlines of this problem, as well as the subtle emotional impact it has on the narrator, are clear from the novel's opening paragraph:

> C'e una ragione perché sono tornato in questo paese, qui e non invece a Canelli, a Barbaresco o in Alba. Qui non ci sono nato, è quasi certo; dove son nato non lo so; non c'è da queste parti una casa né un pezzo di terra né delle ossa ch'io possa dire "Ecco cos'ero prima di nascere." Non so se vengo dalla collina o dalla valle, dai boschi o da una casa di balconi. La ragazza che mi ha lasciato sugli scalini del duomo di Alba, magari non veniva neanche dalla campagna, magari era la figlia dei padroni di un palazzo, oppure mi ci hanno portato in un cavagno da vendemmia due povere donne da Monticello, da Neive o perché no da Cravanzana. Chi può dire di che carne sono fatto? Ho girato abbastanza il mondo da sapere che tutte le carni sono buone e si equivalgono, ma è per questo che uno si stanca e cerca di mettere radici, di farsi terra e paese, perché la sua carne valga e duri qualcosa di più che un comune giro di stagione.
>
> Se sono cresciuto in questo paese, devo dir grazie alla Virgilia, a Padrino, tutta gente che non c'è più.[73]

The style of narration is simple and direct, cast in brief periods with the occasional apocope, inversions, repetitions, rhetorical questions, and common phrases of everyday speech ("dove son nato non lo so"; "magari . . . magari . . . oppure"; "o perché no da Cravanzano. Chi può dire di che carne sono fatto?"; "Ecco cos'ero prima di nascere"). Nonetheless, the occasional non-Italian rhythms and the distinctive lexical registers mark the narrative as a literary artifact. This play of popular and literary forms is apparent in the fables and myths underlying the paragraph: that of the foundling ("in un cavagno da vendemmia") and that of the eternal return ("C'è una ragione perché sono tornato. . . . Ho girato abbastanza il mondo").

It would seem, then, that the narrative may be aiming toward resolution of the problems of alienation and eternal wandering by providing a solution to the problem of origins, since the foundling motif often leads· to revelation of ancestry at the story's conclusion. On the other hand, it is equally possible that the narrator intends to settle in the town of his upbringing, ending his travels by actively reestablishing his roots ("ma è per questo che uno si stanca e cerca di mettere radici, di farsi terra e paese, perché la sua carne valga e duri qualcosa di più che un comune giro di stagione"). This quest for roots could then be seen as a conquest of a homeland, as the foster mother's "Virgilian" name might indicate.

Either of these plots, revelation or conquest, would represent traditionally literary as well as psychologically realistic solutions to the openly stated problems of alienation. It is apparent by the end of the narrative, however, that neither of these plots is utilized to solve the narrator's dilemma. There is a reason for this: there is no solution to the narrator's alienation within the text. The speaker attempts to conceal this lack, but these attempts are mere subterfuge. At first, the lack is indicated only by the sudden displacement of the introductory discourse ("C'è una ragione" is not explained until the second paragraph, "Se sono cresciuto in *questo* paese"), but the failure to resolve this lack remains a problem even during the act of narration, as the speaking subject reflects first on his continuing ignorance of origins ("Qui non ci sono nato, è quasi certo; dove non nato non lo so") and only second on the attempted substitution of a valid home to which he may return ("devo dir grazie alla Virgilia, a Padrino").

As the narrative progresses, the myth of the eternal return mingles with the cyclical myth of the seasons and with that of the moon and the bonfires ("la luna e i falò"). The cycles of birth, growth, death, and rebirth are thus part of the mythic underpinnings of the text as well as the realistic frame of the narrator's return to the land of his past. Again, the point of the text is not merely the affirmation that such cycles exist. Instead, the narrator's project has been and continues to be to insert himself within these cycles in a way that will have special meaning for him as an individual ("perché la sua carne valga e duri qualcosa *di più che un comune giro di stagione*").

Like Faulkner and other even more obviously modernist writers, Pavese openly discusses these questions of belief and of the validity of meaning in his narratives. This procedure creates not only a clear distinction between the realistic and the mythic but also a fundamental doubt about the validity of both. Even as these questions are raised, the novel proceeds by adopting the elements of realism and myth in order to continue its own discourse. In other words, it proceeds even while it questions its own procedure. In part, this accounts for the disturbing effect that Pavese's texts have on the reader even during the most lyrical descriptions of the narrator's return, of his admiration for Nuto, of the natural fruition of the countryside, and of the comforting presence of the hills, which rise and slope like the earth's breasts.

This questioning of validity occurs in the narrator's and Nuto's open and at times contradictory comments on the powers of "destino" (pp. 19, 33, 57, 105 passim). The procedure is even clearer in regard to the central myth of death and rebirth, that of the "falò," which the farmers set on the night of San Giovanni in order to bring rain (according to the narrator, pp. 37-38) and to "awaken" the earth (according to Nuto, p. 39). Immediately after Nuto's explanation, the question of belief is raised:

"Fanno bene sicuro,— saltò. —Svegliano la terra.
    —Ma Nuto,— dissi, —non ci crede neanche Cinto.

Eppure, disse lui, non sapeva cos'era, se il calore o la vampa o che gli umori si svegliassero, fatto sta che tutti i coltivi dove sull'orlo si accendeva il falò davano un raccolto più succoso, più vivace.

—Questa è nuova,— dissi. —Allora credi anche nella luna?

—La luna,— disse Nuto, —bisogna crederci per forza. Prova a tagliare a luna piena un pino, te lo mangiano i vermi. Una tina la devi lavare quando la luna è giovane. Perfino gli innesti, se non si fanno ai primi giorni della luna, non attaccano."[74]

The narrator reacts with disbelief to these myths of rejuvenation and fruition ("Allora gli dissi che nel mondo ne avevo sentite di storie, ma le più grosse erano queste").[75] He upbraids his mentor for believing in such superstitions ("come i vecchi di sua nonna") since at the same time Nuto hopes to demystify the discourse of the Church and the government.[76] Nuto responds that "superstition" is only what brings evil results, such as manipulating myths in order to rob the peasants of the products of their labor or to keep them in ignorance of their own true interests. At this point, the question of the myths' validity is left open; nonetheless, at the end of the chapter, the narrator ambiguously affirms that he had always known the story of the moon and the bonfires, that he had merely forgotten about knowing it: "Anche la storia della luna e dei falò la sapevo. Soltanto, m'ero accorto, che non sapevo più di saperla."[77]

The effect of this concluding notation is the reaffirmation of Pavese's diary entry indicating that the richness of life comes from "ricordi, dimenticati," but the question of belief remains unresolved. Belief was central to Pavese's thoughts on myth during the postwar years, and it also played an important part in his Vichian conception of the poetic "immagine—racconto."[78] Without belief the "simbolo *creduto*," Pavese felt that myth could not exist, yet in *La luna e i falò*, the necessity of belief is not only put in doubt in chapter 9 but openly questioned again in chapter 10. At this point, the narrator manages to take a middle position, discounting the powers of the moon and yet affirming his belief in the powers of the seasons ("Ma io, che non credevo nella luna, sapevo che tutto sommato soltanto le stagioni contano").[79] This knowledge, however, does not provide a point of reentry for the narrator/pilgrim into the society of "le colline," since the seasons, like the life with la Virgilia and Padrino, are portrayed as distant and gone. To be sure, their effects are still felt, but only across the irrecuperable distance of time ("e le stagioni sono quelle che *ti hanno fatto le ossa*, che hai mangiato *quand'eri ragazzo*").[80]

This is still not the end of the narrative's treatment of the moon, the bonfires, and the passage of the seasons. Even though the question of validity is broached again and again by the narrator, the narrative continues to adopt these myths to shape its events. It does so in an odd way, by turning the hope of eternal rebirth into the despair of corrupted fruition, represented by the figure of the fallen woman, Santa, who is the partisans' betrayer. Since she has been regularly depicted by the narrator as the beautiful child of innocence dressed in white ("Santa/Santina"), Nuto's description of her ritual murder at the hands of the partisans carries special force. His words conclude the novel: "[Baracca] fece tagliare tanto sarmento nella vigna e la coprimmo fin che bastò. Poi ci versammo la benzina e demmo fuoco. A mezzogiorno era tutta cenere. L'altr'anno c'era ancora il segno, come il letto di un falò."[81]

The mythic elements of the description—the Edenic vigna (*cf.* p. 31), the purifying fire, the ashes, the bed of the bonfire—coincide with the realistic necessity to hide the body. As Nuto explains, "No, Santo no,—disse, —non la trovano. Una donna come lei non si poteva coprirla di terra e lasciarla così. Faceva ancora gola a troppi" (p. 131).[82] Rather than buttressing the realistic effects of the narration, however, the substructure of myths provides an ironic commentary on the narrator's original hopes for return. As with the "original," formative seasons, the old moral order is gone. Its effects are still felt, but it cannot be revived in the real, postwar world. For the narrator, as opposed to the characters, there is no reentry into the world he had left because, for him, that world no longer exists. The narrator can search for knowledge of himself and his past, he can attempt to "break the seasons" (p. 44) and to wring knowledge from his memories and his narration, but he cannot reenter the life that he had left and in which, even during his childhood, he had been treated as an outcast, tainted by "original" sin ("bastardo"). For the narrator, the mythic cycles of rebirth do not finally obtain. His knowledge of past and present is never to be full.

The obvious question then is whether that old order continues to exist for anyone. The answer, in the terms of both myth and realism, is yes. There are two characters in the novel whose validity is never put' in question on either the mythic or realistic levels. Nuto is idealized throughout the text as "uno grande," a teacher and a mentor. This remains true from the fairy-tale coincidence of his "reintroduction" in America ("—Nuto? Ma lo conosco")[83] to his adoption of Cinto at the narrative's conclusion. At first, some of Nuto's sayings appear too credulous or too simple for the contemporary world, such as his belief in "la luna" or his Wordsworthian pronouncement, "Tuo padre . . . sei tu." Nonetheless, they regularly express and uphold the values of the old moral order. Even Nuto's belief in the powers of the "falò" is sustained, albeit in tragic fashion, by his revelation of the narrative's concluding image, Santina's last "bed."

The other character whose position remains unquestioned is Cinto, the boy who lives where the narrator had lived as a child and who eventually takes the narrator's place in relation to Nuto.[84] Unlike the bitter irony of Santina's naming, Cinto's name is not ironic but allegorical. As Giacinto (Hiacynthus), he represents rebirth in the world even while the narrator represents its difficulties. In this scheme, Nuto thus becomes an Apollonian figure, the one who takes in pupils (p. 12) to protect them and teach them the knowledge of music, books, and nature.[85]

The development of this scheme within the narrative, and the special difficulty it creates for the narrator, are clearest in one of the few dramatic encounters in the story, that of chapter 28. The background for the scene is provided at the end of chapter 26. Cinto comes running up to the narrator and Nuto. The boy is beside himself with terror as he tries to tell them that his father has gone berserk, murdering the family, then burning the house and hanging himself in the vineyard. Only Cinto has escaped, since he had the knife that the narrator had given him earlier as a gift and he used it to protect himself. At first neither the narrator nor Nuto wants to believe Cinto's story, which does seem incredible, as though a Faulknerian scenario of the Garden's destruction were being described by a wild-eyed boy. They begin to believe the boy, however, as they listen to his continuing cries of fear and agony and consider his scratched and dirty body.

At the start of chapter 28, Nuto grabs Cinto by the shoulders and asks him if what he has said is true:

> Nuto lo prese per le spalle e lo alzò su come un capretto.
> —Ha ammazzato Rosina e la nonna?
> Cinto tremava e non poteva parlare.
> —Le ha ammazzate?— e lo scrollò.[86]

Cinto is overcome and can't respond. At this point, the narrator steps in and appears to take charge: "—Lascialo stare,— dissi a Nuto, —e mezzo morto. Perché non andiamo a vedere?"[87] Cinto does not want to return to the site of violence. "—Sta' su,— gli dissi, —*chi venivi a cercare?*"[88] Then the narrator affirms, "*Veniva da me*, non voleva tornare nella vigna."[89] Cinto finally concedes. They all go off, the two men holding the boy by the hand. The boy's acquiescence comes only after the narrator has promised, "Noi non andiamo nella vigna. . . . —Ci fermiamo sulla strada, e Nuto va su lui.'"[90]

This is a crucial passage in the symbolic organization of the novel. It appears initially that the narrator is taking charge and that in doing so he is bringing Cinto under his guidance and protection. This would demonstrate two things; first, that the narrator can act on his own and thus has figuratively outgrown his need for a mentor and, second, that he is in a position to take in pupils in his own right. Such an act would end the reinitiation and repatriation of the narrator in the land of his childhood and complete the progression suggested in chapter 9 ("Mi sembrò di essere un altro. Parlavo con [Cinto] come Nuto aveva fatto con me," p. 38).[91]

This is not, however, what happens. The narrator's continuing inability to act on equal footing with Nuto is indicated by his own suggestion that he and Cinto will remain on the road while *Nuto* goes to check the vineyard. It is ultimately not the narrator but Nuto who takes Cinto in. There is a suggestion that the narrator may eventually find a job for Cinto in Genoa, but this remains only a suggestion; if anything, it indicates the difference between Genoa and the hills. Even in the Langhe, as everywhere else, the narrator is still fundamentally rootless and out of place:

> Cinto se lo prese in casa Nuto, per fargli fare il falegname e insegnargli a suonare. Restammo d'accordo che, se il ragazzo metteva bene, a suo tempo gli avrei fatto io un posto a Genova. . . . *Così Cinto trovò una casa da viverci, e io dovevo ripartire l'indomani per Genova.* . . . Nuto mi stava dietro e mi diceva: —Allora, te ne vai. Non ritorni per la vendemmia? . . . —*Magari m'imbarco,*— *gli dissi,* —*ritorno per la festa un altr'anno.* . . . Io ridevo. —Ti ho perfino trovato un altro figlio. (P. 125)[92]

The implications of the narrator's journey and continued exchange are clear. This is not so much a graduation as a game of exclusion, of odd man out. The problems of roots and authenticity which are posed in the novel's opening passage are never really resolved in the narrative. In part, this absence of solution is obscured by the strong image of Santina's ritual death, which concludes the last chapter. But even this image reaffirms the narrator's alienation from both village life and knowledge, since its presentation by Nuto ("C'ero anch'io," p. 126) reminds the reader that the narrator had been *absent* and so had not shared in the formative events of the Italian Resistenza and civil war. Symbolically, it is important that the narrator's only name is a childhood nickname ("Anguilla," or "Eel"). He remains in this rootless, "slippery" state throughout the entire text. It is Cinto, not the narrator, who makes the move from the farms to the world of trade and production without losing the sense of human fellowship ("Cinto se lo prese in casa Nuto, per fargli fare il falegname e insegnargli a suonare").

The narrator's situation mirrors Pavese's own position in important ways. Pavese, too, had refrained from taking an active role in the fighting of the resistance, even though he had been arrested and incarcerated for possessing politically compromising letters (which were not written either to or by him). Like the narrator, Pavese was never able to establish a lasting relationship with a woman.[93] The text's misogyny is evident in the metaphorical linking "cagnetta"↔"spia." Even during the narrator's adolescence, before his disastrous sexual relationships in a thoroughly demythologized America, "Anguilla" had been at ease only among his male companions or with women who were not sexually threatening ("Mi chiesero se avevo anch'io la mia ragazza. Dissi ch'ero stato *con Nuto,* a guardar suonare," p. 122; my italics).[94] Moreover, the inability to establish valid roots and to act in human society recalls two themes that run throughout Pavese's own diary as well as his fiction.

As is especially apparent in *La luna e i falò*, Pavese's mature realism, unlike Verga's *verismo*, takes shape as a representation of the psychological processes of the individual narrator. (This is one reason why the analyses of class and social institutions in *La casa in collina* and *La luna e i falò*, even when undertaken, are never carried through.) For Pavese, the contemporary world was a place in which the status of the individual subject was constantly in question. His realism could re-create this sense of rootlessness and exclusion from the world's Garden, and it could use its mythic underpinnings to complicate its presentation and even redouble its own questioning. The crisis of Pavese's realism, however, was that it could not finally solve the problems of its own validity, of that of its narrator, or of its worldly creator. The last words of Pavese's diary echo this crisis ("Tutto questo fa schifo. Non parole. Un gesto. Non scriverò più").[95] The themes of personal validity, alienation, and the exclusion of the narrating subject from the world of human life and action also shape the other major narratives of Pavese's last years, *La casa in collina* (1948-49) and *Tra donne sole* (1949). Near the end of his life, the elegiac sorrow of *La luna e i falò* gave over to the diary's despair. The literary cliché "not words/an act," which ends the diary, also ended Pavese's writing. The willful game of odd man out shaping the narrative of *La luna e i falò* was completed in its creator's life by another type of ritualized violence against the irreparably alienated self, in the hotel room in Turin where Pavese took his life. For Pavese, as a man and as a writer, the desacrilization of the contemporary world led not to peace but to the real violence underneath the old myths. The powers of ritual and myth to affirm life and to restore order in the world were simply not sufficient. As in the language of one of the last poems, Death came, and it had the speaker's own eyes.[96] Less than a year after the publication of *La luna e i falò*, as Pavese turned away from the postwar world and its problems, both the myths and the act ended in silence.

Conclusion: The Ends of Realism

Porque en el principio de la
literatura está el mito, y asimismo
en el fin—Borges

Tracing the interaction of realism and myth in modern narrative has meant discussing several of the West's most pressing social problems: alienation; the dissolution of the family and of the individual subject; the function of labor; the ideological valuation of social order; and the tensions between men and women. Even as realism seems content merely to represent these problems, its discourse is never transparent. Realism's necessary interaction with myth assures this complexity, but, at the same time, its need to maintain some point of contact with the world it describes guarantees that its relation to that world will not be purely one of opposition. Thus it should not be surprising that realist literature is at once conservative and visionary, grounded in the fictionalized life of its present yet mindful of both the past and the future.

The dissolution of the familial order and the continuing transformations in our society have entailed changes not only in the historical objects of realist description but also in the techniques of presentation. Both our perception of the world and our means of expressing its appearance have changed and continue to do so. Disruption of the nineteenth-century realist genealogies of social life and events has resulted in major differences in plot and in the assumptions of character formation. Such changes have been accomplished in part by turning the elements of myth against those of realism, as in Faulkner and in Pavese. At the same time, these transformations have been accompanied by the increasing isolation of the narrating subject, as is so apparent in *La luna e i falò*. The sense of isolation, which had left only a trace on the narrative of Boccaccio and the early Renaissance realists, has become especially important in twentieth century realism. This disquieting isolation has pushed realism toward some of the effects of modernism, but crossing into pure abstraction would, of course, mean the end of realism's traditional strategies. These strategies are still at work in contemporary narrative, perhaps less obviously in the academic novel, but with great evidence in journalism and in film.

145

As society changes, then, so does literature; however, these changes never correspond neatly in a one-to-one fashion. This rupture between the fictional locus of meaning and its worldly source accounts, in part, for the problematic nature of realist reference. The difficulty of representation caused by this disjunction means that the primary link between the codes of realism and myth remains the intratextual *perception* of history. The importance of the weight of history holds true, of course, for critical discourse as well. The reader always reads *in* time. As Borges says in the "Parable of Cervantes and the *Quixote*," both myth and literature are functions of the imaginary and of the real. Nevertheless, this does not mean that we are confined to a hall of mirrors with only our own reflection for a guide. Comprehension of the workings of the realistic and the mythic in literary perception as well as in expression should help us to evaluate our own responses as readers and to account for the organization of our texts. In this way, by learning to delineate the layered interactions of realism and myth, we move one step closer· to understanding the historical status of our writers, of their works, and of criticism's own discourse.

Appendix 1: "La Lupa"

Era alta, magra, aveva soltanto un seno fermo e vigoroso da bruna—e pure non era più giovane—era pallida come se avesse sempre addosso la malaria, e su quel pallore due occhi grandi così, e delle labbra fresche e rosse, che vi mangiavano.

Al villaggio la chiamavano *la Lupa* perché non era sazia giammai—di nulla. Le donne si facevano la croce quando la vedevano passare, sola come una cagnaccia, con quell'andare randagio e sospettoso della lupa affamata; ella si spolpava i loro figliuoli e i loro mariti in un batter d'occhio, con le sue labbra rosse, e se li tirava dietro alla gonnella solamente a guardarli con quegli occhi da satanasso, fossero stati davanti all'altare di Santa Agrippina. Per fortuna *la Lupa* non veniva mai in chiesa, né a Pasqua, né a Natale, né per ascoltar messa, né per confessarsi. —Padre Angiolino di Santa Maria di Gesù, un vero servo di Dio, aveva persa l'anima per lei.

Maricchia, poveretta, buona e brava ragazza, piangeva di nascosto, perché era figlia della *Lupa*, e nessuno l'avrebbe tolta in moglie, sebbene ci avesse la sua bella roba nel cassettone, e la sua buona terra al sole, come ogni altra ragazza del villaggio.

Una volta *la Lupa* si innamorò di un bel giovane che era tornato da soldato, e mieteva il fieno con lei nelle chiuse del notaro; ma proprio quello che si dice innamorarsi, sentirsene ardere le carni sotto al fustagno del corpetto, e provare, fissandolo negli occhi, la sete che si ha nelle ore calde di giugno, in fondo alla pianura. Ma lui seguitava a mietere tranquillamente col naso sui manipoli, e le diceva: —O che avete, gnà Pina?— Nei campi immensi, dove scoppiettava soltanto il volo dei grilli, quando il sole batteva a piombo, *la Lupa* affastellava manipoli su manipoli, e covoni su covoni, senza stancarsi mai, senza rizzarsi un momento sulla vita, senza accostare le labbra al fiasco, pur di stare sempre alle calcagna di Nanni, che mieteva e mieteva, e le domandava di quando in quando:

—Che volete, gnà Pina?

Una sera ella glielo disse, mentre gli uomini sonnecchiavano nell'aia, stanchi dalla lunga giornata, ed i cani uggiolavano per la vasta campagna nera: —Te voglio! Te che sei bello come il sole, e dolce come il miele. Voglio te!

—Ed io invece voglio vostra figlia, che è zitella— rispose Nanni ridendo.

147

La Lupa si cacciò le mani nei capelli, grattandosi le tempie senza dir parola, e se ne andò; né più comparve nell'aia. Ma in ottobre rivide Nanni, al tempo che cavavano l'olio, perché egli lavorava accanto alla sua casa, e lo scricchiolio del torchio non la faceva dormire tutta notte.

—Prendi il sacco delle olive,— disse alla figliuola— e vieni con me.

Nanni spingeva con la pala le olive sotto la macina, e gridava "Ohi!" alla mula perché non si arrestasse. —La vuoi mia figlia Maricchia?— gli domandò la gnà Pina. —Cosa gli date a vostra figlia Maricchia?— rispose Nanni.

—Essa ha la roba di suo padre, e dippiù io le do la mia casa; a me mi basterà che mi lasciate un cantuccio nella cucina, per stendervi un po' di paglericcio. —Se è così se ne può parlare a Natale— disse Nanni.

Nanni era tutto unto e sudicio dell'olio e delle olive messe a fermentare, e Maricchia non lo voleva a nessun patto; ma sua madre l'afferrò pe' capelli, davanti al focolare, e le disse co' denti stretti:

—Se non lo pigli, ti ammazzo!

La Lupa era quasi malata, e la gente andava dicendo che il diavolo quando invecchia si fa eremita. Non andava più di qua e di là; non si metteva più sull'uscio, con quegli occhi da spiritata. Suo genero, quando ella glieli piantava in faccia, quegli occhi, si metteva a ridere, e cavava fuori l'abitino della Madonna per segnarsi. Maricchia stava in casa ad allattare i filgiuoli, e sua madre andava nei campi, a lavorare cogli uomini, proprio come un uomo, a sarchiare, a zappare, a governare le bestie, a potare le viti, fosse stato greco e levante di gennaio, oppure scirocco di agosto, allorquando i muli lasciavano cader la testa penzoloni, e gli uomini dormivano bocconi a ridosso del muro a tramontana. *In quell'ora fra vespero e nona, in cui non ne va in volta femmina buona*, la gnà Pina era la sola anima viva che si vedesse errare per la campagna, sui sassi infuocata delle viottole, fra le stoppie riarse dei campi immensi, che si perdevano nell'afa, lontan lontano, verso l'Etna nebbioso, dove il cielo si aggravava sull'orizzonte.

—Svègliati!— disse *la Lupa* a Nanni che dormiva nel fosso, accanto alla siepe polverosa, col capo fra le braccia. —Svègliati, che ti ho portato il vino per rinfrescarti la gola.

Nanni spalancò gli occhi imbambolati, tra veglia e sonno, trovandosela dinanzi ritta, pallida, col petto prepotente, e gli occhi neri come il carbone, e stese brancolando le mani.

—No! non ne va in volta femmina buona nell'ora fra vespero e nona!— singhiozzava Nanni, ricacciando la faccia contro l'erba secca del fossato, in fondo in fondo, colle unghie nei capelli. —Andatavene! andatevene! non ci venite più nell'aia!

Ella se ne andava infatti, *la Lupa*, riannodando le trecce superbe, guardando fisso dinanzi ai suoi passi nelle stoppie calde, cogli occhi neri come il carbone.

Ma nell'aia ci tornò delle altre volte, e Nanni non le disse nulla. Quando tardava a venire anzi, nell'ora fra vespero e nona, egli andava ad aspettarla in cima alla viottola bianca e deserta, col sudore sulla fronte; e dopo si cacciava le mani nei capelli, e le ripeteva ogni volta:

—Andatevene! andatevene! Non ci tornate più nell'aia!

Maricchia piangeva notte e giorno, e alla madre le piantava in faccia gli occhi ardenti di lagrime e di gelosia, come una lupacchiotta anch'essa, allorché la vedeva tornare da' campi pallida e muta ogni volta.

—Scellerata!— le diceva. —Mamma scellerata!

—Taci!

—Ladra! ladra!

—Taci!

—Andrò dal brigadiere, andrò!

—Vacci!

E ci andò davvero, coi figli in collo, senza temere di nulla, e senza versare una lagrima, come una pazza, perché adesso l'amava anche lei quel marito che le avevano dato per forza, unto e sudicio delle olive messe a fermentare.

Il brigadiere fece chiamare Nanni; lo minacciò sin della galera e della forca. Nanni si diede a singhiozzare ed a strapparsi i capelli; non negò nulla, non tentò di scolparsi.

—È la tentazione!— diceva —è la tentazione dell'inferno!

Si buttò ai piedi del brigadiere supplicandolo di mandarlo in galera.

—Per carità, signor brigadiere, levatemi da questo inferno! fatemi ammazzare, mandatemi in prigione; non me la lasciate veder più, mai! mai!

—No!— rispose invece *la Lupa* al brigadiere —Io mi son riserbato un cantuccio della cucina per dormirvi, quando gli ho data la mia casa in dote. La casa è mia. Non voglio andarmene.

Poco dopo, Nanni s'ebbe nel petto un calcio dal mulo, e fu per morire; ma il parroco ricusò di portargli il Signore se *la Lupa* non usciva di casa. *La Lupa* se ne andò, e suo genero allora si poté preparare ad andarsene anche lui da buon cristiano; si confessò e comunicò con tali segni di pentimento e di contrizione che tutti i vicini e i curiosi piangevano davanti al letto del moribondo. E meglio sarebbe stato per lui che fosse morto in quel giorno, prima che il diavolo tornasse a tentarlo e a ficcarglisi nell'anima e nel corpo quando fu guarito.

—Lasciatemi stare!— diceva alla *Lupa* —per carità, lasciatemi in pace! Io ho visto la morte cogli occhi! La povera Maricchia non fa che disperarsi. Ora tutto il paese lo sa! Quando non vi vedo è meglio per voi e per me . . .

Ed avrebbe voluto strapparsi gli occhi per non vedere quelli della *Lupa*, che quando gli si ficcavano ne' suoi gli facevano perdere l'anima ed il corpo. Non sapeva più che fare per svincolarsi dall'incantesimo. Pagò delle messe alle anime del Purgatorio, e andò a chiedere aiuto al parroco e al brigadiere. A Pasqua andò a confessarsi, e fece pubblicamente sei palmi di lingua a strasciconi sui ciottoli del sacrato innanzi alla chiesa, in penitenza—e poi, come *la Lupa* tornava a tentarlo:

—Sentite!— le disse —non ci venite più nell'aia, perché se tornate a cercarmi, com'è vero Iddio, vi ammazzo!

—Ammazzami,— rispose *la Lupa* —ché non me ne importa; ma senza di te non voglio starci.

Ei come la scorse da lontano, in mezzo a' seminati verdi, lasciò di zappare la vigna, e andò a staccare la scure dall'olmo. *La Lupa* lo vide venire, pallido e stralunato, colla scure che luccicava al sole, e non si arretrò di un sol passo, non chinò gli occhi, seguitò ad andargli incontro, con le mani piene di manipoli di papaveri rossi, e mangiandoselo con gli occhi neri. —Ah! malanno all'anima vostra!— balbettò Nanni.

Appendix 2: "The She-Wolf"

She was tall, thin; she had the firm and vigorous breasts of the olive-skinned—and yet she was no longer young; she was pale, as if always plagued by malaria, and in that pallor, two enormous eyes, and fresh red lips which devoured you.

In the village they called her the She-wolf, because she never had enough—of anything. The women made the sign of the cross when they saw her pass, alone as a wild bitch, prowling about suspiciously like a famished wolf; with her red lips she sucked the blood of their sons and husbands in a flash, and pulled them behind her skirt with a single glance of those devilish eyes, even if they were before the altar of Saint Agrippina. Fortunately, the She-wolf never went to church, not at Easter, not at Christmas, not to hear Mass, not for confession. —Father Angiolino of Saint Mary of Jesus, a true servant of God, had lost his soul on account of her.

Maricchia, a good girl, poor thing, cried in secret because she was the She-wolf's daughter, and no one would marry her, though, like every other girl in the village, she had her fine linen in a chest and her good land under the sun.

One day the She-wolf fell in love with a handsome young man who had just returned from the service and was mowing hay with her in the fields of the notary; and she fell in love in the strongest sense of the word, feeling the flesh afire beneath her clothes; and staring him in the eyes, she suffered the thirst one has in the hot hours of June, deep in the plain. But he went on mowing undisturbed, his nose bent over the swaths.

"What's wrong, Pina?" he would ask.

In the immense fields, where you heard only the crackling flight of the grasshoppers, as the sun hammered down overhead, the She-wolf gathered bundle after bundle, and sheaf after sheaf, never tiring, never straightening up for an instant, never raising the flask to her lips, just to remain at the heels of Nanni, who mowed and mowed and asked from time to time:

"What is it you want, Pina?"

One evening she told him, while the men were dozing on the threshing floor, tired after the long day, and the dogs were howling in the vast, dark countryside.

"It's you I want. You who're beautiful as the sun and sweet as honey. I want you!"

151

"And I want your daughter, instead, who's a maid," answered Nanni laughing.

The She-wolf thrust her hands into her hair, scratching her temples, without saying a word, and walked away. And she did not appear at the threshing floor any more. But she saw Nanni again in October, when they were making olive oil, for he was working near her house, and the creaking of the press kept her awake all night.

"Get the sack of olives," she said to her daughter, "and come with me."

Nanni was pushing olives under the millstone with a shovel, shouting "Ohee" to the mule, to keep it from stopping.

"You want my daughter Maricchia?" Pina asked him.

"What'll you give your daughter Maricchia?" answered Nanni.

"She has all her father's things, and I'll give her my house too; as for me, all I need is a little corner in the kitchen, enough for a straw mattress."

"If that's the way it is, we can talk about it at Christmas," said Nanni.

Nanni was all greasy and filthy, spattered with oil and fermented olives, and Maricchia didn't want him at any price. But her mother grabbed her by the hair before the fireplace, muttering between her teeth:

"If you don't take him, I'll kill you!"

The She-wolf was almost sick, and the people were saying that when the devil gets old he becomes a hermit. She no longer roamed here and there, no longer lingered at the doorway, with those bewitched eyes. Whenever she fixed them on his face, those eyes of hers, her son-in-law began to laugh and pulled out the scapular of the Virgin to cross himself. Maricchia stayed at home nursing the babies, and her mother went into the fields to work with the men, and just like a man too, weeding, hoeing, feeding the animals, pruning the vines, despite the northeast and levantine winds of January or the August sirocco, when the mules' heads drooped and the men slept face down along the wall, on the north side. "In those hours between nones and vespers when no good woman goes roving around," Pina was the only living soul to be seen wandering in the countryside, over the burning stones of the paths, through the scorched stubble of the immense fields that became lost in the suffocating heat, far, far away toward the foggy Etna, where the sky was heavy on the horizon.

"Wake up!" said the She-wolf to Nanni, who was sleeping in the ditch, along the dusty hedge, his head on his arms. "Wake up. I've brought you some wine to cool your throat."

Nanni opened his drowsy eyes wide, still half asleep, and finding her standing before him, pale, with her arrogant breasts and her coal-black eyes, he stretched out his hands gropingly.

"No! no good woman goes roving around in the hours between nones and vespers!" sobbed Nanni, throwing his head back into the dry grass of the ditch, deep, deep, his nails in his scalp. "Go away! go away! don't come to the threshing floor again!"

The She-wolf was going away, in fact, retying her superb tresses, her gaze bent fixedly before her as she moved through the hot stubble, her eyes as black as coal.

But she came to the threshing floor again, and more than once, and Nanni did not complain. On the contrary, when she was late, in the hours between nones and vespers, he would go and wait for her at the top of the white, deserted path, with his forehead bathed in sweat; and he would thrust his hands into his hair, and repeat every time:

"Go away! go away! don't come to the threshing floor again!"

Maricchia cried night and day, and glared at her mother, her eyes burning with tears and jealousy, like a young she-wolf herself, every time she saw her come, mute and pale, from the fields.

"Vile, vile mother!" she said to her. "Vile mother!"

"Shut up!"

"Thief! Thief!"

"Shut up!"

"I'll go to the Sergeant, I will!"

"Go ahead!"

And she really did go, with her babies in her arms, fearing nothing, and without shedding a tear, like a madwoman, because now she too loved that husband who had been forced on her, greasy and filthy, spattered with oil and fermented olives.

The Sergeant sent for Nanni; he threatened him even with jail and the gallows. Nanni began to sob and tear his hair; he didn't deny anything, he didn't try to clear himself.

"It's the temptation!" he said. "It's the temptation of hell!"

He threw himself at the Sergeant's feet begging to be sent to jail.

"For God's sake, Sergeant, take me out of this hell! Have me killed, put me in jail; don't let me see her again, never! never!"

"No!" answered the She-wolf instead, to the Sergeant. "I kept a little corner in the kitchen to sleep in, when I gave him my house as dowry. It's my house. I don't intend to leave it."

Shortly afterward, Nanni was kicked in the chest by a mule and was at the point of death, but the priest refused to bring him the Sacrament if the She-wolf did not go out of the house. The She-wolf left, and then her son-in-law could also prepare to leave like a good Christian; he confessed and received communion with such signs of repentance and contrition that all the neighbors and the curious wept before the dying man's bed. —And it would have been better for him to die that day, before the devil came back to tempt him again and creep into his body and soul, when he got well.

"Leave me alone!" he told the She-wolf. "For God's sake, leave me in peace! I've seen death with my own eyes! Poor Maricchia is desperate. Now the whole town knows about it! If I don't see you it's better for both of us . . ."

And he would have liked to gouge his eyes out not to see those of the She-wolf, for whenever they peered into his, they made him lose his body and soul. He did not know what to do to free himself from the spell. He paid for Masses for the souls in purgatory and asked the priest and the Sergeant for help. At Easter he went to confession, and in penance he publicly licked more than four feet of pavement, crawling on the pebbles in front of the church—and then, as the She-wolf came to tempt him again:

"Listen!" he said to her. "Don't come to the threshing floor again; if you do, I swear to God, I'll kill you!"

"Kill me," answered the She-wolf, "I don't care; I can't stand it without you."

As he saw her from the distance, in the green wheat fields, Nanni stopped hoeing the vineyard, and went to pull the ax from the elm. The She-wolf saw him come, pale and wild-eyed, with the ax glistening in the sun, but she did not fall back a single step, did not lower her eyes; she continued toward him, her hands laden with red poppies, her black eyes devouring him.

"Ah! damn your soul!" stammered Nanni.

Notes

Translations will be cited when they are more readily available than originals. Where dates of original publication are unclear, they will be added, if relevant, in parentheses following the title.

Chapter 1

1. On "moral realism" see Jean Piaget and M. N. Maso, *The Moral Judgment of the Child*, trans. Marjorie Gabain (New York: Free Press, 1965), especially chap. 2, "Adult Constraint and Moral Realism," pp. 109-96. Piaget and Maso's concept of "moral realism" —the child's view that all social norms are decreed by the fixed and necessarily incomprehensible laws of the adult world—is a secularized (and critically evaluated) version of the recurrent phenomenon of deterministic realism.

2. Despite its often cited deficiencies, I have used Benjamin Jowett's translation because it is readily available: *The Dialogues of Plato*, 4th ed. (Oxford: Clarendon Press, 1953), vol. 2. There is also an important analysis of imitation in the *Sophistes*, though this later discussion is only tangentially concerned with poetics as such. Of the many current discussions of Platonic mimesis, the most helpful in situating modern commentators (Nietzsche, Heidegger, Girard) in relation to Plato's critique in the *Republic* 10, is Philippe Lacoue-Labarthe's extensive treatment, "Typographie," in Sylviane Agacinski et al., *Mimesis. Des articulations*, "La Philosophie en Effet" (Paris: Aubier-Flammarion, 1975), pp. 165-270.

3. S. H. Butcher, *Aristotle's Theory of Poetry and Fine Art. With a Critical Text and Translation of the "Poetics,"* intro. John Gassner; reprint of 4th ed. (1911; reprint ed., New York: Dover, 1951). All references are to this edition.

4. *Summa Theologiae*, ed. Petri Caramello, vol. 1, pts. 1 and 1-2 (Turin: Marietti, 1952). "What is special here [in Scripture] is that the things signified by the words also have their own significance." My translation.

5. Erich Auerbach, *Mimesis: The Representation of Reality in Western Literature* (1946), trans. Willard R. Trask (Princeton: Princeton University Press, 1953), especially chap. 7, "Adam and Eve," pp. 143-73.

6. See Mikhail Bakhtin, *Problems of Dostoevsky's Poetics*, trans. R. W. Rotsel (Ann Arbor: Ardis, 1973); see also *Rabelais and His World*, trans. Helene Iswolsky (Cambridge: MIT Press, 1968). It should be noted that Bakhtin is more concerned with the carnivalistic as a literary *genre* than as a *mode* of social discourse and comportment.

7. My disagreement with Tzvetan Todorov on the psychological individuation of character within the major novelle—in his *Grammaire du "Décaméron"* (The Hague: Mouton, 1969), pp. 85 ff.—is explained at greater length in my essay, "The Fortunate Fall of Andreuccio da Perugia," *Forum Italicum* 10, no. 4 (December 1976): 344 n. 24. Benedetto Croce discusses the accuracy of the historical details in this story in *La novella di Andreuccio da Perugia* (Bari: Laterza, 1911).

8. Giovanni Boccaccio, *Decameron*, ed. Charles S. Singleton, Scrittori d'Italia, vol. 97 (Bari: Laterza, 1955). All references are to this edition. "But what's the use of crying about it

now? You'll as easily get back a penny of it as the stars in the sky." All translations of the *Decameron* are mine.

9. A related combination of allegorical and realistic elements in Baroque literature and drama was discussed by Fredric Jameson in "The Semiotics of Realism," an address delivered to a conference on narrative at the University of Toronto, Spring 1976.

10. A similar pattern of social change and fictional values in Ihara Saikaku's Japanese tales is discussed by Arthur F. Kunst in "Literatures of Asia," in *Comparative Literature: Method and Perspective*, ed. Newton P. Stallknecht and Horst Frenz, rev. ed. (Carbondale: Southern Illinois University Press, 1971), pp. 312-25. See also Ihara Saikaku, *Five Women Who Loved Love*, trans. William Theodore de Bary, intro. Richard Lane (Rutland, Vt.: Charles E. Tuttle, 1956). The mixture of travel, economic and sexual motivation, worldly knowledge, and ironic humor is clearest in "Gengobei, the Mountain of Love," pp. 195-229.

11. "But what shall we say to those who take such pity on my hunger that they advise me to procure bread? Certainly, I don't know, except that, thinking to myself, I wonder what their reply would be if in my need I were to ask them for it; for I think they would say, 'Go and look for it among the fables.' And yet poets have found more bread among their fables than many rich men among their treasures; and many men by following the examples of fables made their lives flourish, while on the contrary many others, by seeking to procure for themselves more bread than necessary, died prematurely."

12. "They called him and still call him Saint Ciappelletto, and they affirm that God has performed many miracles through him and performs them to this day for those who devoutly invoke his intercession."

13. "And therefore, so that through his grace we may remain safe and sound from these present adversities [i.e., the plague] and in such pleasing company, praising his name, in which we began, and holding him in reverence, we shall beseech him in all our needs, in the certainty that we shall be heard. — Whereupon he [Panfilo] fell silent."

14. See, for example, Velázquez's painting *Las Meninas*. See also Michel Foucault, *The Order of Things: An Archeology of the Human Sciences* (1970; reprint ed., New York: Vintage, 1973), chaps. 1-3.

15. Ian Watt, *The Rise of the Novel: Studies in Defoe, Richardson, and Fielding* (Berkeley and Los Angeles: University of California Press, 1957), pp. 13-15 passim.

16. See Georg Lukács's 1962 preface to *The Theory of the Novel: A Historico-philosophical Essay on the Forms of Great Epic Literature* (1916; 1920), trans. Anna Bostock (Cambridge: MIT Press, 1971). For Lukács's conception of critical realism (with Thomas Mann as a privileged midpoint between Kafka's ideological modernism and Socialist Realism), see *Realism in Our Time: Literature and the Class Struggle*, trans. John and Necke Mander, intro. George Steiner (1964; reprint ed., New York: Harper & Row, 1971).

17. Fredric Jameson, *Marxism and Form: Twentieth-Century Dialectical Theories of Literature* (Princeton: Princeton University Press, 1971), pp. 191-92.

18. "Franz Kafka or Thomas Mann," in Lukács, *Realism in Our Time*, pp. 47-92. For a brief summary of Marx's and Engels's view of the "problem of realism," see Stefan Morawski's introduction to *Marx and Engels on Literature and Art: A Selection of Writings*, ed. Lee Baxandall and Stefan Morawski (St. Louis: Telos, 1973), pp. 30-33. For Engels's later reservations on the poetic viability of types in "Tendenzdrama," see the letter to Minna Kautsky (26 November 1885) excerpted and translated in this selection, pp. 112-13. It should be noted that Lenin's series of articles on Tolstoi serves as a midpoint between the comments of Marx and Engels on Balzac and those of Lukács on Mann, since Lenin viewed Tolstoi as being conscious of the objective need for social change, even while remaining uncertain of the means to accomplish it.

19. Roland Barthes, *S/Z*, Collection "Tel Quel" (Paris: Seuil, 1970), p. 10 passim.

20. For extended discussions of these means of narrative organization see Ramon Fernandez, "The Method of Balzac: The Recital and the Aesthetics of the Novel," in

Messages: Literary Essays, trans. Montgomery Belgion (Port Washington, N.Y.: Kennikat Press, 1964), chap. 2; Auerbach, *Mimesis*, pp. 468-75 (on Balzac's "demonic" representation of the material environment); David Hayman, *"A Portrait of the Artist as a Young Man* and *L'Education sentimentale:* The Structural Affinities," *Orbis Litterarum* 19, no. 4 (1964): 161-75; and Giovanni Cecchetti, "Il 'carro' e il 'mare amaro,'" in *Il Verga maggiore. Sette studi*, Collana critica, vol. 83 (Florence: La Nuova Italia, 1968), pp. 79-113.

21. "Just how honest the quarter might be the name itself demonstrates."

22. Northrop Frye, *The Anatomy of Criticism: Four Essays* (Princeton: Princeton University Press, 1957), pp. 33-67.

23. Auguste Comte, *Partie dogmatique de la philosophie sociale* (1839), vol. 4 of *Cours de philosophie positive*, 5th ed. (1893; reprint ed., Paris: Anthropos, 1969), p. 468.

24. Émile Zola, "Le Roman expérimental," in vol. 10 of the *Oeuvres complètes*, ed. Henri Mitterand, 15 vols. (Paris: Cercle du Livre Précieux, 1968), p. 1178. Page numbers in the text refer to this edition.

25. "Determinism dominates all. It is scientific investigation, it is experimental reasoning, that defeats the hypothesis of the idealists one by one and which replaces the novel of pure imagination with the novel of observation and experimentation." All translations of "Le Roman expérimental" are mine.

26. Hippolyte Taine, "Préface" (1866), in *Essais de critique et d'histoire*, 7th ed. (Paris: Hachette, 1896), p. viii. As has often been pointed out, Taine's theory of historical reflection is even more static and less dialectical than that of Naturalism.

27. "And that is what constitutes the experimental novel: possession of the mechanism of human phenomena, demonstration of the inner workings of intellectual and sensual manifestations according to the way physiology will explain them to us, under the influence of heredity and of environmental circumstances, then demonstration of man as he lives in the social surroundings which he himself has produced, which he modifies every day, and in the midst of which he in turn experiences a continual transformation. . . [as] experimental novelists, going from the known to the unknown, in order to make ourselves masters of nature."

28. "Therefore, the experimental novelist is one who accepts the proven facts, who shows at work in men and in society the phenomenal mechanism of which science is master, and who does not permit his personal sentiment to intrude except in those instances when the determining cause of phenomena is not yet certain, even then trying as much as possible to control this personal sentiment, this a priori idea, by means of observation and experience."

29. Edmund Wilson discusses the Romantic dialectic of the self and the natural world and its subsequent split, with Naturalists asserting the priority of the world and Symbolists withdrawing to contemplate the transcendent mysteries of language itself, in *Axel's Castle: A Study in the Imaginative Literature of 1870-1930* (New York: Charles Scribner's Sons, 1931), pp. 265-67. See also René Girard, *Deceit, Desire, and the Novel: Self and Other in Literary Structure* (1961), trans. Yvonne Freccero (Baltimore: Johns Hopkins Press, 1965), pp. 26-29. This work begins Girard's original and important investigations into the functions of rivalry, violence, and "mimetic desire." Since Girard's theory of mimesis is related to competition and ritual rather than to representation as such, his conception of "mimetic desire" is more properly a component of myth than of realism. It will therefore be treated in the following chapter.

30. Arnold Hauser, *The Social History of Art*, trans. Stanley Goodman, 4 vols. (New York: Random House, Vintage, 1951), 4: 85-88.

31. Comte, *Partie dogmatique de la philosophie sociale*, p. 473; see also pp. 103-5 passim.

32. Giacomo Debenedetti, *Il romanzo del Novecento. Quaderni inediti*, intro. Eugenio Montale, Saggi blu (Milan: Garzanti, 1971; 1976), pp. 688-92. I have retained Debenedetti's

use of the term *myth*, though it does not correspond exactly with my own definitions. Among the treatments of myth in Zola's later novels, see especially Philip Walker, "Prophetic Myths in Zola," *PMLA* 74 (1959): 444-52.

33. Gérard Genette, *Figures III*, Collection "Poétique" (Paris: Seuil, 1972), pp. 147-48 passim.

34. This is true despite the response of the scandalized reading public. For a description of Zola's disgust at the orgiastic entertainments of Maupassant's group (some of whom later joined to pen the "Manifeste des Cinq"), see Matthew Josephson, *Zola and His Time* (London: V. Gollancz, 1929), pp. 275-76. See also Joan Yvonne Dangelzer, *La Description du milieu dans le roman français de Balzac à Zola* (Paris: Presses Modernes, 1938), p. 194.

35. Even in social novels this unity is conventional rather than necessary, as its absence in the great Chinese novel, *The Scholars*, demonstrates. *The Scholars* depicts civil life in eighteenth-century China. Though the narrative is long, it employs neither long-range character focus nor Aristotelian unity of plot: Wu Ching-Tsu, *The Scholars*, trans. Yang Hsien-yi and Gladys Yang, intro C. T. Hsia (New York: Grosset & Dunlap, 1972).

36. For a more detailed account of the literary manifestations of nineteenth-century pessimism, as well as some opposing reactions (especially George Eliot's), see parts 1 and 2 of Maurice Larkin's *Man and Society in Nineteenth-Century Realism: Determinism and Literature* (Totowa, N.J.: Rowman & Littlefield, 1977), pp. 9-110.

37. Foucault, *The Order of Things*, pp. 318-22. Foucault's discussion of Comte's Positivism is especially incisive, though his treatment of competitive (or, in terms of his argument, complementary) positions seems less imaginative.

38. Karl Marx and Frederick Engels, *The Holy Family or Critique of Critical Criticism: Against Bruno Bauer and Company* (1844-45), Vol. 4 of the *Collected Works* (London: Lawrence & Wishart, 1975), pp. 44-46.

39. See Engels's letter of April 1888 to Margaret Harkness (Joan Law), in *Marx and Engels on Literature and Art*, p. 115, in which Engels claims Balzac's realistic critique of post-Revolutionary French society "may crop out even in spite of the author's opinions." To a certain extent, Lukács's work has served to mitigate the materialist critique of Zola in this century; but see the treatment of Zola's inability to focus his inner social sympathies in "The Zola Centenary," in *Studies in European Realism*, intro. Alfred Kazin (New York: Grosset & Dunlap, 1964), pp. 85-96, and the Zola-Tolstoi contrast in "Narrate or Describe?," in *Writer and Critic and Other Essays*, ed. and trans. Arthur D. Kahn (New York: Grosset & Dunlap, 1970), pp. 110-48. See also Jameson's treatment of idealism and mechanically "objective" nondialectical materialism in *Marxism and Form*, pp. 365-66 passim; and Foucault, *The Order of Things*, p. 310. It should be noted that Foucault focuses on the *non-critical* aspects of Marxist thought, in contrast to Jameson's multiple approach.

40. For a description of the development of Asian narrative which suggestively counters Watt's seemingly necessary progression of long-range focus and slowed pace, see Kunst's comments in "Literatures of Asia." As Kunst notes, "the *Tale of Genji* [is] at the start, not the finish of Japanese literary history" (p. 322).

41. Among the studies currently available in English on the theory and history of Socialist Realism, perhaps the most useful, both for its theoretical sophistication and its range, is George Bisztray's *Marxist Models of Literary Realism* (New York: Columbia University Press, 1978). Though at times too schematic, Bisztray's discussion takes care to outline the very different aesthetic assumptions of the positions within his four-model analysis (pp. 197-212). Two recently translated collections of articles show the breadth of the original Russian positions on realism as well as the disappointing lack of imagination in current treatments: *Socialist Realism in Literature and Art: A Collection of Articles*, trans. C. V. James (Moscow: Progress, 1971); and *Marxist-Leninist Aesthetics and Life: A Collection of Articles*, ed. I Kulikova and A. Zis (Moscow: Progress, 1976). See also Henri Arvon, *Marxist Esthetics*, trans. Helen R. Lane, intro. Fredric Jameson (Ithaca: Cornell University

Press, 1973), pp. 83-99; and Georg Lukács, "Critical Realism and Socialist Realism" (1956), in *Realism in Our Time*, pp. 93-135.

42. See Gorky's letter of 19 February 1935 to A. S. Shcherbakov, secretary of the Union of Soviet Writers, in *On Literature: Selected Articles*, trans. Julius Katzer and Ivy Litvinov (Moscow: Foreign Languages Publishing House, 1960): "Much has been written, and is being written, on socialist realism, but no single and clear opinion exists as yet," p. 394. The Brecht-Lukács debate also furnished a pair of dissenting views on realism. Many of these positions had been anticipated by Trotsky. In *Literature and Revolution*, trans. Rose Strunsky (New York: International, 1925), Trotsky managed to champion realism in literature without negating the idealist element of his own aesthetics. He accomplished this by polemically opposing realism not to the Russian Formalists' "abortive idealism" (p. 183), but instead to mysticism: "One may say with certainty that the new art will be realistic. The Revolution cannot live together with mysticism," p. 236. This comment follows both the famous attack, "The Formalist School of Poetry" (pp. 162-83), *and* the denial of simple déterminism in the Party's attitude toward art (pp. 215-27). Trotsky thus managed to stake out a position opposed both to formalism and to the type of administrative realism which did become the "one formula" future of aesthetics in the Soviet Union (p. 227).

43. This temporal and epistemological perspective holds for certain theorists outside the Soviet Union as well, including important dissenters from the poetics of Socialist Realism. See, for example, Bertolt Brecht's insistence on the combination of realism and truth (not mere "stylization") in the notes to *The Caucasian Chalk Circle*, in *Collected Plays*, ed. Ralph Manheim and John Willett (New York: Vintage, 1975), 7: 295.

Chapter 2

1. All references are to Benjamin Jowett's translation, *The Dialogues of Plato*, 4th ed. (Oxford: Clarendon Press, 1953).

2. *Hesiod, the Homeric Hymns, and Homerica*, trans. Hugh G. Evelyn-White, 2nd rev. ed., Loeb Classical Library (Cambridge: Harvard University Press, 1936), pp. 80-81, ll. 27-28.

3. Giambattista Vico, *Opere*, ed. Fausto Nicolini, La Letteratura Italiana, storia e testi, 43 (Milan: Ricciardi, 1953), pp. 365-905. The fullest current criticism of Vico in English is in *Giambattista Vico: An International Symposium*, ed. Giorgio Tagliacozzo et al. (Baltimore: Johns Hopkins Press, 1969), and *Giambattista Vico's Science of Humanity*, ed. Giorgio Tagliacozzo and Donald Philip Verene (Baltimore: Johns Hopkins University Press, 1976). The following are also useful: the special number of *Forum Italicum* devoted to Vico ("A Homage to G. B. Vico in the Tercentenary of His Birth), 2, no. 4 (December 1968); Isaiah Berlin's discussion of Vico and determinism in *Vico and Herder: Two Studies in the History of Ideas* (New York: Viking, 1976), pp. 3-142; and Andrea Bertolini's helpful discussion of the dangers of assuming a stable locus of etymological "truth" in Vichian analysis in "Vico on Etymology: Toward a Rhetorical Critique of Historical Genealogies," *Yale Italian Studies* 1, no. 1 (Winter 1977): 93-106. See also Paul de Man's treatment of chapter 3 of Rousseau's "Essai sur l'origine des langues" ("Que le premier langue dut être figuré," in which the passion of fear is shown to intervene between perception and naming in the relation "homme→géant") in "Theory of Metaphor in Rousseau's *Second Discourse*," *Studies in Romanticism* 12, no. 2 (1973): 475-98. It should be noted that Rousseau's discussion of the metaphorical nature of language is considerably clearer than that of Vico.

4. "Thus every metaphor so formed is a fable in brief" (404). "Imagination is more robust in proportion as reasoning power is weak" (185). "Wonder is the daughter of ignorance; and the greater the object of wonder, the more wonder grows" (184). All translations of the *Scienza nuova* are from *The New Science of Giambattista Vico, Abridged*

Translation of the Third Edition (1744), ed. and trans. Thomas Goddard Bergin and Max Harold Fisch, rev. ed. (Ithaca: Cornell University Press, 1948; 1970). Paragraph numbers of this edition follow the translations.

5. For Vico, "Homer" is not an individual author but rather the collective embodiment of the ancient Greek populace. Like Achilles and Odysseus, such "poets" as Orpheus and Homer represent "fantastic" universals within the historical development of the cultures of Greece.

6. "Irony certainly could not have begun until the period of reflection, because it is fashioned of falsehood by dint of a reflection which wears the mask of truth. Here emerges a great principle of human institutions, confirming the origin of poetry discussed in this work: that since the first men of the gentile world had the simplicity of children, who are truthful by nature, the first fables could not feign anything false; they must therefore have been . . . true narrations.

From all this it follows that all tropes (and they are all reducible to the four types above discussed), which have hitherto been considered ingenious inventions of writers, were necessary modes of expression of all the first poetic nations, and had originally their full native propriety. . . . And here begins the overthrow of two common errors of the grammarians: that prose speech is proper speech and poetic speech improper; and that prose speech came first and afterward speech in verse." (408-9)

By "mondo gentile," Vico means those peoples who exist outside the framework of Jewish and Christian revelation and whose development is, therefore, not directly guided by revealed truth.

The general move from mimicry to irony is discussed by Plato in the *Sophistes* (268a).

7. F. Max Müller, *Contributions to the Science of Mythology,* 2 vols. (London: Longmans, Green, 1897), 1: 42-43. In some respects, discussion of Nietzsche's idea of myth, and of the Apollonian-Dionysian distinction in *The Birth of Tragedy,* would be instructive, but in the present context it would lead too far astray from the question of the origin of myth's signs.

8. Edmund Leach, "Lévi-Strauss in the Garden of Eden," *Transactions of the New York Academy of Science,* ser. 2, vol. 23, no. 4 (February 1961), reprinted in *Claude Lévi-Strauss: The Anthropologist as Hero,* ed. E. Nelson Hayes and Tanya Hayes (Cambridge: MIT Press, 1970), pp. 47-48.

9. See Karl Marx, *A Contribution to the Critique of Political Economy* (1859), trans. S. W. Ryazanskaya, intro. Maurice Dobb (New York: International, 1970), pp. 216-17; Edward B. Tylor, *Primitive Culture: Researches into the Development of Mythology, Philosophy, Religion, Language, Art, and Custom* (London: John Murray, 1871); Sir James George Frazer, *The Golden Bough: A Study in Magic and Religion,* 3rd. ed. (London: Macmillan, 1915; 1955); Lucien Lévy-Bruhl, *La Mentalité primitive* (Paris: Presses Universitaires de France, 1922); and Claude Lévi-Strauss, *La Pensée sauvage* (Paris: Plon, 1962). See also Jean Piaget's assessment of these concepts in *Play, Dreams, and Imitation in Childhood,* trans. C. Gattegno and F. M. Hodgson (New York: Norton, 1951), p. 198; and Lévi-Strauss's treatment of both Jung's archetypes and Piaget's developmentalist assumptions in "The Archaic Illusion" in *The Elementary Structures of Kinship* (1949; 1967), trans. James Harle Bell et al., ed. Rodney Needham, rev. ed. (Boston: Beacon Press, 1969), chap. 7.

10. For a summary of the ritualists' precursors and an overview of the once active "Bennington-Bloomington" debate, see Lord Raglan's, Stanley Edgar Hyman's, and Thompson's essays in *Myth: A Symposium,* ed. Thomas A. Sebeok (1955; reprint ed., Bloomington: Indiana University Press, 1958). Thompson argues against the "monistic," neo-Darwinian approach of the ritualists, but it is difficult to see how his own strategy of postponing theorization till an indefinite future when the collection of data will at last be complete (p. 180) represents any advance over the mechanical cataloguing procedures of nineteenth-century Positivism.

The one-sidedness of such positions is not limited to the various "schools" (e.g., Mircea

Eliade's insistence that all myths are about origins and the eternal return to a past *in illo tempore;* Georges Dumézil's claim that Indo-European myths reflect the tripartite division of society into priests, warriors, and producers; and Frye's neo-Jungian search for archetypes). Attempts to avoid such narrowness include *Myth and Mythmaking,* ed. and intro. Henry A. Murray (New York: Braziller, 1960); and *Myth, Symbol, and Culture,* ed. Clifford Geertz (New York: Norton, 1971). (Both of these appeared as issues of *Daedalus* [88, no. 2, 1959, and 101, no. 1, 1972, respectively], though the volume edited by Murray was expanded substantially in the Braziller edition.) In *Myth and Mythmaking,* the variety of the treatments, which are at times contradictory, indicated the need for definitions even while avoiding overly simplistic polemics. The volume did not, however, really come together into an ordered collection until Murray's conclusion was added to the Braziller edition. Even then, Murray's focus on mythic *events* rather than symbols resulted in an inability to come to terms with the underlying phenomenon of symbol formation itself. Geertz's opening essay in the volume of *Daedalus* which he edited avoids this failure by concentrating on the way symbols function *within* a specific social event ("Deep Play: Notes on the Balinese Cockfight," pp. 1-37). Geertz's treatment of the "use of emotion for cognitive ends" (p. 27) permits him to consider myth as a powerful symbolic "text" rather than as a "rite" or a "pastime," but since his approach is empirical and society-specific, it avoids what Geertz considers the idealist thrust of Lévi-Strauss's cross-cultural procedures (p. 36 n. 38). Geertz's investigation is, of course, limited in its approach. As an anthropologist's version of semiotics with an empirical base, however, his work seems especially fruitful in accounting both for the formation of the mythic sign and for its continuing expressive power.

11. See the following by René Girard: *Deceit, Desire, and the Novel; Self and Other in Literary Structure* (1961), trans. Yvonne Freccero (Baltimore: Johns Hopkins Press, 1965); *Violence and the Sacred,* trans. Patrick Gregory (Baltimore: Johns Hopkins University Press, 1977); *"To Double Business Bound": Essays on Literature, Mimesis, and Anthropology* (Baltimore: Johns Hopkins University Press, 1978); and *Des Choses cachées depuis la fondation du monde* (Paris: Grasset, 1978).

12. C. G. Jung, *Die antike Religion. Eine Grundlegung* (Amsterdam: Pantheon, 1940), chap. 1.

13. C. G. Jung, "The Psychological Aspects of the Kore" (1941) in *The Collected Works,* ed. Sir Herbert Read et al., 2nd ed., 19 vols., Bollingen Series, 20 (Princeton: Princeton University Press, 1953-76), 9, pt. 1, par. 309; emphasis in the original. All references are to this edition, cited subsequently as *CW,* followed by volume and paragraph number. For a later and more complete summary of the archetypes see *Man and His Symbols,* ed. C. G. Jung (1964; reprint ed., New York: Doubleday, 1967).

14. C. G. Jung, "On the Relation of Analytical Psychology to Poetry" (1922), *CW* 15:125; emphasis in the original. See also "Psychology and Literature" (1930-50), *CW* 15:136-62, for Jung's elaboration of the basic modes of artistic creation, the "psychological" and the "visionary," with Goethe's *Faust* as the "best illustration" of both modes; part 1 for the "psychological" and part 2 for the "visionary" (pars. 139 ff.).

15. Jung, "On the Relation of Analytical Psychology to Poetry," par. 127; my italics.

16. C. G. Jung, *Symbols of Transformation: An Analysis of the Prelude to a Case of Schizophrenia* (1911-12; 1952), *CW* 5:130.

17. Jung, "On the Relation of Analytical Psychology to Poetry," par. 125.

18. Jean Piaget, *Play, Dreams, and Imitation in Childhood,* p. 196.

19. Jung, "On the Relation of Analytical Psychology to Poetry," par. 126.

20. C. G. Jung, "The Phenomenology of the Spirit in Fairytales" (1945-48), *CW* 9, pt. 1, par. 451; my italics.

21. Jung, "On the Relation of Analytical Psychology to Poetry," pars. 129-30; my italics.

22. Sigmund Freud, *The Interpretation of Dreams* (1900-30), vols. 4-5 in *The Standard Edition of the Complete Psychological Works of Sigmund Freud,* ed. and trans. James

Strachey in collaboration with Anna Freud, 24 vols. (London: Hogarth Press, 1966-74). Section divisions and page numbers in the text refer to this edition, henceforth abbreviated as *SE*.

23. "Secondary revision" ("sekundäre Bearbeitung") is more often translated as "secondary elaboration" (see p. 488 n. 1).

24. See Otto Rank, "The Myth of the Birth of the Hero: A Psychological Interpretation of Mythology" (1909), in *"The Myth of the Birth of the Hero" and Other Writings*, ed. Philip Freund (New York: Knopf, 1959); Ernest Jones, *Hamlet and Oedipus* (1949; reprint ed., Garden City, N.Y.: Doubleday, 1954); K. R. Eissler, *Discourse on Hamlet and HAMLET: A Psychoanalytic Inquiry* (New York: International Universities Press, 1971); and Melanie Klein, "Some Reflections on 'The Oresteia,'" in *"Our Adult World" and Other Essays* (New York: Basic Books, 1963, pp. 23-54.

Chapter 3

1. Even allowing for the heat of polemical debate, it is difficult to account for the extraordinary number of confusedly negative critiques which the concept of literary realism has inspired. Beginning with Croce's early debunking of "verismo" as a mere "label" and continuing through Jakobson's 1921 broadside, Barthes's treatment in *Le Degré zéro de l'écriture* (1953), and the Wellek-Greenwood debate (1961-62), realism has been periodically condemned as impossible theory, unpalatable practice, or both. See Benedetto Croce, "Giovanni Verga," *La critica*, 1 (1903), reprinted in *La letteratura della nuova Italia. Saggi critici*, Scritti di storia letteraria e politica, 5, 3rd rev. ed. (Bari: Laterza, 1929), 3: 12; Roman Jakobson, "On Realism in Art," trans. Karol Magassy, in *Readings in Russian Poetics: Formalist and Structuralist Views*, ed. Ladislav Matejka and Krystyna Pomorska (Cambridge: MIT Press, 1971), pp. 38-46; Roland Barthes, *Writing Degree Zero* (1953) and *Elements of Semiology* (1964), trans. Annette Lavers and Colin Smith, intro. Susan Sontag (reprint ed., Boston: Beacon Press, 1970), pp. 67-70; René Wellek, "The Concept of Realism in Literary Scholarship," *Neophilologus* (Groningen) 45, no. 1 (1961): 1-20, reprinted in *Concepts of Criticism*, ed. and intro. Stephen G. Nichols, Jr. (New Haven: Yale University Press, 1963), pp. 222-55, and "A Reply to E. B. Greenwood's Reflections," *Neophilologus* 46, no. 3 (1962): 194-96; E. B. Greenwood, "Reflections on Professor Wellek's Concept of Realism," *Neophilologus* 46, no. 2 (1962): 89-97; and René Wellek, "What Is Reality: A Comment," in *Art and Philosophy: A Symposium*, ed. Sidney Hook (New York: New York University Press, 1966), pp. 153-56, in which Wellek again reaffirms his earlier position.

See also Erich Auerbach, *Mimesis: The Representation of Reality in Western Literature* (1946), trans. Willard R. Trask (Princeton: Princeton University Press, 1953), and Ian Watt, *The Rise of the Novel: Studies in Defoe, Richardson, and Fielding* (Berkeley and Los Angeles: University of California Press, 1957). It is especially unfortunate that Auerbach never fully confronts the theoretical implications of his own work, leaving consideration of his methods and perspectives in *Mimesis* to the few guarded comments in the final chapter and the epilogue; nonetheless, his emphasis on shared experience remains especially valuable. Watt's open discussions of "formal realism" (pp. 30-34) and of the broader recuperative functions of "the realism of assessment" are more helpful though very brief; however, Watt's response to subsequent criticisms does little to clarity his theoretical approach: "Serious Reflections on *The Rise of the Novel*," reprinted in *Towards a Poetics of Fiction: Essays from "Novel: A Forum on Fiction," 1967-76*, ed. Mark Spilka (Bloomington: Indiana University Press, 1977), pp. 90-103. For clear enumeration of the problems in the evaluation of verisimilitude, see Wayne C. Booth, *The Rhetoric of Fiction* (Chicago: University of Chicago Press, 1961), pp. 23-64.

The Wellek-Greenwood debate appeared in the midst of other Anglo-American critics' unevenly successful attempts at definition, including, in chronological order: V[ivian] de

Sola Pinto, "Realism in English Poetry," in *Essays and Studies by Members of the English Association* (1939), ed. Percy Simpson (Oxford: Clarendon Press, 1940), 25: 81-100; George J. Becker, "Realism: An Essay in Definition," *Modern Language Quarterly* 10, no. 1 (March 1949): 184-97; Harry Levin, "What Is Realism?," *Comparative Literature* 3, no. 3 (Summer 1951): 193-99; Walter Silz, "Introduction: The Nature of the Novelle and of Poetic Realism," in *Realism and Reality: Studies in the German Novelle of Poetic Realism*, University of North Carolina Studies in the Germanic Languages and Literatures, vol. 11 (Chapel Hill: University of North Carolina Press, 1954), pp. 1-16; Raymond Williams, *The Long Revolution* (New York: Columbia University Press, 1961); George J. Becker, "Introduction: 'Modern Realism as a Literary Movement,'" in *Documents of Modern Literary Realism* (Princeton: Princeton University Press, 1963), pp. 3-38; Harry Levin, *The Gates of Horn: A Study of Five French Realists* (New York: Oxford University Press, 1963); Peter Brooks, "In the Laboratory of the Novel," *Daedalus* 92, no. 2 (Spring 1963): 265-80; Oscar Cargill, "A Confusion of Major Critical Terms" (Address delivered at Upsula College, East Orange, N.J., May 1966), *The Ohio University Review* 9 (1967): 31-38; Peter Demetz, "Zur Definition des Realismus," *Literatur und Kritik* (Salzburg) 16/17 (1967): 333-45; Harry Levin, "On the Dissemination of Realism" in *Proceedings of the Fifth Congress of the International Comparative Literature Association* (1967), ed. Nikola Banesević (Amsterdam: University of Belgrade and Swets & Zeitlinger, 1969), pp. 231-49; Charles Witke, "Conventions of Realism in European and Extra-European Satire," in the preceding volume, pp. 243-49; and David Lodge, "The Novelist at the Crossroads," *Critical Quarterly* (1969), reprinted in *"The Novelist at the Crossroads" and Other Essays in Fiction and Criticism* (Ithaca: Cornell University Press, 1971), pp. 3-34.

   See also René Wellek and Austin Warren, *Theory of Literature*, 3rd ed. (New York: Harcourt, Brace & World, 1948; 1962), pp. 212-25; E. H. Gombrich, *Art and Illusion: A Study in the Psychology of Pictorial Representation*, The A. W. Mellon Lectures in the Fine Arts, 1956, Bollingen Series, 35/5 (New York: Pantheon, 1960); and Damian Grant's disappointingly insufficient distinction between traditional, or "conscientious," and modern, or "conscious," realism in his monograph, *Realism*, The Critical Idiom, vol. 9 (London: Methuen, 1970). Recent treatments include John W. Loofbourow, "Literary Realism Redefined," *Thought* 45, no. 178 (Autumn 1970): 433-43; four essays by Alice R. Kaminsky, George Levine, Loofbourow, and Marvin Mudrick in "Literary Realism and the Facts of Life," in *The Theory of the Novel: New Essays*, ed. John Halperin (New York: Oxford University Press, 1974), pp. 211-93; J. P. Stern, *On Realism*, Concepts of Literature (London: Routledge & Kegan Paul, 1973); George Levine, "Can You Forgive Him? Trollope's *Can You Forgive Her?* and the Myth of Realism," *Victorian Studies* 18 (1974): 5-30; E. L. Epstein, "The Self-Reflexive Artefact: The Function of Mimesis in an Approach to a Theory of Value for Literature," in *Style and Structure in Literature: Essays in the New Stylistics*, ed. Roger Fowler (Ithaca: Cornell University Press, 1975), pp. 40-78; *The Monster in the Mirror: Studies in Nineteenth-Century Realism*, ed. D. A. Williams (Oxford: Oxford University Press [for the University of Hull], 1978); Seymour Chatman's concise summary of structuralist approaches in "Verisimilitude and Motivation," in *Story and Discourse: Narrative Structure in Fiction and Film* (Ithaca: Cornell University Press, 1978), pp. 48-53; Jonathan Arac, "Problems of Realism in *Martin Chuzzlewit*," in *Commissioned Spirits: The Shaping of Social Motion in Dickens, Carlyle, Melville, and Hawthorne* (New Brunswick, N.J.: Rutgers University Press, 1979), pp. 67-93; George Levine, *The Realistic Imagination: English Fiction from Frankenstein to Lady Chatterly* (Chicago: University of Chicago Press, 1981); Marshall Brown, "The Logic of Realism: A Hegelian Approach," *PMLA* 96, no. 2 (March 1981): 224-41; and Elizabeth Ermarth, "Realism, Perspective, and the Novel," *Critical Inquiry* 7, no. 3 (Spring 1981): 499-520.

   For the distinction of metaphor and metonymy (adapted from Frazer and Freud), see Roman Jakobson, "Two Aspects of Language and Two Types of Aphasia Disturbances," in Jakobson and Morris Halle, *The Fundamentals of Language*, part 2 (The Hague, 1956), revised in *Language: An Enquiry into Its Meaning and Function*, ed. Ruth N. Anshen (New York, 1957), reprinted in *Selected Writings* (Mouton: The Hague, 1971), 2: 239-59 (esp. pp. 254, 258). See also Fredric Jameson's useful discussion of these positions in *The Prison-House of Language: A Critical Account of Structuralism and Russian Formalism* (Princeton: Princeton University Press, 1972), pp. 122-23. That metaphor, metonymy, and irony may exist within *one* layered yet united system was foreseen by Vico in the *Scienza nuova*. On the special importance of Vico's formulation see Hayden White, *Metahistory: The Historical Imagination in Nineteenth-Century Europe* (Baltimore: Johns Hopkins University Press, 1973), pp. 31-38, especially n. 13.

For important treatments in French see *Communications* ("Le Vraisemblable"), no. 11 (1968): Gérard Genette, "Vraisemblance et motivation," pp. 5-21; Julia Kristeva, "La productivité dite texte," pp. 59-83; and Roland Barthes, "L'effet de réel," pp. 84-89. Genette treats seventeenth-century cultural motivation; Kristeva deals with the problems of intra-textual and external reference in modern narrative and especially in the works of Raymond Roussel; Barthes discusses primarily the nineteenth-century realist novel. See also Genette, "Métonymie chez Proust," in *Figures III*, Collection "Poétique" (Paris: Seuil, 1972), pp. 41-63; Philippe Hamon's excellent discussions of description and character in "Qu'est-ce qu'une description?," *Poétique* (Paris) 12 (1972): 465-85, and "Un Discours contraint" in the issue of *Poétique* devoted to "Le Discours réaliste," 16 (1973): 411-45; Leo Bersani, "Le Réalisme et le peur du désir," *Poétique* 22 (1975): 177-95, translated and reprinted as "Realism and the Fear of Desire," in *A Future for Astyanax: Character and Desire in Literature* (Boston: Little, Brown, 1976), pp. 51-88; and the fine collection of articles in the issue of the *Revue des Sciences Humaines* (Lille) devoted to "La Représentation," 154, no. 2 (1974). Earlier French treatments appeared in "Le Dialogue de Vézelay" in *Documents* (Paris) ("Le réalisme dans la littérature"), 11, no. 7 (1956).

As regards myth criticism, it is impossible to provide even an overview of current treatments here, but there is a concise, up-to-date bibliography compiled by Albert B. Friedman, *Myth, Symbolic Modes, and Ideology: A Discursive Bibliography* (Claremont, Calif.: Claremont Graduate School, 1976). The most useful history of myth and myth criticism remains Raphael Patai's *Myth and the Modern Man* (Englewood Cliffs, N.J.: Prentice-Hall, 1972).

2. For a suggestive discussion of myth in popular bourgeois ideology, see Roland Barthes, *Mythologies* (Paris: Seuil, 1957), pp. 148-56. Antonio Gramsci's conception of the artistic and social elements of ideological hegemony is also important here, although it seems to me that Gramsci's formulation of ideology itself relies too heavily on conscious manipulation rather than on the nonvolitional aspects of perception.

3. See Italo Calvino, "Appunti sulla narrativa come processo combinatorio," *Nuova corrente* (Milan) 46-47 (1968): 139-48. Calvino is right to argue that a traditional hypothesis of a myth→tale ("fiaba") progression or comixture is inadequate, since "il valore mitico è qualcosa che si finisce per incontrare solo continuando ostinatamente a giocare con le funzioni narrative" (p. 147). It is hardly necessary to argue the converse, that the tale thus precedes myth, since the important point is that the components of myth precede them *both*.

4. In "The Popular and the Realistic" (*Brecht on Theatre: The Development of an Aesthetic*, ed. and trans. John Willett [New York: Hill & Wang, 1964], pp. 107-15), Bertolt Brecht states that "our conception of *realism* needs to be broad and political, free from aesthetic restrictions and independent of convention. *Realist* means: Laying bare society's causal network/showing up the dominant viewpoint as the viewpoint of the dominators/ writing from the standpoint of the class which has prepared the broadest solutions for the most pressing problems afflicting human society/emphasizing the dynamics of development/concrete and so as to encourage abstraction" (p. 109).

5. This is an attempt to separate the various threads of motivation and plotting entwined in Jonathan Culler's discussion of "vraisemblance" in *Structuralist Poetics: Structuralism,*

Linguistics, and the Study of Literature (Ithaca: Cornell University Press, 1975), pp. 144-52.

6. See Roland Barthes's comments on irony and parody in relation to Flaubert and Balzac in *S/Z*, Collection "Tel Quel" (Paris: Seuil, 1970), pp. 51-52 ff; and Culler's treatment of ironic recuperation in *Structuralist Poetics*, pp. 152-60.

7. On the temporality of irony and allegorical self-knowledge (especially in Stendhal), see Paul de Man, "The Rhetoric of Temporality," in *Interpretation: Theory and Practice*, ed. Charles S. Singleton (Baltimore: Johns Hopkins Press, 1969), pp. 173-209.

8. *SE* 17:240. I am indebted to John T. Irwin's discussion of this and subsequent passages from Freud and Nietzsche in regard to William Faulkner in *Doubling and Incest/Repetition and Revenge: A Speculative Reading of Faulkner* (Baltimore: Johns Hopkins University Press, 1975), pp. 82-96. See also *SE* 17:234-38, and Freud's speculations in *Totem and Taboo: Resemblances between the Psychic Lives of Savages and Neurotics*, *SE* 13.

9. See Mircea Eliade, *Patterns in Comparative Religion*, trans. Rosemary Sheed (1958; reprint ed., New York: New American Library, 1963), pp. 392-408; and Claude Lévi-Strauss, "The Effectiveness of Symbols," in *Structural Anthropology*, trans. Claire Jacobson and Brooke Grundfest Schoepf (New York: Basic Books, 1963), pp. 186-205.

10. See also p. 27: "*Protection against* stimuli is an almost more important function for the living organism than *reception* of stimuli." Emphasis in the original.

11. See also "Determinism, Belief in Chance and Superstition—Some Points of View," *SE* 6:239-79.

12. For Freud's depiction of universal narcissistic tendencies, as opposed to the specific disorder of secondary narcissism, see "On Narcissism: An Introduction" (1914), *SE* 16; and, for the basic reality-ego/pleasure-ego distinction, see "Instincts and Their Vicissitudes" (1915), *SE* 14.

13. Peter Brooks, "Freud's Masterplot," *Literature and Psychoanalysis. The Question of Reading: Otherwise*, Yale French Studies, no. 55/56 (1977), pp. 280-300. Brooks is more concerned with the passage from plot to story, or, following the Russian Formalists, from *fabula* to *sjužet*, than with the phenomenology of mythic perception itself.

14. Enrico Castelli, *La critica della demitizzazione: Ambiguità e fede* (Padua: CEDAM, 1972), p. 230: "recounting of the continual request of the supernatural event through the invocation that takes form by contact with an object that continues the timeless narration. A story outside of a determinable time is an 'always' sui generis, because it is itself a part of the origin, the *always has been*, which cannot signify an *always will be*, but instead the original insufficiency. Another aspect of sacred infallibility." My translation; emphasis in the original.

For basic discussions of the problem of belief in regard to mythic forms see Émile Durkheim, *Les Formes élémentaires de la vie religieuse: Le système totémique en Australie* (Paris: Alcan, 1912), especially p. 115; and Guy Rosolato, "The Voice and the Literary Myth," in *The Structuralist Controversy: The Languages of Criticism and the Sciences of Man*, ed. Richard Macksey and Eugenio Donato (Baltimore: Johns Hopkins University Press, 1970; 1972), pp. 208, 218. For treatment of belief as a primary factor in literary *forms*, see Tzvetan Todorov, *Introduction à la littérature fantastique* (Paris: Seuil, 1970); and, for belief as central to the internalized "action" of attitudes, see I. A. Richards, *Principles of Literary Criticism* (New York: Harcourt, Brace & World, 1925), pp. 272-87.

15. A similar distinction, though in different terms, is made by Northrop Frye in *The Critical Path: An Essay on the Social Context of Literary Criticism* (Bloomington: Indiana University Press, 1971), pp. 34-35; see also *The Secular Scripture: A Study of the Structure of Romance* (Cambridge: Harvard University Press, 1976), p. 9.

16. Bruno Bettelheim, *The Uses of Enchantment: The Meaning and Importance of Fairy Tales* (New York: Random House, 1976), pp. 26-27, 34-41, 294.

17. Géza Róheim, "Myth and Folktale," *American Imago* 2 (1941): 266-79, reprinted in *Myth and Literature: Contemporary Theory and Practice*, ed. John B. Vickery (Lincoln: University of Nebraska Press, 1966), pp. 30-32. Róheim's position does not correspond

exactly to Bettelheim's, differing especially in regard to myth's allegorical (here, etiological) specificity of time (p. 30) and in the emphasis on the Eros-Thanatos opposition (pp. 31-32) rather than Bettelheim's ego-superego distinction. There exist, of course, other criteria for myth/tale distinctions. See G. S. Kirk, *Myth: Its Meaning and Functions in Other Cultures* (Berkeley and Los Angeles: University of California Press, 1970), for Kirk's attempt at categorization (based on "seriousness," p. 37) and for his critical presentation of others' views.

18. See T. W. Adorno and Max Horkheimer, *Dialectic of Enlightenment* (1944), trans. John Cumming (New York: Herder & Herder, 1972), especially "Excursus I: Odysseus or Myth and Enlightenment," pp. 43-80.

19. Claude Lévi-Strauss, *La Pensée sauvage*, (Paris: Plon, 1962), chap. 1. On the level of individual cognitive development, for the passion of binding relationships in the personalized symbol as opposed to the cold arbitrariness of the conventional sign, see Jean Piaget, *The Psychology of Intelligence* (1947), trans. Malcolm Piercy and D. E. Berlyne (1950; reprint ed., Totowa, N.J.: Littlefield, Adams, 1960; 1973), pp. 124-26.

20. For this link, explicitly described by Freud, see *Beyond the Pleasure Principle*, p. 38: "*inanimate things existed before living ones."* Emphasis in the original.

21. For a standard formalist statement of this position, see Wellek and Warren, *Theory of Literature*, p. 191. See also Harry Slochower, *Mythopoesis: Mythic Patterns in the Literary Classics* (Detroit: Wayne State University Press, 1970), p. 15; Theodore H. Gaster's hypothesis of the "parallelism" between mythic and realistic realms, in "Myth and Story," *Numen* 1, no. 3 (September 1954): 184-212; and the subtle treatment of myth's interaction with history in Peter Munz, "History and Myth," *Philosophical Quarterly* (Edinburgh) 6, no. 22 (January 1950): 1-16.

22. On fundamental oppositions and other characteristics of proverbs, see A. J. Greimas, *Du Sens. Essais sémiotiques* (Paris: Seuil, 1970), pp. 309-14. For a less schematic and more suggestive treatment see Benjamin's essay on Leskov, "The Storyteller: Reflections on the Work of Nikolai Leskov," in *Illuminations*, trans. Harry Zohn, ed. and intro. Hannah Arendt (1968; reprint ed., New York: Schocken Books, 1969), pp. 83-109: "A proverb . . . is a ruin which stands on the site of an old story and in which a moral twines about a happening like ivy around a wall" (p. 108).

23. See Claude Bremond, "Les rôles narratifs principaux," in *Logique du récit* (Paris: Seuil, 1973), pp. 129-333.

24. Roman Jakobson, "Parts and Wholes in Language," Lecture at the Hayden Colloquium, Massachusetts Institute of Technology, 1960, in *Selected Writings*, 2: 280-84. The levels Jakobson describes are phoneme-morpheme, word, sentence, utterance, and full discourse.

25. E. M. Forster's discussion of character is still useful, despite its obvious limitations. See "People," in *Aspects of the Novel* (New York: Harcourt, Brace & World, 1927), chaps. 3-4.

26. Otto Jespersen, *Language: Its Nature, Development, and Origin* (London: Allen & Unwin, 1922), pp. 123-24. Jespersen describes all the pronouns (including first-person singular), as well as the denomination of personal relationships ("father," "mother") and generic place names ("home"), as shifters.

Chapter 4

1. The most incisive treatment of these debates in Italy remains Giulio Marzot's *Battaglie veristiche dell'Ottocento* (Milan: Principato, 1941). See also Roberto Bigazzi, *I colori del vero. Vent'anni di narrativa: 1860-1880*, Saggi di varia umanità, 10 (Pisa: Nistri-Lischi, 1969).

2. Giovanni Verga, *Tutte le novelle*, ed. Corrado Simioni, 2 vols. (Milan: Mondadori, 1940-70), 1: 145-49. References for all the novelle are to this edition. All italics in "La Lupa," with the exception of the name and the central proverb, are mine. This story is appended, as is Giovanni Cecchetti's translation (which remains by far the most accurate for an American audience), from *"The She-Wolf" and Other Stories*, trans. and intro. Giovanni Cecchetti, 2nd ed. rev. (Berkeley and Los Angeles: University of California Press, 1958; 1973), pp. 3-9.

3. D. H. Lawrence, trans., "Translator's Preface," in *"Cavalleria Rusticana" and Other Stories*, by Giovanni Verga (1928; reprint ed., Westport, Conn.: Greenwood Press, 1975), p. 28.

4. *Verga e D'Annunzio*, ed. Mario Pomilio, Biblioteca dell'Ottocento italiano, 20 (Bologna: Cappelli, 1972), p. 80. It appears to be true that Verga first got the idea for "La Lupa" from his discussions with Capuana. For an account of these conversations and their effect on Verga's writing, see Corrado Di Blasi, *Luigi Capuana originale e segreto* (Catania: Giannotta, 1968), pp. 73-75.

5. The complexity of this operation does not always lead to happy results. Luigi Russo, for one, is less than pleased with Verga's "academic" translation of the central proverb ("In quell'ora"). See *Giovanni Verga*, Universale Laterza, 47 (1919-20; reprint ed., Bari: Laterza, 1976), p. 108. Though it is difficult to determine exactly what Russo finds disturbing about the proverb, it may be the irony of its repetition as much as its form.

6. Giovanni Sinicropi, "La Natura nelle Opere di Giovanni Verga," *Italica* 37, no. 2 (June 1960): 89-108, especially pp. 89-90.

7. See Fredi Chiappelli, "Una lettura verghiana: 'La Lupa,'" *Giornale storico della letteratura italiana* (Turin) 139, fasc. 427 (1962): 370-83. Alberto Asor Rosa claims—and I agree in part—that the story's descriptive effects created an aura of vagueness and thereby protected the sensibilities of the nineteenth-century bourgeois public, which enjoyed titillation but only within certain bounds. See "Il primo e l'ultimo uomo del mondo. Indagine sulle strutture narrative e sociologiche in *Vita dei campi*," *Problemi*, nos. 7-8 (1968), reprinted in *Il caso Verga*, ed. Alberto Asor Rosa, Problemi-Libri, 5, 3rd. ed. (Palermo: Palumbo, 1974), pp. 32-33. See also Vittorio Spinazzola, "Il significato della passione. *La Lupa, Jeli il pastore, Pane nero*," in *Verismo e positivismo*, I Garzanti, Argomenti, 17 (Milan: Garzanti, 1977), p. 92. It is impossible in a brief note to do justice to the subtlety and depth of Spinazzola's treatment of this novella.

8. My conception of the ideological emphasis as falling on individual and universal phenomena at the expense of the factors of class and nation is somewhat broader than that of Romano Luperini (to whose analysis of *Vita dei campi* and *I Malavoglia* I am indebted), who claims "Verga non vede mai l'interesse di classe ma sempre quello dei singoli individui." See "La natura, la società, l'esclusione nel mondo di *Vita dei campi* e dei *Malavoglia*" in *L'orgoglio e la disperata rassegnazione: natura e società, maschera e realtà nell'ultimo Verga*, La nuova sinistra, Saggistica, 61 (Rome: Savelli, 1974), p. 68. Asor Rosa makes a similar point on the side of universality ("destino sociale") in "Il primo e l'ultimo uomo del mondo," p. 77.

9. Spinazzola, "Il significato della passione," p. 91.

10. See the preface to *I Malavoglia* (1881) in Giovanni Verga, *Opere*, ed. Luigi Russo, La Letteratura Italiana, storia e testi, 63 (Milan: Ricciardi, 1968), pp. 177-79, and the dedicatory epistle to Salvatore Farina in "L'amante di Gramigna" (first published as "L'amante di Raya"), in *Tutte le novelle*, 1: 199-201.

11. *Tutte le novelle*, 1: 139. Cecchetti singles out this passage in his introduction to *"The She-Wolf" and Other Stories*, p. xvi.

12. Letter 139, Catania, 29 January 1908, in Giovanni Verga, *Lettere al suo traduttore*, ed. Fredi Chiappelli (Florence: La Monnier, 1954), p. 245.

13. Spinazzola, "Il significato della passione," pp. 84 ff.

14. Livy, *Ab Urbe Condita*. Vol. I (Books I-IV), ed. R. S. Conway and C. F. Walters, corrected ed., 5 vols. (Oxford: Clarendon Press, 1965), 1.4.7.

15. That such rhythms extend throughout the entire text is demonstrated by Chiappelli, "Una lettura verghiana: 'La Lupa,'" p. 372. For a discussion of the organizational effects of repetition—entailing significant difference as well as similarity—see Wido Hempel, *Giovanni Vergas Roman "I Malavoglia" und die Wiederholung als erzählerisches Kunstmittel*, Studi Italiani, 4 (Cologne: Graz Böhlau, 1959), pp. 25-33. Verga's writing continued to demonstrate the effects of popular models. One of the clearest examples of this occurs in "La roba" (*Novelle rusticane*, 1883), in which the introductory paragraph is framed by the familiar, thrice-repeated motif of "Puss in Boots" (Gianfrancesco Straparola's and then Giambattista Basile's "Gagliuso"): "—Qui di chi è? . . . —Di Mazzarò."

16. Russo explains the apparent inconsistency in the time scheme as stemming from the traditional calculation of the hours in rural Sicily: "e qui però bisogna intendere le ore bruciate, che sono dominate dagli spiriti maligni," in his edition of Verga's *Opere*, p. 126 n. 1. Although wolves wander at night, la Lupa appears *perpetually* in motion.

17. Giovanni Cecchetti sees this proverb, in its repetition, as a developing symbol of both la Lupa's power and Nanni's failure. See "Il 'carro' e il 'mare amaro,'" in *Il Verga maggiore. Sette studi*, Collana critica, 83 (Florence: La Nuova Italia, 1968), pp. 95-96.

18. Gérard Genette, *Figures III*, Collection "Poétique" (Paris: Seuil, 1972), pp. 147-49 passim.

19. The Sicilian phrase, as well as the connection between the images of sun and honey, is discussed by Gino Raya in *La Lingua del Verga*, Biblioteca del saggiatore, 16 (Florence: Le Monnier, 1962), pp. 32-33. Claude Lévi-Strauss treats the symbolic wildness of honey in South American mythology in vol. 2 of *From Honey to Ashes: Introduction to a Science of Mythology*, trans. John and Doreen Weightman (New York: Harper & Row, 1973); see pp. 82-103, and especially the Ofaié variant in which the wolf, as one of the canidae, is portrayed as the master of honey (pp. 70-72). The "wolf," in this instance, appears to be a type of fox (p. 83). See also idem, *The Raw and the Cooked: Introduction to a Science of Mythology*, trans. John and Doreen Weightman (New York: Harper & Row, 1969), 1: 66-143. Verga also uses images of possession and lycanthropy, as well as a subtle Christ-Devil opposition, in "L'amante di Gramigna," *Tutte le novelle*, especially pp. 202-4.

20. In all his later writing, Verga was extremely attentive to the details of naming. In the version of "La Lupa" written for the stage (1896), Nanni's child—significantly male—was called Agrippino. See *Opere*, pp. 857-58. Besides the resonance of its Roman origins—both Agrippinas were intimately involved in the ruling of the empire—this name also has an authentically localized Sicilian significance (see Russo's note to the novella in *Opere*, p. 125 n. 1).

21. For a brief assessment of Nietzschean themes in "La Lupa," see Guy Dumas, "A propos de la fin de la 'Lupa' de Giovanni Verga," *Revue des Études Italiennes* (Paris) 7, nos. 2-3 (1960): 241-49.

22. See *Three Essays on the Theory of Sexuality*, in *SE* 7.

23. On the passage from nature to society see Jean-Jacques Rousseau, *Du Contrat social ou principes du droit politique*, in vol. 3 of the *Oeuvres complètes*, ed. Bernard Gagnebin et al., Bibliothèque de la Pléiade (Paris: Gallimard, 1964), sec. 1, subsecs. 5-6, pp. 359-62; see also the "Discours sur l'origine e les fondemens de l'inégalité parmi les hommes," especially on the basic and continual "amour de bien-être," the natural "amour de soi-même," and the fully social "amour-propre," pp. 152-71, 219-20 n. 15.

24. Rousseau, *Du Contrat social*, sec. 1, subsec. 8, pp. 364-65. On the extremely qualified concept of freedom in Rousseau (natural, civil, moral), as well as the difficulties inherent in its rhetorical conceptualization, see Paul de Man, "Theory of Metaphor in Rousseau's Second Discourse," *Studies in Romanticism* 12, no. 2 (1973): 475-98.

25. Rousseau, *Du Contrat social*, sec. 1, subsec. 8, p. 364.

26. .Ibid., p. 365: "Moral liberty, which alone makes man *truly* master of himself; because *the impulsive drive of the single appetite is slavery*, and *obedience to the law which man has prescribed for himself is liberty*." My translation; my italics.

27. *SE* 7: 177-78, 191-92, 225-28, 231.

28. Verga, *Opere*, p. 836; my italics.

29. "From the History of an Infantile Neurosis," *SE* 17:1-123.

30. Spinazzola, "Il significato della passione," p. 94.

31. Lawrence, "Translator's Preface," p. 19.

32. Chiappelli, "Una lettura verghiana: 'La Lupa,'" p. 380.

33. Verga, *Opere*, p. 872.

34. Dumas, "A Propos de la fin de la 'Lupa' de Giovanni Verga," p. 246. Despite the importance of this scene in the story, David Woolf claims that whether or not la Lupa is killed is "immaterial," in *The Art of Verga: A Study in Objectivity* (Sydney: University of Sydney Press, 1977), p. 101.

35. Letter 139, in Verga, *Lettere al suo traduttore*, pp. 244-45. On this internal suspension of the narrative dialectic as one of Verga's standard concluding techniques, see Giacomo Debenedetti, *Verga e il naturalismo. Quaderni inediti*, Saggi blu (Milan: Garzanti, 1976), pp. 45-47.

36. For discussions of the revisions of the text of *Vita dei campi*, see Cecchetti, "Il testo di *Vita dei campi* e le correzioni verghiani," in *Il Verga maggiore*, pp. 47-48; Gaetano Ragonese, "La lingua di Verga e le correzioni di 'Vita dei campi,'" in *Interpretazione del Verga. Saggi e ricerche*, Biblioteca di cultura, 101, 2nd ed. (Rome: Bulzoni, 1965; 1977), pp. 184-286; Olga Ragusa, "Narrative vs. Stylistic Structure in *I Malavoglia*," *Romanic Review* 62, no. 3 (1971) revised in *Narrative and Drama: Essays in Modern Italian Literature from Verga to Pasolini*, De Proprietatibus Litterarum, Ser. Practica, 110 (The Hague: Mouton, 1976), pp. 35-57; Gino Tellini, "Le correzioni di *Vita dei campi*," in *L'avventura di "Malombra" e altri saggi*, Biblioteca de cultura, 41 (Rome: Bulzoni, 1973), pp. 81-111; and Carla Riccardi, "Il problema filologico di 'Vita dei campi,'" *Studi di filologia italiana* (Florence) 35 (1977): 301-36. The only major alteration in "La Lupa" was in Nanni's initial designation of Maricchia, from "vitella" to "zitella" (Cecchetti, *Il Verga maggiore*, p. 55). However, whether the change was due to Verga or to a proofreader or typesetter, as Ragusa suggests (p. 52 n. 3), remains open to speculation. There is also a discussion and a reproduction of an unpublished version of the story in Giancarlo Mazzacurati's "Scrittura e ideologia in Verga ovvero le metamorfosi della Lupa" in *Forma e ideologia. (Dante, Boccaccio, Straparola, Manzoni, Nievo, Verga, Svevo)* (Naples: Liguori, 1974), pp. 142-75.

37. "The simple human fact will always make one think; it will always have the force of what *has really been*, of true tears, of the fevers and sensations that have passed through the flesh. The mysterious process by which passions tie themselves together . . . in their subterranean journey . . . will still constitute for a long time the powerful attraction of that psychological phenomenon which forms the subject of a story, and which modern analysis endeavors to follow with scientific precision." Translation from Cecchetti, *"The She-Wolf" and Other Stories*, pp. 86-87; emphasis in the original.

38. "When in the novel the affinity and cohesion of its every part will be so complete that the creative process will remain a mystery, like the development of human passions, and the harmony of its elements will be so perfect, the sincerity of its reality so evident, its manner of and its reason for existing so necessary, that the hand of the artist will remain absolutely invisible, then it will have the imprint of an actual happening; the work of art will seem *to have made itself*, to have matured and come into being spontaneously, like a fact of nature, without retaining any point of contact with its author, any stain of the original sin." Translation from Cecchetti, *"The She-Wolf" and Other Stories*, pp. 87-88; emphasis in the original. Various elements of this theory extend from Flaubert and Zola to Stephen Dedalus's often-cited theories in James Joyce's *Portrait* (1916). See *A Portrait of the Artist as a Young Man*, ed. Chester G. Anderson (New York: Viking, 1968), p. 215.

39. See Debenedetti, *Verga e il naturalismo*, p. 17; also see pp. 31-33. Though only recently published, these comments were made in the course of Debenedetti's lectures at the University of Messina in 1951-52.

40. Verga, *Opere*, pp. 178-79. "Each one, from the most humble to the most elevated, has played his part *in the struggle for existence, for affluence, for ambition*—from the humble fisherman to the newly rich—to the intruder among the upper classes—to the man of wit and robust will, who possesses the strength to dominate other men, to claim for himself that portion of public consideration which social prejudice would deny him on the basis of unlawful origins, to make the laws, though born outside the law—*to the artist who assumes he is following his own ideal while following another form of ambition*. Whoever observes this spectacle does not have the right to judge it; it is no little accomplishment if he has succeeded *for an instant* in withdrawing from the field *to study the struggle dispassionately*, rendering the scene exactly, with the corresponding colors, in such a manner as to represent reality as it has been, or as it should have been." My translation; my italics.

This published version of 19 January was notably shorter than other discussions of the planned series. (There was also an unpublished preface dated 22 January.) Of the five projected novels, *I Malavoglia, Mastro-don Gesualdo, Duchessa di Leyra, Onorevole Scipioni*, and *Uomo di lusso*, only the first two were completed (1881, 1888-89).

41. A. J. Greimas (with François Rastier), "Les Jeux des contraintes sémiotiques," in *Du sens. Essais sémiotiques* (Paris: Seuil, 1970), pp. 135-55, translated as "The Interaction of Semiotic Constraints," *Game, Play, Literature*, Yale French Studies, no. 41 (1968), pp. 86-105. For a brief discussion of some of the implications of this method of logical analysis for literary studies, see Jameson, *The Prison-House of Language: A Critical Account of Structuralism and Russian Formalism* (Princeton: Princeton University Press, 1972), pp. 161-68.

42. Verga, *Opere*, p. 836; my italics.

43. Erich Neumann catalogues the various forms the goddess assumes and some of the material-psychological functions she represents in *The Great Mother: An Analysis of the Archetype*, trans. Ralph Manheim, Bollingen Series, 47, 2nd ed. (Princeton: Princeton University Press, 1955; 1963). See also E. O. James, *The Cult of the Mother-Goddess: An Archeological and Documentary Study* (London: Thames & Hudson, 1959); and the recent treatment by Paul Friedrich, *The Meaning of Aphrodite* (Chicago: University of Chicago Press, 1978). Neumann's study provides a wealth of information despite its Jungian, and at times polemically idealist, orientation. Representations of this goddess have been found all over the Mediterranean basin; among the best-preserved are the figurines of the serpent goddess discovered at Knossos. Although there are many extensive treatments of the traditional connections between Sicily and both Aphrodite and Persephone (also called *Kore* prior to her abduction), Eugenio Manni's discussion in *Sicilia pagana* (Palermo: S. F. Flaccovio, 1963) is perhaps the most suggestive. The myth of the female earth giving birth to the male sky and then mating with him has variants throughout the Mediterranean and the East. Finally, it should be recalled that Frazer associates the wolf with the corn itself, although this theory has spawned a host of objections.

44. Isis/Osiris could fit into this list except for their traditional brother-sister relationship and Isis's connection with the sky (in still other versions of this opposition, the male represented the sun, whereas the moon, the sky, and the earth were all feminine). Ishtar/Tammuz is another problematical pairing.

45. *Hesiod, the Homeric Hymns, and Homerica*, trans. Hugh G. Evelyn-White, 2nd rev. ed., Loeb Classical Library (Cambridge: Harvard University Press, 1936), pp. 410-11, ll. 68-70, 75-77.

46. Debenedetti claims (in *Verga e il naturalismo*) that the poppies function as a sign of suicidal will ("una volontà suicida," p. 422), though it seems to me there is a strong element of "sfida" here as well. On the overdetermination of the natural detail, see also Asor Rosa, "Il primo e l'ultimo uomo del mondo," pp. 32-33.

47. "The Theme of the Three Caskets" (1913), *SE* 12:301.

48. See J[ohann] J[akob] Bachofen, *Das Mutterrecht*, vols. 2-3 of *Gesammelte Werke*, ed. Max Burckhardt et al. (Basel: B. Schwabe, 1948). The Swiss jurist's *Mutterrecht* (1861)

grew out of a series of lectures delivered in Stuttgart in 1856. It is necessary to remember that Bachofen's analysis was made from the evidence of myths first and society second; therefore, even though its literary application to Verga's text is important, its underlying social hypothesis remains purely speculative.

Many of Bachofen's ideas were affirmed independently by Lewis Henry Morgan's work on American Indian society (*Ancient Society*, 1877). Both these studies have inspired critical appreciation (Engels, Fromm) as well as attacks and also various attempts at modification (Robert H. Lowie, Maurice Godelier). Marx prepared an abstract of Morgan's work, and Engels included an extensive discussion of the work and its implications in *The Origin of the Family, Private Property, and the State*. Early opposition to theories of primitive matriarchies was spurred by Henry Sumner Maine's *Ancient Law* (1861). The matriarchy-patriarchy debate continues in full force today. In many respects the most balanced recent analysis of the problems involved in these discussions is Martin King Whyte's *The Status of Women in Pre-industrial Societies* (Princeton: Princeton University Press, 1978). Even though Bachofen's and Morgan's positions remain in dispute, their basic theses can be retooled for adoption on the level of the individual without too much difficulty, since even in full patriarchy newborn children's initial activities, as well as their perceptions of the world, depend on their mothers. For Verga's text, the important aspect of this phenomenon is therefore patriarchy's *fear* of the threat of continued matriarchal dominion, not the presence of matriarchy itself.

49. Robert Graves's assertions, which are often strikingly polemical, occur in *The Greek Myths*, rev. ed., 2 vols. (Baltimore: Penguin, 1955; 1960), 1: 71. See also Freud, *Totem and Taboo: Resemblances Between the Psychic Lives of Savages and Neurotics*, SE 13:vii-162. Though there is evidence for the historical accuracy of these propositions, it is not conclusive; however, there seems little room for doubt, at least since Frazer, that ritual regicide was practiced in some form throughout the ancient world.

50. Bettelheim, *Uses of Enchantment*, pp. 26-27, 34-41, 294.

51. *SE* 13. Although Freud cites Bachofen and eventually discusses the passage from paganism to Christianity, he acknowledges his own inability to "suggest at what point in this process of development a place is to be found for the great mother-goddesses, who may perhaps in general have preceded the father-gods" (p. 149).

52. In act 2 of the drama, Nanni's penitence is to be demonstrated by the embodied image of Christ in the village's Easter procession (with a crown of thorns that really cut: "la voglio di spine vere! che pungano!" Verga, *Opere*, p. 860).

53. In addition to the symbolic wounding, the association of Christ and the Easter resurrection with the blessing of the crops is made explicit by Nanni in the play's second act ("Avremo una buona annata, se Dio vuole," p. 859).

54. On the connection between the Gorgon's head and the fear of castration, which is allayed, in the case of Verga's narrative, by turning the ax against the other, see Freud, "Medusa's Head" (1922), *SE* 18.

55. This expanded schema for representing thematic development is adapted from Fredric Jameson's "The Vanishing Mediator: Narrative Structure in Max Weber," *New German Critique* 1, no. 1 (Winter 1973): 88.

56. Neumann's outline of similar evaluations in ancient societies is instructive: "Wherever the antivital fanaticism of the male spiritual principle predominates, the Feminine is looked upon as negative and evil. . . . [It] is said to fascinate and hold fast, to lure and enchant. . . . And consequently this male principle of consciousness, which desires permanence and not change, eternity and not transformation, law and not creative spontaneity, 'discriminates' against the Great Goddess and turns her into a demon." *The Great Mother*, p. 233. Cf. the closing line of Verga's drama: "'Ah! . . . ah! . . . Il diavolo siete?'"

57. Verga, *Tutte le novelle*, 1: 332-38. This novella first appeared in *Domenica letteraria* in March 1882, then in *Novelle rusticane*.

58. An important example was Visconti's patently socialist interpretation of *I Malavoglia* in his 1948 film adaptation, *La terra trema.*

59. Verga to Colajanni, 19 November 1891. Quoted by Lina Perroni in "L'attualità politica di Giovanni Verga," in *Dal tuo al mio,* new ed. (Florence: Bemporad, 1929), p. ix. On Verga's growing pessimism in regard to the vulnerability of Italian society in flux, see Olga Ragusa, *Verga's Milanese Tales* (New York: Vanni, 1964), pp. 49-77. For a sympathetic attempt at recuperation of Verga's social analysis, see Gaetano Trombatore, "Arte sociale di Giovanni Verga," *Rinascita* 4, no. 3 (1947): 57-60.

60. Russo describes this procedure as demonstrating "una divinità nascosta nelle cose," in *Giovanni Verga,* p. 251. The complexity of this process and the ideological misapprehension operative in both description and narration indicate the historical inadequacy of Georg Lukács's formula in "Narrate or Describe?" (1936), in *Writer and Critic and Other Essays,* ed. and trans. Arthur D. Kahn (New York: Grosset & Dunlap, 1970), pp. 110-48.

61. The common element between Verga and Frazer would have been Giuseppe Pitrè, whose works on Sicilian customs and folklore were read by both of them.

Chapter 5

1. Verga to Capuana, Milan, 11 April 1881; in Giovanni Verga, *Opere,* ed. Luigi Russo, La Letteratura Italiana, storia e testi, 63 (Milan: Ricciardi, 1968), p. 893. "*I Malavoglia* has been a flop, a complete and utter flop." My translation.

2. The term (which itself has received various interpretations) is Benedetto Croce's. See *La letteratura della nuova Itala. Saggi critici,* Scritti di storia letteraria e politica, 5; 3rd rev. ed. (Bari: Laterza, 1929), 3: 14.

3. For the clearest and perhaps the most regrettable example of this failure, see Antonio Gramsci, *Letteratura e vita nazionale,* Quaderni del carcere, 5 (Turin: Einaudi, 1950; 1974), pp. 90, 179, in which the objectivity of Verga's *verismo* is accepted uncritically and treated as more "*rationally* applied" than Zola's. My italics.

4. Massimo Bontempelli, *Verga, l'Aretino, Scarlatti, Verdi. Nuovi discorsi* (Milan: Bompiani, 1941), p. 9: "Around Giovanni Verga the waters have always been tranquil. A great innovator and destroyer of literary conventions, he never engaged in polemics, and none or few were directed at him." My translation.

5. In Italy, these discussions began with Luigi Russo's 1941 additions to his earlier volume, *Giovanni Verga* (1919-20). Verga's innovative mixture of "choral" discourse, indirect discourse, and the *style indirect libre* has continued to receive critical treatment, much of it polemical in nature. See Vittorio Lugli, "Lo stile indiretto libero in Flaubert e Verga," *Memorie della R. Accademia delle Scienze dell'Istituto di Bologna,* Classe di scienze morali, ser. 4, vol. 5 (1942-43): 131-43; Giacomo Devoto, "Giovanni Verga: i piani del racconto" (1954), in *Itinerario stilistico,* intro. Gianni A. Papini, Biblioteca di letteratura e d'arte, n.s. (Florence: Le Monnier, 1975), pp. 200-212; Nicola Vita, "Genesi del 'discorso rivissuto' e suo uso nella narrativa italiana," *Cultura neolatina* 14, fasc. 1-2 (1955): 5-34; Leo Spitzer, "L'originalità della narrazione nei 'Malavoglia,'" *Belfagor* 11, no. 1 (January 1956): 37-53; Ivo Franges, "Su un aspetto dello stile di Giovanni Verga (Il dialogo interiore)," *Studia Romanica* 1, no. 2 (December 1956): 3-43; Giulio Herczeg, *Lo stile indiretto libero in italiano,* Biblioteca della lingua nostra, 13 (Florence: Sansoni, 1963); Francesco Nicolosi, *Il "Mastro-don Gesualdo": dalla prima alla seconda redazione* (Rome: Ateneo, 1967); Giovanni Cecchetti, "I] 'carro' e il 'mare amaro,'" in *Il Verga maggiore. Sette studi,* Collana critica, 83 (Florence: La Nuova Italia, 1968); Antonio Lanci, "*I Malavoglia:* Analisi del racconto," *Trimestre,* no. 253 (1971): 357-408; Olga Ragusa, "Narrative vs. Stylistic Structure in *I Malavoglia,*" *Romanic Review* 62, no. 3 (1971), revised in *Narrative and Drama: Essays in Modern Italian Literature from Verga to Pasolini,* De Proprietatibus Litterarum, Ser. Practica, 110 (The Hague: Mouton, 1976); and Michal Peled Ginsburg, "*I Malavoglia* and Verga's

'Progress,'" *MLN* 95, no. 1 (January 1980): pp. 96-97. The seminal discussion of this topic was that by Werner Günther, *Probleme der Rededarstellung Untersuchungen zur direkten, indirekten, und "erlebten" Rede im Deutschen, Französischen, und Italienischen* (Marburg: D. Lahn, 1928), pp. 133-34.

6. Gaetano Ragonese, *Interpretazione del Verga. Saggi e ricerche*, Biblioteca di cultura, 101, 2nd ed. (Rome: Bulzoni, 1965; 1977), p. 52.

7. Verga criticism in English, which began with William Dean Howells, has always been sparse; however, it may at last be developing, as is indicated by Alfred Alexander's fine biography, *Giovanni Verga: A Great Writer and His World* (London: Grant & Cutler, 1972), and Giovanni Cecchetti's recent survey, *Giovanni Verga*, Twayne's World Authors Series, 489 (Boston: G. K. Hall, 1978).

 8. Giuseppe Petronio, "Interventi," in *Il caso Verga*, ed. Alberto Asor Rosa, Problemi-Libri, 5, 3rd ed. (Palermo: Palumbo, 1974), p. 121. This work has in turn been integrated into the most recent assessments of Verga studies. See especially Salvatore Rossi, *L'età del verismo*, Scuola e cultura, 8 (Palermo: Palumbo, 1978).

9. Verga, *Opere*, pp. 187-88. All references are to this edition of *I Malavoglia*. "So Master 'Ntoni, to keep the boat running, had put through a deal with Uncle Crocifisso, nicknamed 'Dumbbell,' to buy some lupin beans on credit and sell them at Riposto, where Compare Cinghialenta said there was a ship from Trieste taking on cargo. To tell the truth, the lupins were a bit spoiled; but they were the only ones you could get at Trezza, and that foxy old Dumbbell also knew that sun and water were uselessly eating up the *Provvidenza*, tied up below the wash shed, completely idle; so that's why he kept on pretending that he was a little dense. 'What's that?' he said. 'You think it's too much? Don't take them! But I can't do it for a cent less, on my conscience, because I have a soul that must meet its Maker!—and he swayed his head, which really looked like a bell without a clapper" (pp. 25-26). All translations of *I Malavoglia* are from Raymond Rosenthal's *The House by the Medlar Tree* (New York: New American Library, 1964).

10. "All this was said in front of the church door at Ognina, on the first Sunday in September, which was the feast day of the Holy Virgin and had brought a great throng of people from all the nearby villages" (p. 26).

11. For a full discussion of this extremely complex issue, see Patricia Drechsel Tobin, *Time and the Novel: The Genealogical Imperative* (Princeton: Princeton University Press, 1978).

12. "In the parish register they were in truth called *Toscano*." My italics.

13. "There was a time when the Malavoglia were as thick as the stones on the old Trezza road." "C'era una volta" is the standard equivalent of "Once upon a time."

14. "But that [i.e., the confusion] didn't mean a thing, *for ever since this world was a world* they'd been known from father to son as Malavoglia at Ognina, Trezza, and Aci Castello, and they had *always* had their own boats in the water and their own roof tiles in the sun." My italics.

15. Russo, *Giovanni Verga*, p. 155.

16. "All seagoing folk, good, upright, the exact opposite of what you would think from their nickname. *And this is as it should be.*" My italics.

17. Vittorio Spinazzola, "Legge del lavoro e legge dell'onore nei *Malavoglia*," in *Verismo e positivismo*, I Garzanti, Argomenti, 17 (Milan: Garzanti, 1977), pp. 126-212.

18. "The sayings of the old folks never lie."

19. "'Without a man at the tiller the boat can't sail.' —'You've got to be a sexton before you can be the Pope.' —Or: 'Stick to your trade, you may not get rich but you'll earn your bread.' —'Be satisfied to be what your father made you, if nothing else you won't be a rascal.' And many other wise maxims."

20. "'Here! What about this? Instead of paying so much a month, pay up at Christmas, and so you'll save a tarì for every salma!' .... And he [Piedipapera] started filling the bags. 'In the name of God,' he cried, 'there's one bag that's filled.'"

21. "And those were *the last* words of his they heard." My italics.

22. Mena's namesake, the Catanian Saint Agatha, suffered a metaphorically similar fate at the hands of the Roman senator Quintanius. She refused to marry him, since she did not love him, and in return he rendered her unfit for relations with any man (he ordered that she be tortured, and in the process her breasts were torn off).

23. "The fatal incessant journey . . . to arrive at the conquest of progress." My translation.

24. " 'Ntoni took a stroll on the sea every blessed day, and he had to travel on his oars, breaking his back."

25. "That boy had a heart greater than the sea. 'It's the Malavoglia blood,' his grandfather said."

26. " 'My home is my mother' " (p. 93). "The worst thing . . . is to leave your own town, where even the stones know you, and it must break your heart to leave them behind on the road. 'Blessed is the bird that makes his nest his home' " (p. 177).

27. "But, luckily for the woman, all of a sudden it got around that Master 'Ntoni had returned at night, on a ship from Catania, and that he was ashamed to show his face because he didn't even have shoes on his feet" (pp. 199-200).

28. "But his grandfather, his brother, and his sisters gave him a warm welcome, as though he had really returned loaded with money, and his sisters clung to his neck, laughing and crying. . . . And they said to him: 'Now you won't leave us again, isn't that so?' " (p. 200).

29. See Spinazzola, "Legge del lavoro e legge dell'onore nei *Malavoglia*," pp. 153 passim.

30. "Goodbye!' 'Ntoni repeated. 'You see that I'm right to go away! I can't stay here. Goodbye, and *forgive me*, all of you' " (p. 269; my italics).

31. " 'The sea is bitter, and the sailor dies at sea' "; " 'He who has goods at sea has nothing!' "

32. "At Aci Trezza it grumbles in a special way"; "because the sea is homeless too, and *belongs* to all those who listen to it, here and there, wherever the sun rises and sets . . . and it seems the voice of *a friend*." My italics.

33. It should be noted that this is not a simple, straightforward progression from realism to myth (as is demonstrated by the *realistic* frame of *Lady Chatterly's Lover*, 1928).

34. D. H. Lawrence, *Women in Love* (1920; reprint ed., New York: Modern Library, 1948). All page references in the text are to this edition. Despite important textual problems, there still does not exist a definitive critical edition.

35. The long conversations in *Women in Love* made Norman Douglas complain that the narrative at times seemed like "realism gone crazy." See *D. H. Lawrence: A Composite Biography*, ed. Edward H. Nehls, 3 vols. (Madison: University of Wisconsin Press, 1957-59), 2: 11.

36. *The Complete Poems of D. H. Lawrence*, ed. and intro. Vivian de Sola Pinto and F. Warren Roberts (New York: Viking, 1971), p. 697; see also pp. 958-60 for variants.

37. *D. H. Lawrence and Italy: "Twilight in Italy," "Sea and Sardinia," "Etruscan Places,"* intro. Anthony Burgess (New York: Viking, 1972), p. 31. All page numbers in the text are to this edition.

38. There is an account of Lawrence's use of Frazer's work in John B. Vickery, *The Literary Impact of "The Golden Bough"* (Princeton: Princeton University Press, 1973), pp. 280-325. Vickery's discussion is especially perceptive on the individual narratives, but I cannot agree with his conclusion that the progress of Lawrence's *works* merely recapitulated, in allegorical and deterministic fashion, Frazer's sequence of the dying and reviving god (p. 325). It seems to me that the important question involves not only the works but also Lawrence's feelings about reincarnation and the artist's creation of his own life as a god-like creator. This multiple approach is suggested (though not in relation to Lawrence) by Anton Ehrenzweig in "The Theme of the Dying God," part 4 of *The Hidden Order of Art: A Study in the Psychology of Artistic Imagination* (Berkeley and Los Angeles: University of California Press, 1967), pp. 171-256.

39. The question of phallic as opposed to some other type of love remains as confused today (in fiction and in psychoanalytic writing) as it was in Lawrence's work. See, for example, the suggestive but hardly definitive attempt by Jacques Lacan to describe a type of "jouissance" (orgasm) that would obviate the simple phallic-vaginal opposition and, at the same time, help to explain mystic communion and ecstasy: "Dieu et la jouissance de la femme" in *Le Séminaire de Jacques Lacan, Livre XX, Encore, 1972-1973*, ed. Jacques-Alain Miller (Paris: Seuil, 1975), pp. 61-71.

40. Anaïs Nin, in her brief but extremely perceptive comments on *Twilight in Italy* in *D. H. Lawrence: An Unprofessional Study*, intro. Harry T. Moore (1932; reprint ed., Chicago: Swallow Press, 1964), notes Lawrence's ability to make us feel the unity of mysticism "*through our senses*," and she concludes that "he restated mysticism in modern terms" (p. 76; emphasis in the original).

41. Lawrence began reading Verga in 1916 and later translated two collections of Verga's stories and one of his novels (*Mastro-don Gesualdo*), though there is a long-standing debate on the accuracy of Lawrence's translations (including treatments by Giovanni Cecchetti, Armin Arnold, Olga Ragusa, and Mary Corsani). The most thorough study of Verga's complex influence (both positive and negative) on Lawrence remains Maria Motta Vaccarelli's "'Nostalgia for Sicily': The Fictional Modes of Giovanni Verga and D. H. Lawrence" (Ph.D. diss., Catholic University of America, 1972). Other treatments include Piero Nardi, "Ciò che Lawrence deve a Verga," *L'Italia letteraria* 12, n.s. 3 (9 February 1936): 5, and *La Vita di D. H. Lawrence*, vol. 1 of *Tutte le opere*, I classici contemporanei stranieri (Milan: Mondadori, 1947); Armin Arnold, "D. H. Lawrence, the Russians, and Giovanni Verga," *Comparative Literature Studies* 2, no. 3 (1965): 249-58; Mary Corsani, *D. H. Lawrence e l'Italia*, Civiltà letteraria nel Novecento, Sezione inglese-americana, 2 (Milan: Mursia, 1965); Patrizio Rossi, "'The Fox' e 'La Lupa': D. H. Lawrence lettore di Verga," *English Miscellany* (Rome) 24 (1973-74): 299-320; Judith G. Ruderman, "Lawrence's *The Fox* and Verga's 'The She-Wolf': Variations on the Theme of the 'Devouring Mother,'" *MLN* 94, no. 1 (January 1979): 153-165; and the general discussion by Barbara Bates Bonadeo, "D. H. Lawrence's View of the Italians," *English Miscellany* (Rome) 24 (1973-74): 271-97. There is also a brief comment on Lawrence's reading of Verghian "emotional" psychology in Sandra M. Gilbert's *Acts of Attention: The Poems of D. H. Lawrence* (Ithaca: Cornell University Press, 1972), pp. 137-38.

42. "Spirit of place" is Lawrence's term (in *Studies in Classic American Literature*). The notion unites the timelessness of the genius loci with the place-specific effects of historical and cultural realism.

43. At times Lawrence also pairs chapters and even larger segments by using notably similar dialogues, such as the discussions of male love ending "A Chair" (pp. 415-16) and "Exeunt" (pp. 347-48).

44. This description of *Women in Love* occurs in Keith Sagar's *The Art of D. H. Lawrence* (Cambridge: At the University Press, 1966), p. 226.

45. The Vintage edition, to which all page numbers in the text refer, is set in small type and runs to forty-eight pages: *"St. Mawr" and "The Man Who Died"* (New York: Random House, 1953).

46. There have been very few critical treatments of the narrative; however, some article-length discussions have recently appeared. Of these, the ones I have found most useful are those that deal openly with the narrative's intricate web of mythic allusions. See Evelyn J. Hinz and John J. Teunissen, "Savior and Cock: Allusion in Lawrence's *The Man Who Died*," *Journal of Modern Literature* 5, no. 2 (April 1976): 279-96; and Robert H. MacDonald, "The Union of Fire and Water: An Examination of the Imagery of *The Man Who Died*," *D. H. Lawrence Review* 10, no. 1 (Spring 1977): 34-51. See also Joyce Carol Oates's suggestive comments at the conclusion of "Lawrence's *Götterdämmerung*: The Tragic Vision of *Women in Love*," *Critical Inquiry* 4, no. 3 (Spring 1978): 559-78. Her assertion that tragedy is "transcended" in myth (pp. 566-576) is, however, open to question. The important

point seems to me to be whether in Lawrence's work myth actually transcends tragedy or merely serves as a way to obfuscate the human history Lawrence could not and would not accept. This type of question served as the basis of Caudwell's [Christopher St. John Sprigg's] polemically Marxian attacks in the 1930s and remains an important problem in Lawrence criticism.

47. On Lawrence's later pessimism, specifically in connection with his own progressive illness and this story (discussed in a letter to Earl Brewster), see Harry T. Moore, *The Priest of Love: A Life of D. H. Lawrence*, rev. ed. of *The Intelligent Heart: The Story of D. H. Lawrence*, 1954; 1962 (reprint ed., New York: Farrar, Strauss & Giroux, 1974), p. 430. It is important that even though Lawrence, like the reborn Jesus, is sick of man's world as it is, he still revels in the potentials of the phenomenal world and in what it could become. The necessity of male-female relationships is also reflected in Lawrence's continuing imagery of failed *Blutbrüderschaft*, which frames the description of the relationship between the "man who died" and Judas (p. 205).

48. This imagery of the internalized sun appears in its reverse aspect (setting rather than rising) in the fine poem "November by the Sea," in *The Complete Poems*, p. 455. It also appears as a positive image of mankind's social and moral revitalization at the conclusion of *Apocalypse*: "Start with the sun, and the rest will slowly, slowly happen." *Apocalypse*, intro. Richard Aldington (1931-32; reprint ed., New York: Viking, 1966), p. 200.

49. The question is posed but left unanswered in Mark Schorer's introduction to Harry T. Moore's *Poste Restante: A Lawrence Travel Calendar* (Berkeley and Los Angeles: University of California Press, 1956), p. 17. For Schorer, "The question forces itself. . . . But no answer comes, it lies in the still undefined history and character of our times."

50. This combination of hope and fear is especially evident in the open mix of pagan and Christian iconography in Lawrence's series of poses as both Pan and Christ (recorded on film and in portraits) in the 1920s.

51. All references are to the third edition of William Faulkner, *The Hamlet* (New York: Random House, 1964). For a thorough discussion of the various editions and their shortcomings, see James Everett Kibler, Jr., "A Study of the Text of William Faulkner's *The Hamlet*" (Ph.D. diss., University of South Carolina, 1970).

52. The historical accuracy of Faulkner's depiction of what was then the new South is open to question. Many writers have assumed the essential accuracy of Faulkner's portrayal, but Myra Jehlen, in her Marxist study, *Class and Character in Faulkner's South* (New York: Columbia University Press, 1976), claims that Faulkner's narratives ignore the all-pervasive importance of Northern-financed industries in the postwar South. According to Jehlen, this allows Faulkner to place undue emphasis on individualism rather than industrial capitalism. Gary Lee Stonum's recent approach is an attempt to reconcile such opposing perspectives by claiming Faulkner's attitude in the trilogy is not so much that of the historical observer as of the elegist. See his chapter, "Elegy as Meta-fiction," in *Faulkner's Career: An Internal Literary History* (Ithaca: Cornell University Press, 1979), pp. 153-99. See also Evans Harrington and Ann J. Abadie, eds., *The South and Faulkner's Yoknapatawpha: The Actual and the Apocryphal* (Jackson: University Press of Mississippi, 1977).

53. Olga Vickery first pointed out the importance of love and money as objects of exchange in the trilogy in "The Profit and the Loss," in *The Novels of William Faulkner: A Critical Interpretation* (Baton Rouge: Louisiana State University Press, 1959), pp. 167-92. Since the appearance of Vickery's work, there have been many discussions of these two aspects of the narrative, but none has surpassed either the subtlety or the perspicacity of her treatment. Florence Leaver pointed out the structural importance of the narrative's "war of minds" in "The Structure of *The Hamlet*," *Twentieth Century Literature* 1, no. 2 (July 1958): 77-84. (I do not, however, subscribe to her conclusions regarding Mrs. Littlejohn's moral supremacy.)

54. There are three book-length treatments of myth in Faulkner's work, including the trilogy: Richard P. Adams, *Faulkner: Myth and Motion* (Princeton: Princeton University Press, 1968); Walter Brylowski, *Faulkner's Olympian Laugh: Myth in the Novels* (Detroit: Wayne State University Press, 1968); and Lynn Gartrell Levins, *Faulkner's Heroic Design: The Yoknapatawpha Novels* (Athens: University of Georgia Press, 1976). See also Michael Rice's suggestive but very brief treatment, "Myth and Legend: The Snopes Trilogy: *The Hamlet, The Town* and *The Mansion*," *UNISA English Studies* 4, no. 1 (April 1976): 18-22.

55. The heroic horse swap between Ab and Pat Stamper is similar to one in Longstreet's *Georgia Scenes*. The legend of the treasure hidden in the land derives from a series of ancient tales, one of which was retold by William Buttler Yeats in *The Celtic Twilight:* "The Three O'Byrnes and the Evil Faeries," reprinted in *Mythologies* (New York: Collier Books, 1969), pp. 86-87.

Outside the frame of the battle of wits, other portions of the narrative also depend on the interweaving of myth, romance, and irony. The romantic pairing of Ike and the cow, with its Ovidian overtones and passages of lush natural description, is treated both as a moral anecdote and as a parody of the myth of Io and Jove. (For Faulkner's own parody of his material, in which "Mr. Faulkner" appears in the role of Ike, see "Afternoon of a Cow," reprinted in *Uncollected Stories of William Faulkner*, ed. Joseph Blotner [New York: Random House, 1979, pp. 424-32].) The McCarron-Eula affair represents a travesty of the valiant knight's battle for his lady fair, with both knight and lady fighting off the ludicrously naïve competitors. The fable of the "Hound of Hell" shapes Mink Snopes's grotesque struggle to dispose of the body of Jack Houston. The "Spotted Horses" episode contains elements of the myth of the Centaurs, as has occasionally been noted in the criticism of the narrative.

56. Cleanth Brooks summarizes the deal (in which Ratliff is only partially victorious) and provides a detailed ledger in an appendix to *William Faulkner: The Yoknapatawpha Country* (New Haven: Yale University Press, 1963), pp. 402-6.

57. An avatar of this yarn is recounted by Thomas D. Clark in *Pills, Petticoats, and Plows: The Southern Country Store* (1944; reprint ed., Norman: University of Oklahoma Press, 1964), p. 286.

58. For a discussion of Faulkner as both modernist and traditionalist, see Hugh Kenner's chapter, "The Last Novelist," in *A Homemade World: The American Modernist Writers* (New York: William Morrow, 1975), pp. 194-221.

59. Faulkner's own views of the South's development, as well as the myths he used to focus on the corruption of nature and of the human community, were doubtless affected by the South's position of economic dependency on the industrialized North (as both the dominant place and the dominant mode of American production). Nonetheless, to claim that dependency was (even unconsciously) the *determining* factor in Faulkner's views and in his narrative strategies, as Susan Willis does in "Aesthetics of the Rural Slum: Contradictions and Dependency in 'The Bear,'" *Social Text* 1, no. 2 (Summer 1979): 82-103, seems naïve. Willis's argument—her description of the South's shift from a "peripheral" to a "semi-peripheral" status in relation to the North and her discussion of the formal effects of this shift *within* Faulkner's developing mythology—is extremely suggestive; however, she tends to slight the very real problems within current dependency theory itself and the difficulties of its application outside the primary object of her discussion, the fourth section of "The Bear." It seems to me that from the late 1930s on, Faulkner was, if anything, more conscious of the South's dependency than Willis's treatment suggests, but that nonetheless this was not the central concern informing his use of myth, at least not in the trilogy.

60. These words are from Faulkner's Nobel Prize Address (10 December 1950), reprinted in *Essays, Speeches and Public Letters*, ed. James R. Meriwether (New York: Random House, 1965), pp. 119-21.

61. Ratliff remained one of Faulkner's favorite creations. In April 1962, during one of his last public appearances, Faulkner was asked if he reread his own works. In his response, the one character he mentioned by name was Ratliff: "I like my sewing machine agent, Ratliff, I will go back to read about him, to laugh again quite often." See *Faulkner at West Point*, ed. Joseph L. Fant III and Robert Ashley (New York: Random House, 1964), p. 115.

62. As was the case for Lawrence, it is finally impossible to calculate the influence that translating had on Pavese's own work. Absorption of another novelist's techniques and strategies by reading and translating is never an immediate, one-step process, and Pavese himself insisted in an often-cited 1950 radio interview that the primary lesson of translation is one of resistance, of learning how *not* to write. It is nonetheless clear that the influence that the writers he translated had on the style and temporal organization of Pavese's narratives was of special importance (perhaps most clearly Lewis, Anderson, and Steinbeck in the early, highly realistic prose; Melville, Dos Passos, and Faulkner in the middle and later works). See Pavese's comments in "Intervista alla radio" (1950), in *Saggi letterari*, 2nd ed., *Opere di Cesare Pavese* (14 vols.), vol. 12 (Turin: Einaudi, 1951), p. 264: "Il tradurre—parlo per esperienza—insegna come *non* si deve scrivere. . . . Alla fine di un periodo intenso di traduzioni—Anderson, Joyce, Dos Passos, Faulkner, Gertrude Stein —*io sapevo* esattamente quali erano i moduli e le movenze letterarie che non mi sono consentiti, che mi restano esterni, che mi lasciano freddo." Emphasis in the original. "Translation—I am speaking from experience—teaches one how *not* to write. . . . At the end of an intense period of translating—Anderson, Joyce, Dos Passos, Faulkner, Gertrude Stein—I *knew* exactly which were the literary forms and movements that are not meant for me, that remain external, that leave me cold." My translation. A full analysis of the influence of translating among modern writers, such as Lawrence-Verga and Pavese-Faulkner, would be extremely instructive, but it would require far more space than the present study permits.

For treatment of the influence of American writers on Pavese, see Patrizia Lorenzi Davitti, *Pavese e la cultura americana. Fra mito e razionalità* (Messina: D'Anna, 1975). There is also an ample and perceptive discussion of Pavese's language in Anco Marzio Mutterle's *L'immagine arguta. Lingua, stile, retorica di Pavese*. La ricerca letteraria, Serie critica, 38 (Turin: Einaudi, 1977).

63. Pavese, "Intervista alla radio," pp. 266-67. My translation.

64. Though *Dialoghi con Leucò* was one of Pavese's favorite works, the abandonment of realism and the heavy-handedness of the mythic treatment often give rise to the same type of unintended ironies that mar Lawrence's works in a similarly mythic mode. The Faulknerian influence on Pavese has often been discussed, but Lawrence's influence, though less direct, was also acknowledged by Pavese. See *Il mestiere di vivere (Diario 1935-1950)*, 2nd ed., *Opere di Cesare Pavese*, vol. 10 (1952), 1 Dec. 1949, p. 343: "Scoperto l'altra sera quanto mi abbia plasmato la lettura di *Sun* e *The Woman who rode away* di Lawrence ('36-'37?)," "Discovered the other night to what an extent the reading of *Sun* and *The Woman Who Rode Away* shaped me." My translation.

65. It is tempting to portray this division into uniformly short chapters as a lesson learned from Dos Passos, or even from the Faulkner of *As I Lay Dying;* but it might as easily have been Pavese's means of maintaining control over a narrative that he wrote with extreme rapidity (the manuscript is dated "18 settembre-9 novembre 1949"). For a discussion of Pavese's means of patterning narrative time, see Louis Kibler, "Patterns of Time in Pavese's *La luna e i falò*," *Forum Italicum* 12, no. 3 (Fall 1978): 339-49.

66. Pavese, *Il mestiere di vivere*, 13 February 1944 (p. 251): "The richness of life is created by memories [which one has] forgotten." My translation.

67. "But where could I go? I'd come to the end of the world, to the last shore [i.e., America], and had enough of it. Then I began to think that I could go back across the mountains." All translations of *La luna e i falò*, except for occasional emendations of my own, are from *The Moon and the Bonfires*, trans. Marianne Ceconi, foreword by Paolo Milano (1953; reprint ed., Westport, Conn.: Greenwood Press, 1975).

68. Pavese, *Il mestiere di vivere*, 27 May 1944 (p. 256): "Who knows how many things have happened to me. . . . You mean: who knows in how many different ways I have still to view my own past, and so have still to discover there unsuspected events." My translation.

69. "So I began to understand that you don't just talk, to say, 'I've done this, I've done that, I've eaten and drunk,' but you talk to get an idea, to understand how the world works. I'd never thought of it before. And Nuto knew a lot, he was like a grownup" (p. 105).

70. The best known of the Left's polemics against Pavese, whose relationship with Marxism and the Italian Communist party was always uneasy, was Alberto Moravia's early article on "Pavese decadente" in *Corriere della sera* (December 1954), expanded in his later "Fu solo un decadente," *L'Espresso* (Rome) 16, no. 28 (12 July 1970): 14. This type of *ad hominem* attack has recurred on occasion, though the extreme nature of Moravia's position resulted in creating more sympathy than animosity for Pavese's works, even on the left. See Carlo Salinari's early response to Moravia, "La poetica di Pavese" (1955), reprinted in *Preludio e fine del realismo in Italia*, Nobiltà dello spirito, 12 (Naples: Morano, 1967), pp. 87-97; Davide Lajolo, "Un raffronto Pavese-Moravia," *L'Europa letteraria* 5, no. 27 (March 1964): 75-80; Giovanni Caserta, *Pavese, un problema. Testo di una conferenza tenuta il 3 ottobre 1970 nella sede del circolo "Rinascita" di Matera* (Matera: Rinascita, 1971); and Gian Carlo Ferretti's interestingly ambivalent description of Pavese's social thought in two essays: "Pavese e la scelta del silenzio," in *Studi in memoria di Luigi Russo* (Pisa: Nistri-Lischi, 1974), pp. 477-85; and "Il fascino pericoloso dei ritorni," *Rinascita* 34, no. 1 (7 January 1977): 32-33.

71. Among the studies of Pavese in English, perhaps the most helpful for approaching *La luna e i falò* are Louis Tenenbaum, "Character Treatment in Pavese's Fiction," *Symposium* 15, no. 2 (Summer 1961): 131-38; John Freccero, "Mythos and Logos: The Moon and the Bonfires," *Italian Quarterly* 4, no. 16 (Winter 1961): 3-16; Peter M. Norton, "Cesare Pavese and the American Nightmare," *MLN* 77, no. 1 (January 1962): 24-36; Donald Heiney, *America in Modern Italian Literature* (New Brunswick, N.J.: Rutgers University Press, 1964), pp. 171-86, and *Three Italian Novelists: Moravia, Pavese, Vittorini* (Ann Arbor: University of Michigan Press, 1968), pp. 83-146; Gian-Paolo Biasin, *The Smile of the Gods: A Thematic Study of Cesare Pavese's Works*, trans. Yvonne Freccero (Ithaca: Cornell University Press, 1968); Bruce Merry, "Artifice and Structure in *La luna e i falò*," *Forum Italicum* 5, no. 3 (September 1971): 351-58; Kibler, "Patterns of Time"; and Sergio Pacifici, *The Modern Italian Novel: From Pea to Moravia*, pref. Harry T. Moore (Carbondale: Southern Illinois University Press, 1979), pp. 118-59.

72. "Virgilia wanted me because she already had two girls, and they hoped to settle on a big farm when I was a bit older, *where we'd all work together and get ahead*" (p. 4; my italics).

73. "I came back to this village and not to Canelli, Barbaresco or Alba because I had a reason to. I wasn't born here, that's almost certain. I don't know where I was born. Around here there isn't a house or piece of land or bones that could make me say 'This is what I was before I was born.' I don't know whether I came from a hill or a valley, from the woods or from a house with balconies. Maybe the girl who left me on the steps of the Cathedral at Alba wasn't a country girl at all. Perhaps her people owned a palace, or perhaps two poor women from Monticello brought me in a grape picker's basket, or someone from Neive—or why not even from Cravanzana? Who knows what flesh I come from? I've traveled enough through the world to know that all flesh is equally good and worth the same, but you get tired of it and that's why you try to sink your roots in the ground to make land and a country for yourself, so that your flesh will mean something and last a little longer than just the simple round of the seasons.

If this is the village where I grew up, I owe it to Virgilia and Padrino—my foster parents, people who aren't here any longer."

74. "'Why, of course they're right to do it,' he burst out. 'They wake up the earth.'
'But, Nuto,' I said, 'not even Cinto believes that.'

And yet, he said, he didn't know what it was, whether it was the heat or the blaze or that the saps were running, anyhow all the fields where the bonfires were lit at the edges had juicier and livelier crops.

'That's a new one,' I said. 'So you believe in the moon, too?'

'The moon,' Nuto said, 'you can't help believing in. Try to cut down a pine tree when the moon's full—the worms will eat it up. You have to wash a grape vat when the moon's young. Even grafting doesn't take unless you do it when the moon's only a few days old'" (p. 56).

75. "Then I said I'd heard many stories in this world but these topped them all."

76. ("Old grandmothers' tales").

77. "I also knew of the moon and the bonfires. But I realized that I'd forgotten I knew."

78. For Pavese's discussions of various kinds of symbols and of the mythic sign (for which belief is a necessity), see *Saggi letterari*, pp. 272-73 and 316-18.

79. "But I, who didn't believe in the moon, knew that when everything added up, only the seasons count."

80. "It's the seasons that *made your bones strong*, that you fed on *when you were a boy*." My italics.

81. "[Baracca] made them cut a lot of dry branches in the vineyard, and we piled them on her until there were enough. Then we poured gasoline on the pile and set fire to it. By noon, it was all ashes. Last year the mark was still there like the bed of a bonfire."

82. "'No, not Santa,' he said. 'They won't find her. You couldn't cover *her* with earth and just leave her that way. There were too many men who still wanted her'" (p. 206; emphasis in the translation).

83. "Nuto? Why, I know him."

84. Merry notes the folktale simplicity of the novel's characters as well as the parallels between Cinto and the narrator in "Artifice and Structure in *La luna e i falò*."

85. Nuto also resembles another mentor, Chiron, who appears in Pavese's *Dialoghi con Leucò*. Like the good Centaur, Nuto embodies the best qualities of nature and reason, and he also teaches the young initiate how to drink.

86. "Nuto grabbed him by the shoulders and lifted him up like a little goat.
'You mean he killed Rosina and your grandmother?'
Cinto was trembling and he couldn't talk.
'He really killed them?' and he shook him."

87. "'Leave him alone,' I said to Nuto. 'He's half dead. Why don't we go and see?'"

88. "'Get up,' I said. '*What did you come here for?*'" My italics.

89. "*He'd come to see me* and didn't want to go back to the vineyard again." My italics.

90. "We won't go to the vineyard. . . . We'll stay by the road and let Nuto go on up."

91. "I seemed to be someone else. I was talking to him as Nuto had talked to me" (p. 53).

92. "Nuto took Cinto into his house to show him carpentry and to teach him to become a musician. We agreed that if the boy did well, later on I would find him a job in Genoa. . . . *Cinto found a house to live in, and I had to go back to Genoa the next day.* . . . Nuto was after me and said, 'So you're leaving? Will you be back for the grape harvest?' . . . . '*Perhaps I'll ship to sea,*' I told him. '*I'll be back for the fair another year*' . . . . I laughed. 'I even found you another son'" (pp. 194-95; my italics).

93. The fullest attempt at a psychological portrait of Pavese through his works is Dominique Fernandez's *L'Échec de Pavese* (Paris: Grasset, 1967). See also Michel David, *La psicanalisi nella cultura italiana* (Turin: Boringhieri, 1966), pp. 511-26.

94. "They asked me if I didn't have a girl, too. I said I'd been *with Nuto* watching him play" (p. 193; my italics).

95. Pavese, *Il mestiere di vivere*, 18 August 1950. "All of this is disgusting. Not words. An act. I won't write any more." My translation.

96. "Verrà la morte e avrà i tuoi occhi" (March 1950). This is the poem that compares death to an absurd vice, "un vizio assurdo," and repeats the theme of suicide ("Sarà come smettere un vizio"), which recurs throughout Pavese's letters, poems, and prose from early in his life until his death.

Index

The Johns Hopkins University Press

This book was set in Alphatype Palatino text and display by David Lorton from a design by Alan Carter. It was printed on 50-lb. Bookmark and bound by Thompson-Shore, Inc.